I0109507

Citizens, Courts, and Confirmations

Citizens, Courts, and Confirmations

POSITIVITY THEORY AND THE JUDGMENTS OF THE AMERICAN PEOPLE

James L. Gibson
and Gregory A. Caldeira

PRINCETON UNIVERSITY PRESS
PRINCETON AND OXFORD

Published by Princeton University Press, 41 William Street, Princeton, New Jersey 08540
In the United Kingdom: Princeton University Press, 6 Oxford Street, Woodstock, Oxfordshire OX20 1TW

LIBRARY OF CONGRESS CATALOGING-IN-PUBLICATION DATA

Gibson, James L.
Citizens, courts, and confirmations : positivity theory and the judgments of the American people / James L. Gibson and Gregory A. Caldeira.
p. cm.
Includes bibliographical references and index.
ISBN 978-0-691-13987-6 — ISBN 978-0-691-13988-3
1. Judges—Selection and appointment—United States. 2. United States. Supreme Court—Officials and employees—Selection and appointment. 3. Alito, Samuel A., 1950– 4. Public opinion—United States. 5. Alito, Samuel A., 1950——United States Supreme Court confirmation hearings, 2006. I. Caldeira, Gregory A. II. Title.
KF8776.G53 2009
347.73′14092—dc22 2008055155

British Library Cataloging-in-Publication Data is available

This book has been composed in Sabon

Printed on acid-free paper. ∞

press.princeton.edu

Printed in the United States of America

10 9 8 7 6 5 4 3 2 1

This book is dedicated to the memory of Mark Andrew Kinsella.

Contents

Figures and Tables

Figures

Tables

Preface

Upon returning from the annual meeting of the American Political Science Association, waiting for a flight at D.C. National, we first learned of the death of Chief Justice William Rehnquist. With Rehnquist's death came another vacancy on the Supreme Court, and the very real possibility that a highly disputatious fight over the nominee would materialize. Rehnquist's demise immediately stimulated us to think about the role of the mass public in confirmation processes, and how the upcoming events might provide an opportunity to test some interesting theories about how Americans view the Supreme Court and how those views change in response to contentious nominations to the high bench.

But a study of change must, perforce, have measures before and after the event hypothesized to drive opinion evolution. When the timings of important political events are not predictable, it is typically impossible to find relevant data preceding the event (t_1), just as it is logistically demanding to secure funding for survey work during the event itself (t_2) and after the dispute has subsided (t_3). Thus, the optimal research design has never before been used to study public opinion during the course of a nomination to the United States Supreme Court.

In this case, we were fortunate that a t_1 survey existed, fielded several months before the nomination, and that the survey included a number of highly relevant measures of attitudes toward the Supreme Court. That survey was not designed to have anything to do with the nomination and confirmation of judges to the Supreme Court, but the questionnaire did include crucial measures of institutional support. In addition, the general measures of political knowledge included in that survey were directed toward the Supreme Court. Thus, the t_1 survey provided sufficient baseline indicators to make a study of opinion change interesting and feasible.

But where could funding be found quickly enough to be able to mount a second interview of the t_1 respondents during the course of the nomination battle itself? Few funding agencies exist that can decide within the course of just a few months to allocate significant research support to time sensitive projects. Fortunately, the National Science Foundation (NSF) is one such agency.

NSF has a program designed to fund worthy projects of this sort. Proposals for small-scale, exploratory, and high-risk research in the fields of science, engineering, and education normally supported by NSF may be submitted to individual programs, including social behavioral and economic sciences. Such research is characterized as preliminary work on untested and novel ideas; ventures into emerging research ideas; the application of new expertise or new approaches to "established" research topics; having extreme urgency with regard to availability of or access to data, facilities, or specialized equipment, including quick-response research on natural disasters and similar unanticipated events; and efforts of similar character likely to catalyze rapid and innovative advances. Fortunately for us, NSF was willing to consider a proposal for research on the Alito nomination under this SGER program, and even more fortunately, the Law and Social Sciences Program, directed by Isaac Unuh, found our proposal worthy of funding. "Firehouse studies" of this type are not common in political science, not because of their lack of value, but because funding is so difficult to secure in a timely manner. We are fortunate that NSF has the foresight to appreciate that important research proposals require expeditious consideration if valuable opportunities are not to be lost, and we appreciate even more the support of the Law and Social Sciences Program for this research.

Thus, this project employs a three-wave panel study and is an effort to assess how public opinion affects and is affected by controversial nominations to the Supreme Court. Our research discovers a number of unexpected findings about all aspects of the process, ranging from the extent of knowledge that Americans possess about the Supreme Court to their perceptions and assessments of Judge Alito to the consequences of the confirmation battle for longer-term attitudes toward the Court. Just as our research design is unprecedented, so too are our principal findings.

Given the unusual nature of the design of this project, we are uncommonly indebted to a number of people and institutions. Support for the 2005 survey (t_1) was provided by the Atlantic Philanthropies in a grant to the Center for Democracy and the Third Sector (CDATS) at Georgetown University. The 2005 survey was also funded in part by the Weidenbaum Center on the Economy, Government, and Public Policy at Washington University, St. Louis. Marc Morjé Howard, with the assistance of James L. Gibson, was primarily responsible for executing that survey. We greatly appreciate Howard's untiring efforts on the 2005 project, as well as the support for this research provided by Steven S. Smith and the Weidenbaum Center.

As we have noted, the nomination surveys were supported by the Law and Social Sciences Program of the National Science Foundation (SES-0553156). Any opinions, findings, and conclusions or recommendations expressed in this material are those of the authors and do not necessarily reflect the views of the National Science Foundation. Additional funding for the 2006 survey was provided by the Mershon Center for

International Security Studies at the Ohio State University ("The Legitimacy of the Supreme Court and Critical Nominations"), to whom we are much indebted. Finally, questions in the 2006 surveys relating to the U.S. Congress were added with the support of a Congressional Research Award from The Dirksen Congressional Center.

Various portions of this book have profited from presentations at professional conferences. Chapter 2 is a revised version of a paper delivered at the 65th Annual National Conference of the Midwest Political Science Association, April 12–15, 2007, Palmer House Hilton, Chicago, Illinois. In addition to the 2005–2006 panel data, that research relies upon multiple data sets, gathered with the support of various agencies. Collection of the 2001 data would not have been possible without the support of the Weidenbaum Center on the Economy, Government, and Public Policy, Washington University, St. Louis, and The Ford Foundation (Grant Number 1015–0840). We are especially indebted to Steve Smith, Director of the Weidenbaum Center, for his encouragement of this work. We also appreciate the research assistance of Marc Hendershot, Jessica Flanigan, and Christina Boyd on that project. We are thankful for the most useful comments on an earlier version of that paper from our colleagues, including Bert Kritzer, Markus Prior, Kent Tedin, Marc Hendershot, Jan Leighley, C. Neal Tate, Michael X. Delli Carpini, Jon Krosnick, Skip Lupia, Gary Segura, Elliot Slotnick, Jeff Mondak, Chris Claassen, Tali Mendelberg, and the Workshop on Empirical Research in Law at Washington University Law School.

For comments on chapter 3, we are indebted to Damon Cann, Jeffrey Yates, Gerhard Loewenberg, and Robert Y. Shapiro. We also appreciate the research assistance of Marc Hendershot, Jessica Flanigan, and Christina Boyd.

Chapter 4 is a revised version of a paper delivered at the 64th Annual National Conference of the Midwest Political Science Association, April 20–23, 2006, Palmer House Hilton, Chicago, Illinois. We also appreciate the research assistance of Marc Hendershot and Christina L. Boyd, both of Washington University, and the comments of Jonathan To, Carissa van den Berk Clark, Amy Overington, Thomas G. Hansford, Barry Friedman, Lee Walker, and Jeff Yates on an earlier version of that paper.

Chapter 5 is a revised version of a paper presented at the 2007 Annual Meeting of the American Political Science Association. In that chapter, we make use of information about the advertisements run during the Alito confirmation process that was made available by the Brennan Center at New York University. We appreciate the counsel of Deborah Goldberg on various aspects of those data.

Chris Claassen and Rachel Berland provided most useful research assistance on various aspects of this project.

Finally, we appreciate President Bush for his decision to name a controversial candidate for a seat on the Supreme Court. Had Bush nominated a centrist judge, our project might have been jeopardized. By naming one of the most conservative candidates available, Bush ensured that the confirmation process would be controversial and politicized, thereby giving us an opportunity to learn more about how citizens update their views toward the nation's highest judicial institution.

James L. Gibson
Cape Town, South Africa
August 2007

Gregory A. Caldeira
Columbus, Ohio
August 2007

Citizens, Courts, and Confirmations

CHAPTER ONE

Introduction

THE PUBLIC AND SUPREME COURT NOMINATIONS

The processes by which nominees are confirmed to a seat on the United States Supreme Court have changed rather dramatically over the past fifty years. It is not just that confirmation struggles are more disputatious today; perhaps more important is the expansion of the numbers of actors involved in such disputes. In the past, it was relatively rare for the mass public to play much of a role. Today, one of the crucial elements in confirmation strategies concerns how public opinion will be managed and manipulated. We do not gainsay that elite groups have great influence over whether a nominee is to be confirmed (and that is another important part of how the process has changed). But at least since the days of the Bork defeat and Thomas victory, the preferences of the mass public have been influential in determining who goes on the Supreme Court.

The role of ordinary people has increased in part owing to the far greater availability of information about nominees and the confirmation process. In recent times, cable television has provided extensive coverage of the Senate hearings, and the public's pulse is often taken by media polls during the confirmation period. Evidence from many sources indicates that Americans are remarkably attentive to and even informed about the actors and issues involved when a president puts forth a nominee to the nation's highest court.

And there is little doubt that the stakes of confirmation politics have increased as well. The Supreme Court is divided on many salient sociolegal issues, as are the American people and their elected representatives. Indeed, the whole question of who gets on the Supreme Court has become one of the most important political issues of our time. And even beyond any given issue, debates over the proper role of the judiciary within the American democratic framework are becoming increasingly vocal, even strident. Confirmation politics have entered a new era in which the process is more open than ever before; the public is more engaged than it has been in the past; and nearly everyone believes that confirmation fights are entirely worth fighting.

More generally, the process of nominating and confirming judges to the federal bench has become more intensely politicized than in the recent past.[1] Perhaps this era can be demarcated by the failed Bork nomination (e.g., Epstein et al. 2006), but the period of the Clinton presidency (and indeed any instance of divided control of the Congress and the presidency) also represents a high-water mark in the politics of contested confirmations. Recent nominations to the Supreme Court have been divisive and controversial. These politicized circumstances constitute a potentially volatile brew.

Many questions arise from this mix of ingredients, questions that scholars heretofore have been unable to address. Perhaps most important is that of ascertaining the effect of politicized confirmation battles on the legitimacy of the Supreme Court and the broader court system in the United States. Many fear that politicization undermines judicial legitimacy: that once the judiciary is seen as just one more political plum, the special reverence Americans hold for their courts will be eroded. The assumption is that whenever Americans are exposed to the politics that has always provided a backdrop for the judiciary, the respect accorded to courts diminishes. The process is fairly simple:

- Americans dislike many of the inherent processes of democratic politics—logrolling, bargaining, compromise, deal making, et cetera.
- The legitimacy of institutions profits when policy makers dissociate themselves from ordinary political processes.
- The great strength of courts is that their decision-making processes are grounded in principle and logic, not politics, and that they are to some considerable degree opaque.
- Any process that associates courts with ordinary politics does so at the risk of considerable damage to the legitimacy of the judiciary.

This set of arguments is widely heard when it comes to campaigning by judges holding elected positions in the state judiciaries (e.g., Geyh 2003). Many fear exactly the same dynamics will undermine the legitimacy the Supreme Court and other federal courts if the politicization of the selection process continues along its current trajectory.

Indeed, the process envisaged by critics is well represented in a somewhat different but related context by the extremely controversial decision the United States Supreme Court made in the 2000 presidential dispute. In *Bush v. Gore*, a perfectly divided Supreme Court—and one divided by political party affiliation as well—awarded the election to George W. Bush. The justice casting what many consider to be the deciding vote (Sandra Day O'Connor) was reported to have proclaimed at a cocktail party "this is terrible" when told that a Gore victory in the election was

[1] On the worldwide tendency toward the politicization of law and the legalization of politics, see Tate and Vallinder 1996.

likely (Gillman 2001, 18, citing Thomas and Isikoff 2000). Various law professors proclaimed in an advertisement in the *New York Times* that the Supreme Court had sacrificed a significant portion of its institutional legitimacy through its ruling in *Bush v. Gore*.[2] It is difficult to imagine how a set of circumstances could arise that would constitute a greater threat to the legitimacy of the Supreme Court than its (so-called self-inflicted) involvement in settling the presidential election in Florida and therefore for the nation.

Yet things are not always as they seem. It turns out that the available evidence is that the Court's involvement in the election did *not* damage its legitimacy. In a comparison of data from a survey conducted at the height of the controversy with survey data from 1995 and 1987, Gibson, Caldeira, and Spence (2003a) found no evidence whatsoever that the Court's legitimacy took a dip owing to its decision. Other scholars report similar findings; for instance, Price and Romantan (2004, 953, emphasis added) draw the following conclusion from their research: "On the whole our findings are consistent with the hypothesis that the election—even with the vituperative disputes in its wake—served to *boost* public attachment to American political institutions."[3] Many academic understandings of the impact of *Bush v. Gore* seem to be considerably off the mark.

How is it that the United States Supreme Court avoided any harmful consequences of the election imbroglio? Again, Gibson, Caldeira, and Spence (2003a) have proffered an answer: the theory of positivity bias. According to this theory, discussed more completely below, anything that causes people to pay attention to courts—even controversies—winds up reinforcing institutional legitimacy through exposure to the legitimizing symbols associated with law and courts. The theory suggests a bias in favor of developing positive feelings for the institution, even during conflicts, and even among losers in such conflicts. While there are many elements to this theory, its central prediction is that legal controversies tend to reinforce judicial legitimacy by teaching the lesson that courts are different from the other institutions of the American democracy, and are therefore worthy of respect.

Does the theory of positivity bias apply to confirmation hearings? No one knows, and it is therefore the purpose of this research to test the theory in that context. Specifically, our objectives in this book are to assess the hypothesis that confirmation hearings are not injurious to institu-

[2] On 13 January 2001, 585 law professors placed an advertisement in the *New York Times* condemning the Court's decision in *Bush v. Gore* as illegitimate. The advertisement, as well as much additional material and criticism, can be found at *http://www.the-rule-of-law.com* (accessed 12/7/2001).

[3] See also Yates and Whitford 2002; Kritzer 2001, 2005; Gillman 2001; Nicholson and Howard 2003.

tional legitimacy, owing to the fact that increased exposure to the judicial process, whatever the circumstances and even when citizens are displeased, results in collateral exposure to the symbols of judicial legitimacy, thereby tending to reinforce rather than undermine institutional support. As Gibson, Caldeira, and Baird (1998, 356) explain: "Generally, to be aware of a court is to be supportive of it. This positivity bias may be associated with exposure to the legitimizing symbols that all courts so assiduously promulgate."

This theory of positivity bias relies heavily upon the preexisting attitudes people hold toward the United States Supreme Court, and in particular on theories of institutional legitimacy and what some refer to as "diffuse support." Social scientists now generally agree that few forms of political capital are as useful to political institutions as legitimacy, and no institution is more dependent upon legitimacy than the judiciary. The conventional view is that courts have neither the power of the purse nor of the sword and are therefore dependent upon the voluntary compliance that typically springs from legitimacy. But the truth is that, however useful legitimacy may be to courts, no political institution could be effective without some mechanism for inducing citizens to believe that accepting their policy outputs, even disagreeable ones, is the right thing to do (Tyler 1990, 2006). Indeed, it is perhaps not hyperbole to claim that the concept of legitimacy has become one of the most important building blocks of contemporary theories of institutional stability and efficacy.

But how is it that events come to shape attitudes toward institutions? Many assume such orientations are learned early in life, and are obdurate and resistant to change. Fortunately, some research exists that is directly relevant to the question of how citizens update their views toward institutions like the Supreme Court.

Changes in Attitudes toward Judicial Institutions

From the initial empirical studies of legitimacy came the view that beliefs about institutions were inculcated early in the life-cycle, perhaps even in adolescence, and changed little over time (hence the great interest in research on political socialization—see, for example, Caldeira 1977). The understanding that public attitudes toward institutional legitimacy are highly resistant to change, however, seems no longer tenable.[4] While be-

[4] We equate several terms in this book: institutional legitimacy, diffuse support, and institutional loyalty. This is the same concept Caldeira and Gibson (1992) refer to as "institutional support." For a full explication of the conceptual and theoretical foundations of this concept, see the discussion in Caldeira and Gibson (1992, 636–42). For a recent review, see Gibson 2008c.

liefs and values acquired early in life may shape perceptions and evaluations of institutional outputs to some degree, legitimacy is nonetheless not immune to forces of change. We know, for instance, that the views of African Americans toward the United States Supreme Court evolved over time from strong support to considerable suspicion (Gibson and Caldeira 1992). We also know that attitudes are to some degree responsive to policy outputs, be it through highly salient decisions (e.g., Grosskopf and Mondak 1998; Gibson, Caldeira, and Spence 2003a) or through decisions with particular local relevance (e.g., Hoekstra 2003). Indeed, the very theory upon which so many studies of legitimacy rely (Easton's theory of diffuse support) acknowledges that sustained disappointment with the outputs of an institution can in the long-term empty the "reservoir of goodwill." Like interpersonal trust and loyalty, a single incident may not destroy a relationship, but repeated violations of expectations over time can entirely deplete loyalty. Few social scientists today believe that support for political institutions is impervious to influence from institutional performance or exogenous shocks and events.

What we do *not* know, however, is whether/why/how/under what conditions change takes place. Did, for instance, the controversies over the Bork and Thomas nominations to the United States Supreme Court have a lasting effect on public perceptions of the institution? We do not know. Moreover, it is even unclear from the research literature whether sizeable short-term reactions to individual judicial decisions have lasting effects (Grosskopf and Mondak 1998). As we have noted, from available evidence it seems that the United States Supreme Court may actually have enhanced its institutional legitimacy via its ruling in *Bush v. Gore* (e.g., Gibson, Caldeira, and Spence 2003a), but even that conclusion is based only on a comparison of aggregate statistics over time, and some recent evidence (which we present below) suggests that the Court's legitimacy has surrendered any gains it might have made from the disputed presidential election of 2000. *When it comes to the question of how legitimacy is created, maintained, and destroyed, social scientists have some theories and conjectures, but precious little data, and scant understanding of processes of opinion updating and change.*

There are many good reasons why we know so little about the dynamics of change, but perhaps the most exculpatory is that longitudinal data are woefully scarce. Consider the data most widely used to understand changing attitudes toward the United States Supreme Court: Apart from one-shot surveys, scholars rely on aggregate time series data from the General Social Survey (measuring confidence in the leaders of the Supreme Court—e.g., Caldeira 1986; Durr, Martin, and Wolbrecht 2000; Ura and Wohlfarth, with Sill 2007); some small collections of individual surveys conducted over time (e.g., our data from 1987, 1995, 2001, and 2005);

a handful of before and after media polls (e.g., Grosskopf and Mondak 1998) and short-term time series (e.g., Kritzer 2001); simulations and mathematical models (e.g., Mondak and Smithey 1997); and a tiny number of studies (outside the laboratory/campus, that is) that directly assess individual-level change (e.g., Tanenhaus and Murphy 1981; Hoekstra 2003). Of course, the major impediment to panel studies of individual-level stability and change lies in the unwillingness of most scholars (and funders) to mount t_1 surveys *prior to* important events taking place. Change can only be assessed when baseline data are available, which means that measurements must be taken well in advance of highly salient controversies. Unlike the periodicity of elections, the events that shape institutional legitimacy occur irregularly and are often difficult to predict in advance. Hence, data and knowledge deficits are enormous when it comes to understanding how legitimacy waxes and wanes.

The purpose of this book is therefore specifically to test hypotheses about the causes and consequences of changes in attitudes toward the United States Supreme Court. Based on a three-wave nationally representative panel survey, this project is centered around the controversy over the nomination of Judge Samuel Alito to the U.S. Supreme Court. Confirmation fights are valuable for testing theories of change because they provide a fecund opportunity to understand how citizens revise and update their attitudes toward the Supreme Court and its institutional legitimacy.

Our contention is that these confirmation processes "wake up" dormant attitudes toward law and courts in the United States by providing a salient window into the operation of the Supreme Court. To take just a simple example, the theory of mechanical jurisprudence—according to which, judges make decisions not on the basis of their ideologies but rather strictly according to the syllogisms of *stare decisis*—is placed under strain during confirmation hearings since nearly all actors focus (to at least some degree) on the ideology of the nominee. Debates are certainly clouded by confused discussions over "judicial activism and restraintism," but few close observers of the process doubt that ideologies are important. Thus, the central legitimizing symbols upon which the Court relies—its impartiality and its strict adherence to the law—are potentially compromised during politicized confirmation processes. Consequently, although confirmation battles have been rare in recent American politics (Epstein et al. 2003, 352–58), when they occur, they provide a telling opportunity for understanding how citizen attitudes toward courts are formed and shaped.

Typically, courts are thought to be relatively low salience institutions, and the attitudes of people reflect heavily their basic and more general values (e.g., support for democratic institutions and processes, including minoritarian institutions like the Supreme Court; see Caldeira and Gibson 1995). When a flood of new information becomes available—as is true of politicized confirmation hearings—citizens must somehow incorporate the new information into existing belief systems.[5] The purpose of this study is thus to determine how citizens "update" their views of the Supreme Court on the basis of exposure to highly salient and most likely partisan confirmation disputes.

Although the data necessary to investigate change are rarely available, some recent theoretical advances make it propitious for launching a major new inquiry into institutional legitimacy. The theory of positivity bias has much to say about how events shape public assessments of the judiciary.

The Theory of Positivity Bias

What theories are useful for understanding processes of opinion change when it comes to the United States Supreme Court? As we have developed it, the theory of institutional loyalty and positivity bias suggests that standing commitments to an institution generate a bias in expectations and perceptions of confirmation struggles that predispose people to accept judicial nominees. Because the theory of positivity bias is so central to this project, we consider it in some detail

What is positivity bias?

As Gibson, Caldeira, and Spence (2003a) explain it, positivity bias is a frame through which contemporary political conflicts are judged. In their theory, the process goes something like the following. People become attentive to courts in the context of policy controversies (e.g., *Bush v. Gore*) or events like confirmation hearings. In such circumstances, judicial symbols proliferate—in part because elites and interest groups realize the power of such symbols and attempt to manipulate them—so it is impossible for attentive citizens to avoid exposure to them.[6]

[5] For instance, Gimpel and Wolpert (1996) report that fully 95 percent of the American people had an opinion about whether Clarence Thomas should be appointed to the Supreme Court.

[6] Gimpel and Ringel (1995, 146) advance a quite contrary hypothesis: "The more one knows about a nominee, the more one is likely to disapprove of him or her." This conjecture is based on the finding that opposition to a nominee tends to focus on policy disagreements, and that knowledge generally produces more awareness of the policy positions of candidates. (On negativity bias—the argument that displeasure with Court opinions has greater consequences for institutional attitudes than pleasure—see Grosskopf and Mondak 1998.) While this may be so, their argument discounts another extremely important consequence of exposure to courts: As people pay attention to salient judicial events, they become ex-

Legitimizing symbols likely activate preexisting loyalty toward the institution (where it exists), as well as reinforce the understanding that courts are different from other political institutions. Consequently, although policy concerns may have provided the initial impetus for attention to a court, a second dimension, which we term "judiciousness" (Gibson and Caldeira 2006), is often activated and, for some, becomes the dominant frame for judging the events.

Caldeira and Gibson (1995) further suggest that the legitimacy of courts is *not* undermined by the disagreeable opinions issued by the institutions. This is in part related to the ability to shirk responsibility for decisions by reference to the dictates of precedent. If more knowledgeable people are more likely to accept the theory of *stare decisis* and mechanical jurisprudence, just as they are more likely to be attentive to courts, then it follows that they are also more likely to be persuaded by the justices' denials of responsibility for the decision. This argument stands in sharp contrast to the position of Grosskopf and Mondak 1998, who hypothesize a strong negativity bias in how citizens react to Supreme Court opinions. Such a bias implies that citizens hold the justices accountable for undesirable decisions. The extremely high level of legitimacy the Supreme Court enjoys (and has enjoyed for several decades—see Gibson 2007) seems to be incompatible with the Grosskopf/Mondak theory of negativity.

Is positivity bias associated with any substantive views of the judicial process?

We believe that positivity bias is closely connected to the view that courts are different from other political institutions, and that judicial decision making is largely a nonpolitical process. This conception is quite similar to what Scheb and Lyons refer to as the "myth of legality," by which they mean "the belief that judicial decisions are based on autonomous legal principles" and "that cases are decided by application of legal rules formulated and applied through a politically and philosophically neutral process of legal reasoning" (Scheb and Lyons 2000, 929).[7] We hypothesize that those characterized by strong loyalty to courts tend to subscribe more

posed to the potent legitimizing symbols that tend to define courts as nonpolitical institutions worthy of respect and deference. Perhaps the findings of Gimpel and Ringel are peculiar to the extreme cases they study (Bork and Thomas).

[7] In referring to this as a "myth" we are only deferring to the term of art that has emerged in the literature (e.g., Baird and Gangl 2006). We suspect that most political scientists view legalistic depictions of Supreme Court decision making as generally empirically inaccurate, but we are not required in this analysis to accept or reject any particular view about how decisions *actually get made* on the Court.

strongly to the myth of legality, and therefore are more likely to view courts as relatively distinct, non-political institutions.

How does positivity bias arise?

Our understanding of the origins of positivity bias begins by positing that citizens do *not* naturally differentiate between the judiciary and the other branches of government. That courts are special and different must be learned. For example, long ago, Casey (1974) demonstrated that the more one knows about law and courts, the *less* realistic are perceptions of judicial decision (i.e., the more one is likely to believe in the theory of mechanical jurisprudence). Something about being exposed to information about courts contributes to people embracing this traditional mythology of judicial decision making (Scheb and Lyons 2000; Brisbin 1996). Thus, those most ignorant about politics—and with little exposure to judicial politics—are likely to hold views of courts and other political institutions that are quite similar: Courts are not seen as special and unique.[8]

Exposure to legitimizing judicial symbols reinforces the process of distinguishing courts from other political institutions. The message of these powerful symbols is that "courts are different," and owing to these differences, courts are worthy of more respect, deference, and obedience—in short, legitimacy. Because courts use nonpolitical processes of decision making (and since the American people do not necessarily approve of the decision-making procedures common to political institutions—Hibbing and Theiss-Morse 1995, 2002), and since judicial institutions associate themselves with symbols of impartiality and insulation from ordinary political pressures, those more exposed to courts come to accept the "myth of legality."

This process of social learning explains why citizens who are more aware of and knowledgeable about courts tend to adopt less realistic views of how these institution make decisions and operate (e.g., Scheb and Lyons 2000). For instance, Hibbing and Theiss-Morse (1995) have shown that greater awareness of the Supreme Court leads to *more* support for it, whereas greater awareness of the Congress is associated with *less* support for that institution. Kritzer and Voelker (1998) offer a similar argument. Caldeira and Gibson (1992, 1995) have shown in several contexts that greater awareness of judicial institutions is related to a greater willingness to extend legitimacy to courts. Gibson, Caldeira, and Baird (1998) have confirmed this finding in research in roughly twenty

[8] This conjecture is certainly true of many countries other than the United States, as in the former East Germany, for instance (see Markovits 1995). See also Walker 2006.

countries. Something about being exposed to the institution increases support for it, and there is apparently something unique about exposure to judicial institutions.

But does this mean that Court legitimacy is immutable?

We do not use positivity theory to imply that the Supreme Court can never under any circumstances lose its legitimacy. We can imagine that a sustained series of unpopular decisions could alienate multiple, successive constituencies, resulting in a precipitous decline in support for the Court, coupled with growing support for altering the structure and the function of the institution.

Our contention, however, is that the effects of popular and unpopular decisions are asymmetrical. Popular decisions generate unadulterated support for the Court, just as they do for any institution. But the effects of unpopular decisions are discounted, both by processes of shirking and by association with the legitimizing symbols of judicial power. We acknowledge that the decline of institutional legitimacy could become a nonlinear, cascading process in the sense that as the Court's reservoir of support becomes shallower, the impact of unpopular decisions grows. We know of no such cascade in American history, however.[9] Our objective in this book is to determine whether politicized confirmation processes can have a delegitimizing effect on the Supreme Court by providing an image of the Court incompatible with the processes undergirding positivity theory.

How does positivity bias influence perceptions of decisions and events?

A positivity bias is actually little more than a frame through which events are perceived and evaluated (on framing, see Druckman 2004). "Issue framing effects refer to situations where, by emphasizing a subset of potentially relevant considerations, a speaker leads individuals to focus on these considerations when constructing their opinions" (Druckman 2004,

[9] In all of our thinking about these processes, we are much influenced by Roosevelt's attacks on the Supreme Court in the 1930s. If an enormously popular president, stimulated to action by a continuous string of unpopular and crippling Supreme Court decisions, cannot succeed in changing the Court, it is difficult to imagine a scenario in which such attacks would succeed. At the same time, however, Gibson and Caldeira (1992) point to declining support for the Supreme Court among some segments of the African American community from roughly the Warren Court era to the Rehnquist Court, so clearly a diminution of Court support is possible. Gaining a greater understanding of the processes of change in Court support is precisely the objective of this book.

672). Framing is a process by which the salience or accessibility of different criteria or dimensions by which an event or case might be judged varies according to preexisting characteristics of the individual. A stimulus activates a frame, and the frame influences how the world is perceived and judged. Elites often compete in proffering frames for the mass public (e.g., Sniderman and Theriault 2004), which typically results in alternative frames being available in the marketplace. Framing effects are not inevitable (Druckman 2004), preexisting attitudes do not always exist, and it is never easy to predict which particular frames will become dominant, but the battle for public opinion is often (if not typically) a battle of one frame against another.

Confirmation battles provide a prime example of competing frames.[10] On one hand, the frame of legality is advanced, typically by proponents of the nominee. Their argument is that the nominee ought to be judged primarily (if not exclusively) on legalistic criteria like judiciousness. On occasion, the opposition will engage the judiciousness battle, but more likely is an attempt to substitute a frame defined by political considerations such as ideology, partisanship, and policy. Which frame comes to dominate depends in part on the nominee and the elements of the specific context, but also in part on whether citizens have preexisting commitments (loyalty) to the institution that can be activated. In the case of the United States Supreme Court, the outcome of a confirmation controversy depends in significant part on the degree to which citizens subscribe to the myth of legality, which is of course a central element of positivity bias. Figure 1 portrays these processes of positivity bias in schematic and stylized form.

For example, Nicholson and Howard (2003) provide a useful earlier effort to use framing theory to account for how the Americans viewed the Supreme Court's decision in *Bush v. Gore*. They analyze three competing frames for the decision: partisan, legal, and election. One of their more interesting findings is that the partisan frame (through which they tried to persuade their respondents that the Supreme Court's decision was made on the basis of partisanship and politics) failed entirely to influence the legitimacy of the Supreme Court, even though the election frame (stressing the role of the Supreme Court in bringing the election to an end) had some limited effect. Their research also strongly confirms Druckman's argument that scholars ought to focus on the conditions under

[10] In an extremely insightful paper, Sniderman and Theriault (2004) argue that research on framing is generally flawed because the typical research design does not employ alternative frames for events. In virtually all important political controversies, multiple, competing frames are typically proffered. As Sniderman and Theriault put (2004, 158), "[T]his whole body of studies on framing has gone terribly wrong by overlooking politics itself."

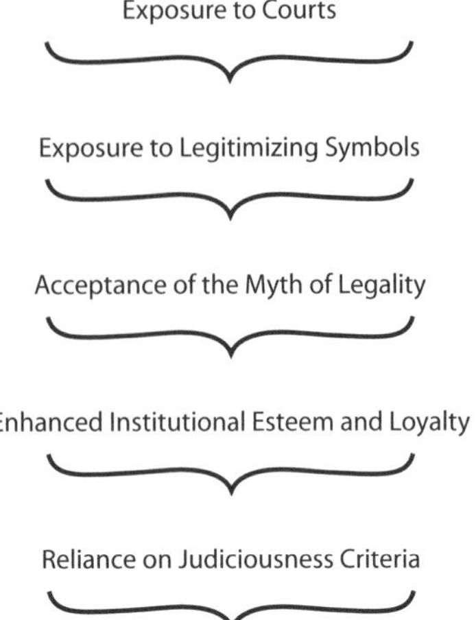

Figure 1.1. The Consequences of Positivity Bias

which issue frames are effective. Perhaps one such condition is related to whether the frame activates well-established, but often dormant, political beliefs and attitudes.

Whether positivity frames are able to override attempts to politicize confirmation processes is an important question both for theory and for the practical politics of confirmations.[11] The job of the successful nominee is to activate the legal rather than political frame through which ordinary citizens perceive and judge the confirmation process. We hypothesize that to the extent that legal expectations are satisfied, the influence of ideology, policy, and partisanship is minimized, which is typically the preferred strategy of policy-minded presidents.

Thus, a central hypothesis emerging from the theory of positivity frames is that preexisting institutional loyalty plays a crucial role in how confirmation processes are perceived and judged. Of course, facts and contexts are not unimportant; how people perceive the details of confirmation fights is crucial to the formation of their preferences. We hypothesize that loyalty interacts with events surrounding the confirmation, causing citizens with a sense of loyalty toward the Court to rely primarily upon criteria of judiciousness in judging the nominee. In contrast, those without a sense of institutional loyalty are likely to judge the confirmation process in terms of ordinary political criteria.

[11] This sentence should not be taken to mean that we believe that any nominations are anything but political. Presidents always seek to advance their political goals (whatever they may be at the moment) through their nominees to the Supreme Court. When we refer to the politicization of a process, we simply mean that some parties to the controversy attempt to substitute a political frame for a legal frame and thus to change the criteria (or dimensions) on which the process is judged.

Updating Processes: Theories of Individual-Level Change

Institutional loyalty provides a positivity frame through which confirmation events are perceived and judged. But that is not the end of the causal process: Instead, while preexisting attitudes shape perceptions of events, perceptions of events in turn influence attitudes. We propose that salient judicial events, like contentious confirmation processes, stoke hibernating attitudes, bringing them alive, and potentially changing them. Thus, while one portion of our analysis focuses on events as "dependent variables," another portion treats them as "independent variables" embedded within a theory of individual-level attitude change.

A theory of change must include two components. First, an understanding of cross-sectional differences is necessary. Such a theory provides an explanation of why citizens differ in their attitudes at any given point in time. For instance, Caldeira and Gibson (1995) have shown that the tendency to extend legitimacy to courts is in part a function of support for democratic values more generally. That theory has proven to be quite valuable in understanding and predicting individual difference in attitudes toward courts.

Second, a theory of *change* must also be grafted onto the cross-sectional theory. For instance, it is unlikely that changes in levels of legitimacy are due to alterations in support for democratic values inasmuch as the latter is usually thought to be formed early in life and to be resistant to change (e.g., Gibson 1995). The cross-sectional theory must identify causal factors that are themselves subject to exogenous influences.

Bendor, Diermeier, and Ting (2003) have proposed a simple but powerful theory that can be modified and made useful for understanding change in levels of legitimacy. The model posits that citizens are "adaptively rational," by which they mean that people are susceptible to basic processes of reinforcement learning. They then add "aspirations" to the model. Aspirations are essentially expectations against which experiences are measured; the relationship between expectations and experiences defines encounters as either successful and unsuccessful. Over time, aspirations adjust to experience. In short, "adaptation combines reinforcement learning and endogenous aspirations" (2003, 263).

Learning about the Supreme Court is a dynamic process involving the interaction of experiences and aspirations. Citizens hold expectations of judges and judicial institutions that interact with exposure to messages from the confirmation process.[12] To the extent that perceptions satisfy expectations, attitudes toward the institution are unlikely to change. Dis-

[12] As we note below, these expectations cannot be assumed but rather must be directly measured. And expectations of judges, of course, are well understood within the context of role theory (e.g., see Gibson 1981).

appointment, however, can be a powerful engine for change, especially to the extent that the disappointment emerges from the acceptance of a politicized confirmation frame. To the extent that people come to view nominees to the high bench as "politicians in robes," the distinctive, non-political character of the Supreme Court can be undermined, opening the door for reconsideration of loyalties toward the institution itself. Because challenges to nominees to the Supreme Court so often focus on ideology, partisanship, and highly realistic views about how the justices go about the business of making the law, these events have great potential to reshape attitudes toward courts.[13] The processes are without doubt complicated, involving interactions between preexisting attitudes and perceptual frames, the availability of highly salient alternative views of the operation of the judiciary, and poorly understood "tipping" processes when the presumption of judiciousness begins to quickly melt away. Whether attitudes toward the legitimacy of the institution change depends in part on the relationship between expectations and perceptions. Where dissatisfaction arises, its impact is strong because it threatens the view that courts are nonpolitical institutions. Thus, confirmation processes have considerable potential for reordering attitudes toward the U.S. Supreme Court. But only by measuring each of the concepts independently (loyalty, before and after, expectations, perceptions, beliefs about the process of judging, et cetera) can these complex causal relationships be unraveled.

Thus, to address the impact of the nomination processes on the legitimacy of law and courts requires a pre- and post-research design centered on a highly salient confirmation event. Such a design, on a somewhat limited and less-than-perfect basis, we implemented in conjunction with the nomination of Judge Alito to the Supreme Court (see appendix A for the methodological details of the survey). This book reports the results of those surveys.

Outlining the Chapters That Follow

We begin this analysis by confronting directly the oft-heard doubts about the relevance of a study of mass opinion when it comes to courts in general and confirmation debates in particular. Critics often contend that the American people know nothing about law and courts and therefore at-

[13] It is at this point that the Grosskopf and Mondak (1998) theory of negativity may be useful. We doubt that negativity bias has much to do with how people evaluate individual Court decisions. But when people are forced to rethink processes of decision making—indeed, the very function of the Supreme Court within the American political system—negative conclusions (e.g., that the institution is politicized) may indeed have the disproportionate influence of a negativity bias.

tempts to understand their views are both irrelevant and doomed to failure since the bulk of mass attitudes can be best described as random error. We present in chapter 2 evidence rebutting the conventional wisdom, relying on our confirmation survey, a similar survey in 2001, and the American National Election Surveys. We conclude from this chapter that the American mass public is vastly more informed about the Supreme Court than heretofore thought, and, therefore, that something can be learned by studying how Americans react to politicized confirmation processes.

Chapter 3 focuses on public attitudes prior to the Alito nomination. Here, we discuss in detail our theory of institutional loyalty, the predispositions that are so central to the theory of positivity bias. David Easton referred to institutional support as a "reservoir of goodwill," and theories of legitimacy ever since have stressed the importance of courts not having to attend slavishly to majority opinion. We offer our conceptualization of loyalty, as well as a measurement strategy that has served us well in the past. We contrast loyalty with the well-known measures of confidence in the leaders of the Court, as well as with other approaches to measuring institutional attitudes.

Following our earlier research, we also assess the degree to which support for the Supreme Court is grounded in ideological and partisan divisions within the American people. We find no evidence of a polarized mass public in the contemporary United States when it comes to fealty to the Supreme Court. Instead, support for the Court is more closely associated with general support for democratic institutions and processes, which is an important finding because it suggests that court support is relatively obdurate (since support for democratic values is a core political attitude for most Americans). This chapter largely focuses on the calm before the Alito storm, and provides the baseline data from which change in attitudes can be assessed.

We focus in chapter 4 on the Alito nomination itself. Our survey was in the field immediately after public testimony on the nomination ended, so we are able to examine in more detail than has been possible in the past the attentiveness of people to the process and their expectations and perceptions of it. Much in this chapter will be surprising to most readers—for instance, Judge Alito was seen on average as only slightly to the right of center on the ideological continuum, despite the fact that he promises to be one of the most conservative judges to sit on the High Bench in modern times. Most important, we use the confirmation fight to flesh out positivity theory, testing the hypothesis that preexisting support for the Court led to a predisposition to weight particular criteria heavily in assessing Judge Alito. We refer to this criterion as "judiciousness," and argue that those who would defeat a nominee must overcome a high barrier in convincing court supporters to rely more heavily on ideological factors in assessing a nominee. We also examine in this chapter the advertising campaigns for and against Alito's confirmation, based on a systematic analysis of data collected on the broadcasts sponsored by interest groups. We know of no other study of the role of the mass public in a confirmation process that is as comprehensive and theoretically grounded as this one.

The most innovative chapter in this book is undoubtedly chapter 5, for it is here that we actually assess change in attitudes. The simple hypothesis is that change in loyalty toward the Supreme Court is a function of perceptions of the degree of politicization of the confirmation process. For some respondents, the process rendered the "myth of legality" mythical, causing a diminution in support for the Court. For others, paying attention to the process was tantamount to taking a college-level course in the uniqueness of the judiciary in the American political system, and support for the institution was buoyed. Throughout this analysis, we make comparisons to the effect of controversial decisions on court support, considering in particular the fabled *Bush v. Gore* decision. With the possible exception of Hoekstra's analysis, no earlier research has been able to focus so thoroughly on individual-level change (which of course necessitates microlevel panel data), so this chapter makes a substantial empirical contribution to our understanding of positivity bias.

In the final chapter, we take a few steps away from the data and think somewhat more broadly about courts, democracy, and legitimacy. Here, we also outline what we consider to be the next research step for those interested in how understanding how institutional legitimacy is acquired and expended.

Thus, this analysis examines public attitudes and values prior to, during, and after the confirmation struggle, and treats institutional support as both an independent and dependent variable. In the final analysis, we present a new perspective on the importance of the American people for the performance of the country's judicial institutions.

CHAPTER TWO

Knowing about Courts

One of the old chestnuts of political science is that the American mass public is remarkably ignorant of courts, including the U.S. Supreme Court. For instance, an oft-cited survey in 1989 reported that 71 percent of the Americans could not name a single member of the Supreme Court; in contrast, 54 percent of the same sample was able to name the judge on the television show "The People's Court" (Judge Wapner; see Morin 1989). Similarly, a Zogby poll found that 77 percent of the American people were able to identify two of Snow White's Seven Dwarfs; only 24 percent could name two Supreme Court justices.[1] Evidence of this sort is typically used to document—and decry—the public's woeful levels of knowledge when it comes to the American judiciary.

Many important implications flow from the finding of widespread ignorance among the mass public. Some argue that analysts should therefore focus their energies mainly (if not exclusively) on the views and expectations of elite publics. Perhaps more politically significant are the oft-heard pleas to reduce the role of the mass public in selecting judges—whether in the election of judges in the states or in the process of nominating and confirming federal judges at the national level. In this view, if the American people are irretrievably ignorant of law and courts, elites—preferably legal elites—should be given the task of determining who should, and should not, be a judge. Thus, a panoply of crucial political considerations rides on the back of the empirical finding of mass ignorance.

From a more theoretical vantage, an important finding from earlier research is that knowing about high courts goes along with enhanced esteem for the judiciary (e.g., Gibson, Caldeira, and Baird 1998). This is a robust finding, since it is based on surveys conducted in about two dozen countries (see Gibson 2007b). From this perspective, low knowledge of courts is politically significant since it threatens the legitimacy of judicial institutions.

Even though widely accepted, the image of the American people as ignorant about courts rests upon a remarkably thin layer of empirical evidence. And, as we will demonstrate in the analysis in this chapter, the

[1] See http://www.zogby.com/Soundbites/ReadClips.dbm?ID=13498 (accessed 12/20/2006).

measurement approach used to document mass ignorance is itself seriously flawed. Because, as we have suggested, important theoretical and policy implications flow from our understanding of the political competence of the American people in this realm, it is crucial that the empirical record be thoroughly examined and evaluated.

Consequently, our purpose in this chapter is to revisit the question of the ignorance of the American mass public about the United States Supreme Court. In doing so, we rely primarily upon two data sets. The first is a nationally representative telephone survey conducted in early 2001 in the midst of the controversy over the Supreme Court's decision in *Bush v. Gore*. Because that survey most likely captures public knowledge of the Court at its apogee, we follow with a more extensive, nationally representative, three-wave panel study conducted in 2005–2006. The first interview in that panel (t_1, 2005) was conducted face-to-face; the follow-up interviews were via telephone during the debate over whether Judge Samuel Alito should be confirmed to the United States Supreme Court (t_2, 2006) and several months thereafter (t_3, 2006). We know of no other data bases that address the issue of knowledge of the nation's highest court in so thorough a fashion. (See appendixes 2.A and A for the details of these surveys.)

Our contributions here go considerably beyond the quality of the data on which we rely. By using closed-ended indicators of judicial knowledge, we take a different operational tack than have many previous researchers. In doing so, we follow an extensive body of literature indicating that knowledge is more reliably and validly measured using closed-ended multiple-choice questions (for a summary see Mondak 2006). Our empirical findings run deeply contrary to most extant research: the American people know orders of magnitude more about their Supreme Court than most other studies have documented. And, although knowledge of the Court was indeed particularly high during the litigation surrounding the disputed presidential election of 2000, our findings from the 2005 survey reveal only a slight diminution in the levels of information people hold about the Court. Moreover, levels of knowledge are quite stable over time and do not merely reflect information gained (and perhaps not retained) during salient judicial controversies. Empirical findings such as these have never before been reported.

We conclude by suggesting that the American people may be more competent than is ordinarily thought at performing the role in the socio-legal process assigned to them by democratic theory. Those who lampoon ordinary people for their supposed ignorance and who would rearrange the legal system to compensate for this perceived incompetence ought, we submit, to carefully consider our arguments and results.

Assessing Public Information about Law and Courts

A conversation with virtually any judge in the United States (and, in our experiences, all judges in Europe) about whether judges ought to be elected inevitably elicits the view that the American people know much too little about judges, law, and courts to be able to exercise their democratic duty as electors.[2] Evidence is often marshaled to document the woeful levels of knowledge ordinary people have about things judicial and legal, and the conclusion typically drawn is that the legal system ought to be more insulated from that ignorance. Based on the belief that the American people are irretrievably ignorant when it comes to law and courts, a variety of interest groups have taken on the charge of limiting the role of the mass public in the legal system.[3]

Some have situated this critique of citizen ignorance within the larger context of intellectual and academic elitism. Lupia (2006), for instance, argues that contemporary criticisms of mass political ignorance are misplaced because research tends to focus on measuring what scholars think citizens *ought to know*, rather than what is practically *necessary to know* about politics. Thus, he asserts (2006, 22): "Until critics can offer a transparent, credible, and replicable explanation of why a particular set of facts is necessary for a particular set of socially valuable outcomes, they should remain humble when assessing the competence of others."

Another important voice in dissent is that of Caldeira and McGuire (2005), who argue that public knowledge of courts is more nuanced and complicated than typically thought. For instances, citizens tend to know about court decisions of local interest and those that directly affect them (e.g., Hoekstra 2000, 2003); highly salient controversies often penetrate the consciousness of the American people (e.g., contentious battles over nominations to the U.S. Supreme Court—see Caldeira and Smith 1996, and Gimpel and Wolpert 1996); and most black Americans know that Clarence Thomas is a justice on the U.S. Supreme Court. Moreover, some portion of public ignorance of courts is surely a direct function of court-made policies that inhibit the flow of relevant political information about judges and courts, as in the pre-*Minnesota v. White* (2002) prohibition

[2] Thus, Kritzer (2001, 34) remarks that political scientists "have long documented the minimal knowledge most citizens have about the Court." Perhaps the most comprehensive investigation of the knowledge of the American people is that of Delli Carpini and Keeter 1996.

[3] Many interest groups and organizations seek to minimize the role of ordinary people in the selection and retention of judges at both the state and federal levels. We count in this group the Brennan Center at New York University, the interest group Justice at Stake Campaign (see http://www.justiceatstake.org/ [accessed 3/9/2007]), as well as the American Bar Association.

on making policy pronouncements in campaigns for public office.[4] Thus, blanket indictments of the American people for knowing little or nothing about law and courts are far too simplistic.[5]

As we have noted, one consequence of the belief that the American people are congenitally ill-informed is that many elites question whether ordinary people should play much role in the nomination and confirmation of justices to the U.S. Supreme Court. Perhaps more significant is that, according to positivity theory (e.g., Gibson, Caldeira, and Spence 2003a), ignorance of the judiciary is associated with the failure to distinguish courts from ordinary political institutions (see Mondak et al. 2007), and the failure to acknowledge that courts are in some sense nonpolitical institutions undermines judicial legitimacy. Following our reconsideration of the empirical evidence on knowledge, we will have more to say about this theory, but a considerable body of research now documents the relationship between being knowledgeable about courts and extending those institutions respect and legitimacy (e.g., Gibson, Caldeira, and Baird 1998). Thus, if the conventional wisdom about Americans' political ignorance is wrong, myriad consequences for the structure and function of the judiciary follow. The empirical question of mass ignorance therefore has broad implications for normative theories of democracy and the American judiciary.

Empirical Evidence of Mass Ignorance

The Conventional Wisdom

How ignorant *are* the American people? A highly influential survey finding is the claimed inability of the American people to identify the (then) Chief Justice of the United States, William Rehnquist. The American National Election Study (ANES), for instance, regularly asks the following question: "Now we have a set of questions concerning various public figures. We want to see how much information about them gets out to the public from television, newspapers and the like." What about "William

[4] Of that situation, Justice Marshall observed: "the greater power to dispense with elections altogether does not include the lesser power to conduct elections under conditions of *state-imposed voter ignorance*. If the State chooses to tap the energy and the legitimizing power of the democratic process, it must accord the participants in that process . . . the First Amendment rights that attach to their roles." *Republican Party v. White*, 122 S. Ct. 2528 (2002), at 2541 (quoting *Renne v. Geary*, 501 U.S. 312, 349) (emphasis added) (1991) (Marshall, J., dissenting) (alteration in the original).

[5] Hojnacki and Baum (1992) demonstrate that, even in the 1980s in Ohio, at least some judicial races were quite salient to voters (e.g., almost as salient as the race for the U.S. Senate; 927).

Rehnquist—What job or political office does he NOW hold?" This question is embedded in a list of other items asking about leaders such as Dennis Hastert, Dick Cheney, and Tony Blair. In the postelection survey of 2004, only 27.9 percent of the respondents correctly identified Rehnquist as the Chief Justice, a figure that compares dismally to Dick Cheney (84.5 percent) and Tony Blair (62.0 percent), although it is considerably higher than the percentage able to identify Dennis Hastert as Speaker of the House (9.3 percent). If the American people cannot get such basic and elementary facts right, the elitist argument goes, how can they be trusted to select their political and legal leaders and hold them accountable for their actions?[6]

Beyond the ANES data are a number of studies by the mass media and interest groups, all of which point to low levels of information and knowledge.[7] For instance, according to a survey conducted by Findlaw (2005), only 43 percent of the American people can name at least one justice who was serving on the U.S. Supreme Court at the time.[8] Unfortunately, however, details on the methodologies of such studies are rarely presented—for example, it is not clear whether these results are in response to an open-ended or closed-ended question (see http://public.findlaw.com/ussc/122005survey.html [accessed 10/22/2006])—rendering suspect the value of such polls.

In general, the research literature on the legal and judicial knowledge of Americans is not particularly robust. By any accounting, the recall approach, on which so much rides, suffers from a number of striking flaws and limitations. Open-ended questions requiring the recall of factual information are among the most demanding measures of political knowledge (Lupia 2006). No frame of reference is provided. Or worse, as in the entire ANES survey, the interview is defined by a partisan/political context—and therefore we wonder whether the frame of partisan politics makes it difficult for some to switch from that context to a single individual associated with the judicial system.

But these are not the only limitations plaguing this approach to measuring political knowledge. Most worrisome, in one instance, the ANES re-

[6] It is fairly common to find law review articles that cite the ANES findings as evidence of the deplorable ignorance of the American people about the judicial process. For examples, see Herzog (2005), Gewirtzman (2005), and Somin (2004).

[7] For a collection of polls on knowledge of the Supreme Court, see William Ford's blog at http://www.elsblog.org/the_empirical_legal_studi/2006/02/supreme_court_a.html (accessed 12/20/2006).

[8] According to the survey, Sandra Day O'Connor is the most widely recognized justice, with 27 percent of the sample able to recall her name. Chief Justice Roberts was recalled by only 16 percent of the respondents. See http://public.findlaw.com/ussc/122005survey.html (accessed 10/22/2006).

quired its interviewers to code the accuracy of the respondents' answers to the knowledge question during the interview itself,[9] apparently using highly simplistic and extremely literalist criteria.[10] Thus, if one replies that William Rehnquist is "the Chief Justice of the United States Supreme Court," the interviewer would, according to ANES coding rules, record the answer as "correct," even though the official title of the leader of the United States Supreme Court is the "Chief Justice of the United States." References to Rehnquist as a Supreme Court judge who is the head honcho or main guy or the main one are,[11] according to ANES rules, scored as incorrect.[12] According to these strict procedures, only 10.5 percent of the respondents "correctly" identified Rehnquist in the 2000 ANES.[13]

In addition to the closed-ended responses, however, the interviewers recorded the respondents' verbatim answers in all years except 2004. These responses are of some interest for assessing the degree of knowledge people have about politics and the national judiciary. For instance, if one were to accept answers in the 2000 ANES that identify Rehnquist as a Supreme Court judge/justice without reference to his role as chief justice, the figures change dramatically. An additional 22.5 percent of the respon-

[9] According to an e-mail communication with Pat Luevano of ANES (January 31, 2007), in nearly all surveys since 1986, the ANES interviewers were required to record the verbatim responses of the interviewee. These replies were then coded as correct or incorrect by either SRC or ANES staff. In 2004, however, in-the-field coding by interviewers took place. The coding instructions were: "We are strict regarding acceptable answers: We will accept ONLY 'Chief Justice'—'Justice' alone is definitely *NOT* acceptable. (The court must be 'the Supreme Court'—'Chief Justice of the Court' won't do. Note: applies only if R would specifically say 'the Court,' a rare phrasing, rather than 'the Supreme Court'). If unsure whether correct, code as best you can and record R's response as a remark." According to Luevano, very little verbatim material was recorded in 2004, so it is not possible to review the coding decisions of the interviewers.

[10] Jeffrey Mondak in a personal communication first suggested to us that there might be considerable coding problems in the ANES data (see also Mondak 2001).

[11] We are precluded by the terms of our agreement with ANES granting us access to the verbatim open-ended responses from directly quoting any specific replies from the respondents.

[12] Moreover, the interviewers are told that the ⌊DK KEY IS NOT ALLOWED FOR THIS QUESTION⌋, but in fact large numbers of respondents are recorded as making "no attempt to guess," and virtually every respondent has successfully claimed a de facto "don't know" reply prior to hearing the Rehnquist question. Thus, with this approach to measuring knowledge, error variance is introduced because the respondents differ in their understandings of the availability of the "don't know" option with any given question.

[13] For obvious reasons, we focus in this analysis on the coding of knowledge about the U.S. Supreme Court. Similar issues arise with scoring as correct and incorrect replies about the other political leaders asked about in the survey. ANES has released an important report on this matter: see http://www.electionstudies.org/announce/newsltr/20080324PoliticalKnowledgeMemo.pdf (accessed June 13, 2008).

dents fall into this expanded knowledgeable category.[14] If replies identifying Rehnquist simply as a judge are counted as correct, this percentage grows even more. It is still true that a majority of the respondents cannot say what Rehnquist's job is in response to the open-ended query, but the way the ANES codes this variable significantly underestimates the knowledge of the American people.[15] Indeed, by our analysis of the open-ended ANES data, 71.8 percent of the respondents the ANES coded as giving incorrect answers (this excludes the sizeable portion of respondents saying they don't know Rehnquist's job) could in fact be considered to have given "incomplete or nearly correct" answers. Of these 349 respondents, 91 identified Rehnquist as a Supreme Court justice, 54 as a Supreme Court judge, and for 61 the only recorded reply was "Supreme Court." Thus, what ANES typically codes as incorrect answers are not wildly erroneous replies (e.g., Rehnquist is a Senator from Idaho), but instead are incorrect only because they do not satisfy the extremely rigid requirements of the coding in that survey. In our view, the ANES data are so problematic that we believe only the simplest and grossest inferences can be drawn from these data.[16]

Moreover, from the more general vantage of survey research, open-ended questions such as these constitute rigorous and difficult tests of public knowledge. A more reasonable, perhaps fairer, approach is to determine whether people can *recognize* the names of justices, rather than whether citizens can be *remember* their names (e.g., Tedin and Murray 1979).[17] After all, it is difficult to envisage an actual political scenario in which it would be necessary for citizens to be able to recall a judge's name without any prompting. The external validity (or "mundane real-

[14] This analysis is based upon our categorization of the open-ended replies collected by the interviewers. Dave Howell at ANES was extremely helpful in providing the data necessary to conduct the analysis reported here.

[15] It is not clear to us how seriously the interviewers took the instruction to record the verbatim responses, since there seems to be considerable variability across respondents in the amount of detail recorded. Consequently, we doubt that these open-ended data can be subjected to a sustained, serious analysis, even if one can have substantial confidence in the general conclusion that the ANES estimates of political knowledge are quite biased.

[16] Thus, for example, we are prepared to accept the conclusion that more Americans can recall the name of the vice president than the chief justice of the United States.

[17] Prior and Lupia (2006) show that open-ended measures of knowledge significantly underestimate the true levels of information within the mass public. Their experiments reveal that the respondents registers much higher scores if a) an incentive for giving the correct answer is provided (thereby encouraging the respondents to devote more energy to trying to answer the questions), and b) knowledge is reconceptualized not as the ability to recall facts from memory, but rather as the ability to find information by consulting reliable sources.

ism")[18] of the ANES measure is low in the sense that the question seems to posit a set of circumstances that are quite foreign to the experiences of most Americans (see Lupia 2006). Imagine, for example, the following conversation among three voters.

> VOTER 1: The Supreme Court is out of control, what with its decision to give Bush the presidency, the threats to a woman's right to choose whether to have an abortion, et cetera.
> VOTER 2: Yes, I agree. I bet it has to do with the chief justice, who I think is a staunch Republican.
> VOTER 1: Yeah, I agree. What *is* his name? I can't remember.
> VOTER 2: Neither can I, but the guy ought to be impeached.
> VOTER 3: I think his name is Rehnquist, Ringgold, or something like that.
> VOTER 1: Maybe. But whatever his name is, we need a new judge on the Supreme Court. I guess I'll have to vote for the Democrats next time so as to get a better Supreme Court.

It is difficult for us to see that this conversation would be any more politically meaningful were the discussants able to remember the name of the chief justice. And, after all, even Richard Nixon, as he was about to nominate him to the Supreme Court, had difficulty remembering the assistant attorney general's name, referring to him instead as "Renchburg," at least according to John Dean (2001)!

Thus, the principal methodology used to document the ignorance of the American people is flawed in both conceptualization and operationalization. Even more worrisome is the way in which the ANES implements these measures. We need another approach to measuring knowledge of the judiciary.

2001 Closed-Ended Results

Even were the ANES coding scheme improved, we would have serious reservations about the utility of open-ended questions that ask respondents to recall information in the context of an interview which, we contend, never has a real-world political context. More useful approaches rely upon closed-ended multiple-choice questions (see Mondak 2001; Tedin and Murray 1979). Our 2001 national survey adopted such a measurement strategy.

[18] Aronson et al. (1990) distinguish between "experimental realism" (the content of an experiment being realistic to the subjects so that they take the task seriously) and "mundane realism" (the similarity of the experimental context and stimuli to events likely to occur in the real world—in short, verisimilitude). An open-ended question of the type used by ANES seems to profit from neither type of realism, but especially not from mundane realism.

In our 2001 survey, conducted in the midst of the dispute over the Supreme Court's decision in *Bush v. Gore,* we asked several questions about knowledge of the U.S. Supreme Court. For instance, we queried our respondents about whether they thought any of the justices on the Supreme Court is an African American, and, in a separate question, whether they knew if any of the justices is a female. In both instances, *nearly 80 percent of the respondents* (79.7 and 79.1 percent, respectively) correctly responded that at least one of the justices is black and that at least one of the justices is female. Only a very small portion of the American people believes that there is no woman or no African American on the Court.

Of course, when asked in this fashion, respondents can easily profit from guessing the correct answer.[19] Consequently, we followed both of these questions with a test of whether the respondents could recognize the name of a specific justice. In the instance of the African American justice, we asked the respondents to identify an African American from among the following list of names: Clarence Thomas, Nathaniel R. Jones (judge, U.S. Court of Appeals for the Sixth Circuit), and Damon Keith (judge, U.S. Court of Appeals for the Sixth Circuit).[20] For the question about female justices, we asked about Sandra Day O'Connor, Patricia Wald (chief judge, retired, U.S. Court of Appeals for the District of Columbia), and Karen J. Williams (judge, U.S. Court of Appeals for the Fourth Circuit).[21] To what degree are Americans able to identify black and female justices sitting on the Supreme Court?

The top portion of table 2.1 reports our findings regarding an African American on the Court. A large majority of the respondents recognizes that there is an African American on the Court (79.7 percent), and most of these people (88.4 percent) identify Clarence Thomas as the African

[19] Franklin, Kosaki, and Kritzer (1993, 13) assert that, in their survey, little evidence can be found that respondents are giving socially desirable answers to their questions (e.g., claiming to know that the Court has decided an issue when it has not).

[20] We randomly varied the order of presentation of these three names. Order of presentation is not significantly related to correctly identifying Clarence Thomas as the African American Supreme Court justice. Note that, on the basis of a review of the literature on testing (e.g., Tversky 1964), Mondak (2001) recommends that multiple-choice items use at least three alternatives. He also concludes from a review of the testing literature that using more than three possible responses is, on balance, of little value.

[21] These stimuli were also randomly varied. A chi-square test of the difference in correctly identifying Sandra Day O'Connor is significant at .002, even though gamma is only .09. Across all respondents, when O'Connor was mentioned first, 60.3 percent of the respondents recognized her name; when she was mentioned second, the percentage giving a correct answer was 71.1 percent; and when hers was the last name presented, 66.2 percent recognized her as a female Supreme Court justice. Since there is no clear explanation for these results—and in light of the extremely weak relationship—we treat this finding as substantively insignificant.

American Supreme Court justice. Very significant minorities of Americans recognize Thomas's name, *even when they initially claimed not to know whether an African American sat on the Court* (see the first data column of the table).[22] For instance, 41.3 percent identify Clarence Thomas even though in response to the previous question they said that they thought there was no African American on the Court. Overall, 78.4 percent of Americans correctly identify Clarence Thomas as the African American Supreme Court justice (data not shown).[23]

Our findings concerning a woman on the Court are similar (see the lower portion of Table 2.1). Again, nearly 80 percent of the respondents claim to know that there is a woman on the Supreme Court, although the percentage able to identify Sandra Day O'Connor correctly is significantly smaller than the percentage able to identify Clarence Thomas. One obvious explanation of this finding is that some of the respondents were thinking of Ruth Bader Ginsberg when they answered our question about a female justice. Still, a large majority of those who responded that there is a woman on the Court recognized O'Connor's name, and, overall, 65.9 percent of all of the respondents identified Sandra Day O'Connor as a female justice on the Supreme Court (data not shown). The most important difference between the questions about African American and female justices is that those who did not know whether a woman is on the Court are generally unable to recognize Sandra Day O'Connor's name when questioned further, whereas Clarence Thomas is much more recognizable to all respondents.[24] Perhaps the ANES is simply asking its question about the wrong Supreme Court justice when it focuses on Rehnquist.[25]

The mere ability to identify a justice by name is not, we argue, a sufficiently rigorous test of knowledge (despite the emphasis in the literature on the inability of Americans to do this). Consequently, we queried our

[22] This finding seems consistent with the evidence of Prior and Lupia (2006) to the effect that when citizens expend greater effort in answering knowledge questions they tend to answer more questions correctly.

[23] No difference exists between the percentages of African Americans and whites who can identify Clarence Thomas.

[24] No difference exists between the percentages of men and women who can identify Sandra Day O'Connor.

[25] Although we do not want to engage in serious debate about which justice ought to be used in knowledge questions, we do recognize that some citizens most likely learn about the institution and its incumbents via processes of symbolic representation. We do not assume, however, that an African American knowing about Clarence Thomas is necessarily uninformed about the Court more generally, just as we do not assume that a resident of Arizona knows nothing further than that Rehnquist hails from that state. Indeed, symbolic representation may be useful precisely because it stimulates citizens to pay attention to an institution and learn more about how it functions.

TABLE 2.1.
Recognition of an African American and a Woman on the Supreme Court, 2001

Believes there is an African American on the Court		79.7 %
Recognizes Clarence Thomas	88.4 %	
Does not	11.6 %	
Total	100.0 %	
Believes there is no African American on the Court		5.3
Recognizes Clarence Thomas	41.3 %	
Does not	58.7 %	
Total	100.0 %	
Does not know if there is an African American on the Court		15.1
Recognizes Clarence Thomas	39.3 %	
Does not	60.7 %	
Total	100.0 %	
Total		100.0 %
N		1418
Believes there is a woman on the Court		79.1 %
Recognizes Sandra Day O'Connor	77.2 %	
Does not	22.8 %	
Total	100.0 %	
Believes there is no woman on the Court		5.9
Recognizes Sandra Day O'Connor	16.9 %	
Does not	83.1 %	
Total	100.0 %	
Does not know if there is a woman on the Court		15.0
Recognizes Sandra Day O'Connor	25.4 %	
Does not	74.6 %	
Total	100.0 %	
Total		100.0 %
N		1418

respondents about three structural and functional attributes of the Supreme Court: how the justices are selected, the length of their terms, and which institution has the "last say" when it comes to interpreting the Constitution. Table 2.2 reports their replies. Since the same questions were asked in both 2001 and 2005, we report data from both surveys.

Remarkably large percentages of Americans correctly answer these questions about the Court. In 2001, nearly three out of four knew that the justices of the Court are appointed; and, despite having to choose from among the Court, the Congress, and the president, more than 60

TABLE 2.2.
Knowledge of the U.S. Supreme Court, 2001, 2005

	Percentages (Rows Total to 100 %, except for rounding errors)		
	Correct Answer	*Incorrect Answer*	*Don't Know*
Justices are appointed			
2001	73.9	10.4	15.7
2005	65.4	14.9	19.7
Justices serve a life term			
2001	66.4	16.1	17.4
2005	60.5	19.5	20.0
Court has "last say" on the constitution			
2001	60.7	28.4	10.9
2005	56.8	27.7	15.5

Note: 2001 N ≈ 1418.
2005 N ≈ 1000.

The questions read:

Some judges in the United States are elected; others are appointed to the bench. Do you happen to know if the justices of the United States Supreme Court are elected or appointed to the bench?

Some judges in the United States serve for a set number of years; others serve a life term. Do you happen to know whether the justices of the United States Supreme Court serve for a set number of years or whether they serve a life term?

Do you happen to know who has the last say when there is a conflict over the meaning of the Constitution—the United States Supreme Court, the United States Congress, or the president?

percent answered that the Supreme Court has the ultimate "say" on the Constitution. Only 13.6 percent of the respondents got none of these questions correct; 44.4 percent answered all three accurately. Were the respondents doing nothing more than simply guessing at the answers to these questions, one would expect that only 8.25 percent would answer all three questions correctly (.50 × .50 × .33). Our data thus suggest that Americans are far more knowledgeable about the Supreme Court than many scholars and commentators suggest or imply and than most previous researchers have reported.[26]

[26] Kritzer's survey work (2001) is an important exception to this generalization. He found that the average number of correct answers in reply to six Supreme Court knowledge questions is 3.15 (2001, 37). For instance, large proportions of the American people knew that the Supreme Court does not use juries and that it is not obliged to hear all cases brought before it, information that strikes us as much more relevant and politically significant than knowing the names of some sitting justices. In contrast, only 19.8 percent knew the name of the chief justice.

The evidence from the 2001 survey indicates that Americans know far more about the U.S. Supreme Court than is typically supposed. But perhaps this is not surprising since the survey was conducted during a period of American politics in which the Court may well have been as salient as at any time in its history. Media coverage of the Court and its decisions was massive; the political stakes in the dispute were as high as they get; the political and legal issues generally accessible to ordinary people (e.g., voting rights); and the drama was unsurpassed. A survey conducted in the heat of such an important political battle risks providing an atypical view of the knowledge of the American people, even if such a survey suggests that people can learn about the Supreme Court when it becomes important and relevant to do so.

We therefore repeated many of these questions in a survey we conducted in 2005 (see appendix A for details), and these data are also reported in table 2.2. The data reveal that in fact knowledge as indicated by all three questions declined from 2001 to 2005. Yet, the decline is small, and even in 2005, substantial majorities of Americans held correct information about their Supreme Court.[27] Thus, it seems that people learn from salient controversies involving the Supreme Court, but that the knowledge of a substantial proportion of Americans does *not* depend upon an attention-catching controversy.

The final set of questions assessing knowledge of the Court focuses on its decisions.[28] We asked the 2001 respondents whether they knew if the Court had issued decisions in three areas of public policy: abortion, the voting rights of African Americans, and the maximum tax rate people have to pay on their income. Table 2.3 reports their answers.

Once more, the data indicate a substantial amount of knowledge about the Court. Two-thirds of the respondents know that the Court has made decisions on abortion and African American voting rights, and even 42 percent know that the Court has *not* made decisions on the maximum income tax rate (a very difficult test indeed). We do not necessarily claim that Americans have a great deal of substantive knowledge about the Court's involvement in these issues, but only 13 percent of the respon-

[27] Kritzer (2001) reports a similar finding about change in opinions pre- and post–*Bush v. Gore*.

[28] Based on a survey conducted in St. Louis, Missouri, Franklin and Kosaki (1995) examine awareness of individual Supreme Court decisions, focusing on the role of the mass media in promoting awareness and how the media interacts with the characteristics of individual citizens. They document a great deal of variability in awareness of different Court rulings, much of which can be attributed to the extent of media coverage of the decisions. They also rely upon the familiar two-step flow of information, with elites playing an important mediating role. See also Franklin, Kosaki, and Kritzer (1993), who conclude that awareness of Court decisions is relatively high.

TABLE 2.3.
Knowledge of Supreme Court Decisions, 2001

Has Court Made Decisions On . . .	*Percentages (Rows total to 100 %, except for rounding errors)*		
	Correct	*Incorrect*	*Don't Know*
Abortion (Has ruled)	68.4	7.0	24.6
Rights of Black Americans (Has ruled)	65.6	9.0	25.4
Maximum Income Tax Rate (Has not ruled)	41.7	12.3	46.1

N ≈ 1418.
Note: The correct answer to each question is shown in parentheses.

dents got all of these questions wrong, even if only 26 percent got all of them right.

With data from closed-ended questions, we draw dramatically different conclusions about how informed the American people were in both the 2001 and 2005 surveys. Whether question form actually "caused" these results can still be debated, however, given the post hoc nature of our data and analysis we have adduced. More direct, and causally persuasive, evidence is available from an experiment we conducted in a survey fielded in 2006.

The 2006 Question-Wording Experiment

In the last wave of our study of the Alito confirmation (conducted several months after the confirmation fight was concluded), we included an experiment on the way in which political knowledge is measured. The respondents were randomly assigned to one of two conditions: (1) knowledge was measured via short answer, open-ended questions, or (2) knowledge was measured by closed-ended, multiple-choice questions. In both instances, we asked about three political figures: William Rehnquist, John G. Roberts Jr., and Bill Frist.

When asked in the third-wave interview of the Alito confirmation study what job or political office John G. Roberts Jr., now holds, only 7.0 percent of the respondents replied "chief justice of the United States Supreme Court"; another 8.1 percent said he was a Supreme Court justice. Fully 74.2 percent of the respondents did not know who Roberts was (and most could not even formulate a guess). This finding comports well with conventional wisdom about the ignorance of the American people.

A second question asked about the job or office of "William Rehnquist, who is now dead." Although only 12.1 percent of the respondents correctly said that Rehnquist was the chief justice of the U.S. Supreme Court, another 30.1 percent said that Rehnquist was a Supreme Court justice. Obviously, since at the time of the survey Roberts was a newly minted Supreme Court justice, while Rehnquist had served on the Court for thirty-five years, the recently deceased chief justice was much more likely to be in the respondents' accessible memories. This finding reinforces the view that not all political facts should be treated as equally useful measures of public knowledge.

At the same time, information about the identity of Bill Frist was not much more widespread. Only 11.6 percent correctly identified him as majority leader of the U.S. Senate, while another 4.2 percent replied that Frist is a senator. If citizens are too ill-informed to play a responsible role in the judicial process, perhaps they are also too ill-formed to be involved in selecting and evaluating legislators as well. Thus, this portion of our experiment strongly confirms the conventional wisdom about the ignorance of the American people, with perhaps the slight caveat that their ignorance is not limited to the U.S. Supreme Court.

Only 7.0 percent of the respondents hearing the open-ended versions of the question replied that Roberts is the chief justice. But when the other half of the sample (randomly assigned) was asked to identify the chief justice from a list of three names, 46.3 percent correctly selected John G. Roberts Jr.[29] When asked to identify the majority leader from a list of three names, 43.7 percent correctly identified Frist.[30] Finally, 71.1 percent of the respondents were able to identify Rehnquist as the former chief justice when presented with three names.[31] According to these data, which rely upon fairly difficult questions with foils requiring the ability to differentiate individuals occupying the same or similar roles, the American people are *vastly* more knowledgeable about politics than is typically portrayed. Thus, with respect to the political knowledge experiment, there is enormous variance that depends upon whether open-ended or closed-ended questions are asked of the respondents; and, given random assignment to question form, we are entitled to considerable confidence that the *cause* of the answers we recorded is the form of the question asked.[32] We

[29] The two foils were "J. Harvie Wilkinson, III" and "Theodore Olson."

[30] The two foils were "Mitch McConnell" and "Ted Stevens."

[31] The two foils were "Lewis F. Powell" and "Byron R. White."

[32] In the closed-ended version of the questions, we randomly varied the order in which the names were presented to the respondents. In no instance is a chi-square test for differences in the distribution of correctly identifying the name statistically significant. Some variability does exist across the three order conditions—when Rehnquist's name is mentioned second, 77.1 percent of the responses are correct; when his name is first on the response set list, 64.4

contend that the open-ended recall measures of political knowledge are not particularly useful or valid indicators of the level of information ordinary Americans hold about politics.[33] In the end, we agree with Mondak's conclusion that "researchers have explored numerous considerations regarding item format, but the bottom line is that multiple-choice questions are highly resistant to response sets, meaning that use of multiple-choice questions maximizes our capacity to form valid inferences regarding respondents' levels of knowledge" (2001, 228).

Temporal Stability: The Role of Context

Earlier research has documented that the percentage of respondents correctly answering political knowledge questions increases as an election approaches (e.g., Johnston, Hagen, and Jamieson 2004). The data reported above on the relative salience of Rehnquist and Roberts suggest a similar contextual phenomenon: the longer information is available in a political system, the more likely are citizens to acquire it. Finally, our data on the 2001 election also suggest that context matters (see also Kritzer 2001).

Consequently, it is reasonable to hypothesize that the Alito nomination raised levels of information about the Court among the mass public. Our panel survey is particularly well designed for assessing this hypothesis since we asked knowledge questions during the t_1, t_2, and t_3 interviews, with the t_2 survey conducted during the debate over whether to confirm Judge Alito.

Is knowledge at the individual level stable over time? Figure 2.1 provides the descriptive frequencies on the items asked in the 2005 and 2006 panel surveys.

---

percent recognized him as the chief justice—but the variability is relatively small and the pattern of variability across the three people (Rehnquist, Roberts, and Frist) is not consistent (e.g., when Roberts's name is listed second, the percentage correctly answering the question is the lowest, not highest). Given the lack of statistical significance and the absence of any clear pattern of recency or primacy effects, we conclude that the order of presentation of the responses had little systematic impact on the ability of the respondents to identify these political leaders.

[33] At a later point in the t_3 interview, we asked the respondents to tell us which of three definitions of judicial activism they considered correct. The percentages identifying the concept as meaning "that judges rely on their own judgments of what is fair in the case rather than allowing the constitution, the legislature or prior Court decisions to dictate what the outcome of the case will be" according to the number of correct answers to the knowledge items are: 54.5, 64.3, 79.7, and 74.3, from 0 to 3 correct answers, respectively. These findings contribute to our confidence in the validity of the knowledge indicator.

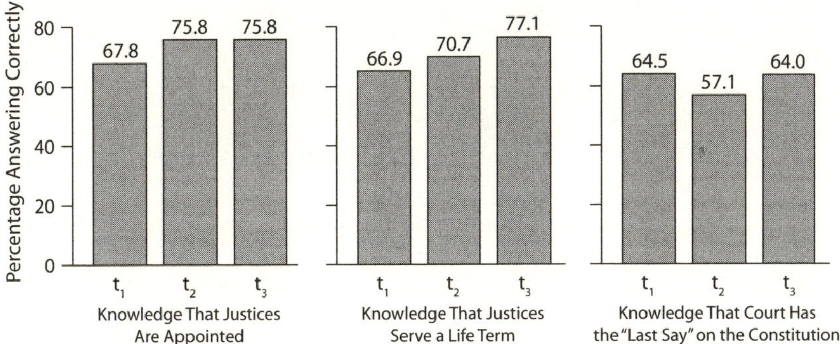

Figure 2.1. Change in Levels of Knowledge across the 2005–2006 Panel Survey

Of the individuals interviewed at all three waves in the panel survey, the mean number of correct answers to the three Court questions in the first survey was 2.13; in 2006, the means were about the same—2.15 at t_2 and 2.27 at t_3 (with standard deviations of around 1.0). Thus, at the aggregate level, little change occurred. One can see this pattern in the individual knowledge items as well (see figure 2.1). There is some slight increase in knowledge over the course of the three interviews (most likely reflecting some degree of reactivity to the interviews),[34] but generally the percentages change only marginally. Knowledge of the Court is high, and was not appreciably raised by the Alito hearings.[35]

Perhaps these findings are influenced by the relative ease of the questions we asked of the respondents. Large majorities answered each of these three questions correctly at the t_1 interview, most likely reflecting the wide diffusion throughout society of information about the basic structure and function of the Court. Moreover, those who did not already know such basic information were unlikely to become very attentive toward the Supreme Court during the nomination process and therefore this opportunity to learn something about the Supreme Court passed them by.

Of course, aggregate-level stability often masks microlevel change. But, in this case, the correlations between the indicators of the numbers of correct Court answers for each survey pair (t_1t_2, t_2t_3) are .60 and .71. Furthermore, 53.7 percent of our respondents did not increase or decrease their knowledge between the first and last interviews; 28.6 percent had

[34] For the three items, the following percentages answered correctly at t_3 but not at t_1: 12.0, 15.2, and 13.5 percent, for the selection, term, and function items, respectively. The comparable figures for "unlearning" from t_1 to t_3 are: 7.2 percent, 3.6 percent, and 15.9 percent.

[35] See chapter 4, below, for evidence that the Alito nomination was quite salient to the American people.

more knowledge in 2006 than in 2005, but for 17.7 percent of the respondents, knowledge decreased from the initial interview to the last. This observed stability, of course, reflects in part a ceiling effect, since 52.1 percent of the t_1 respondents got all three answers correct.

Thus, these data indicate that the American people are better informed than suggested by conventional wisdom, that their level of information is not unduly shaped by salient but ephemeral events, and that at the individual level, political knowledge is quite stable. These findings add confidence to both the validity and reliability of our conclusions to this point.

Discussion and Concluding Comments

The most important finding of this chapter runs strongly counter to existing understandings of public knowledge of law and courts: these respondents demonstrate relatively high levels of information about the Supreme Court. To our knowledge, few prior studies have documented this level of information about the Court. We contend that this finding is in part a function of the method by which knowledge is measured, and we are consequently critical of most earlier efforts to document what citizens know about the Supreme Court. When citizens are asked reasonable questions about what they understand about the Supreme Court, most can answer accurately.

We certainly do not want to overclaim from our findings on how knowledgeable the American people are about the Supreme Court. The questions we asked are relatively easy ones (indeed, the evidence is that we did not ask enough hard questions, since there is so much bunching of the data at the highest level of knowledge). Nor are we at all certain that most Americans recognize and appreciate the distinction between institutions designed to cater to the preferences of the majority (e.g., legislatures) and those primarily serving the interests of minorities (e.g., courts), even if these are typically privileged minorities.

But we do assert that the image of the American people as entirely bereft of information about courts, as ignorant of their role in the American democracy and their importance as makers of public policy, and as oblivious to the nature of judicial institutions and processes most likely undercredits ordinary people. Certainly there is little in our data to suggest that the views of the American citizenry are too ill-informed to be worthy of any serious consideration, both from the political process and from scholars of the judiciary. It seems that the American people may know enough about law and courts to be able to perform their assigned function as constituents of the contemporary judicial system in the United States.

Appendix 2.A

Survey Design, The 2001 Survey

This research is based on a survey conducted in early 2001 by the Center for Survey Research (CSR) at Ohio State University. The survey is based on a typical Random-Digit-Dial (RDD) sample of the American mass public and an oversample of African Americans. The fieldwork in the primary sample was conducted from January 5 through January 19, 2001, with 1,006 interviews completed during this period. Telephone interviewing was employed, utilizing an RDD sample purchased from Genesys Sampling Systems. The sample is representative of English-speaking households in the forty-eight contiguous U.S. states (and Washington, D.C.). Within households, respondents were selected by the "last birthday" technique (see Lavrakas 1993, 111–13). The median length of interview was about twenty minutes.

Using the AAPOR standards (American Association for Public Opinion Research 2000), several response rates were calculated. According to AAPOR Response Rate 5, our survey had a rate of 35 percent; according to AAPOR Response Rate 1, the rate was 26 percent. Using AAPOR's Cooperation Rate 3, our "cooperation rate" was 49 percent; modifying this rate by taking into account all households in which it is certain that an interviewer spoke with the selected respondent, the cooperation rate climbs to 78 percent.

We also surveyed an oversample of African Americans. We sampled from census tracts in which the concentration of African American households was 25 percent or greater. The field work was conducted from January 22, 2001, through February 12, 2001. In all respects, the methods employed in the oversample were identical to those employed in the primary sample.

A total of 409 interviews with African American respondents were completed in the oversample. The response rates for the oversample are: AAPOR Response Rate 1: 30 percent; AAPOR Response Rate 5: 40 percent; AAPOR Cooperation Rate 3: 55 percent; and Modified AAPOR Cooperation Rate 3: 80 percent.

We have weighted these data to adjust for the unequal probabilities of selection (i.e., the oversample), and nonresponse (following the convention of the American National Election Study—see Survey Research Center n.d.).

CHAPTER THREE

The Popular Legitimacy of the United States Supreme Court

The period of the early twenty-first century in the United States is judged by many to be an era of rather intense partisan and ideological polarization. From abortion rights to the war in Iraq, Democrats disagree with Republicans, just as liberals joust with conservatives. The primary colors of contemporary America seem to be red and blue. On a variety of important political issues, partisan and ideological differences are substantial and profound.[1]

Implicated in many of the issues dividing the Americans is the United States Supreme Court. For a variety of reasons, the Court often finds itself at the center of intense political disputes: be it the right to abortion, the right to burn an American flag in protest, the degree to which church and state must be separated, and conflicts between rights of privacy and national security. These issues clearly divide Americans of different ideological and partisan persuasions, and much of the contemporary debate focuses on what the Supreme Court has, or has not, ruled.

What is less obvious, however, is whether this same sort of polarization exists with regard to the basic institutional legitimacy of the Supreme Court. Have divisions over public policy been exacerbated to the point that they have undermined the very legitimacy of the institutional author of such policy: the U.S. Supreme Court? If so, then the divisiveness of the current era may have more profound and lasting consequences than even the most pessimistic analysts currently imagine.

There are indeed signs that threats to the institutional integrity of the Supreme Court abound. Certainly, the justices of the Court have complained about this matter, often couching their arguments in terms of the preservation of one of the most distinctive, essential, and cherished attributes of courts: judicial independence. In 2006, former Justice Sandra

[1] The literature on how divided the Americans are is itself somewhat divided. Fiorina (2006) does not believe such differences to be profound, but many (if not most) draw different conclusions from the available data (e.g., Abramowitz and Saunders 2005; McCarty, Poole, and Rosenthal 2006; Sinclair 2006). Others suggest that even areas such as foreign policy—once thought to be the last bastion of nonpartisanship—have become highly disputatious (e.g., Shapiro and Bloch-Elkon 2006).

Day O'Connor delivered a series of speeches decrying those who would limit the independence of the American judiciary.[2] There can be no doubt that certain members of Congress have attacked the U.S. Supreme Court, and no shortage exists of legislation designed to "curb" the Court's decision-making authority. These range from the "Safeguarding Our Religious Liberties Act" (H.R. 4379), introduced by Ron Paul (TX-14) with the purpose of eliminating federal court jurisdiction over state and local policies regarding the free exercise or establishment of religion, any privacy claim related to issues of sexual practices, orientation, or reproduction, and any equal protection claim based on the right to marry without regard to sex or sexual orientation, to the "Congressional Accountability for Judicial Activism Act of 2004" (H.R. 3920), introduced in the House of Representatives by Representative Ron Lewis (KY-2) and twenty-six co-sponsors, and which would empower Congress to reverse by a two-thirds vote any judgment of the U.S. Supreme Court that concerns the constitutionality of an act of Congress.[3]

Specific, high-stakes Court decisions have drawn vicious and legitimacy-challenging criticism—as in the direct attack by various law professors on the Court's legitimacy after its ruling in *Bush v. Gore*— and there is no shortage of threats to the judiciary from the religious right, right-wing terrorists and murderers, and fanatics.[4] Serious proposals to change the structure of the judiciary have been floated—e.g., various plans to convert the life tenure of Supreme Court judges to a fixed term.[5] For instance, Farnsworth (2004, 2, footnotes omitted) asserts: "In recent years at least ten distinguished scholars (as well as two distinguished judges and a distinguished journalist) have proposed abolishing life tenure for Supreme Court Justices and replacing it with fixed terms of years in office." While not all dissatisfaction with judges in the United States is focused on the Supreme Court, there can be little doubt that the justices of the Court are correct to worry about the implications of the current political climate in the country for the legitimacy of law and courts in general and their court in particular. Finally, some longitudinal studies of trust in the United States

[2] For an unofficial transcript of one of these speeches, see http://www.law.ufl.edu/dedication/speechtext.shtml (accessed June 8, 2006). In his 2005 report on the federal judiciary, Chief Justice Roberts asserted what has become another familiar refrain: "A more direct threat to judicial independence is the failure to raise judges' pay." See http://www.uscourts.gov/ttb/jan06ttb/yearend/index.html (accessed May 26, 2006).

[3] For a discussion of earlier Court-curbing efforts in the American case, see Friedman 2005, 314–15. For European examples, see Schwartz 2000.

[4] See, for example, http://www.judgesgonewild.com/ (accessed 5/26/2006).

[5] That paper provides full citations to support this claim. See also Eskridge and Levinson 1998; Levinson 2006.

Supreme Court argue that partisan polarization in Court attitudes has risen significantly in recent times (e.g., Mate and Wright 2006).[6]

Nonetheless, earlier research on the legitimacy of the Supreme Court has generally found that the institution enjoys a fairly substantial "reservoir of goodwill" among the American people (e.g., Caldeira and Gibson 1992; Gibson, Caldeira, and Baird 1998). That research is dated, however, and certainly predates the emergence of strong ideological and partisan cleavages in the United States, especially as the dust (and unity) of the 9/11 attack has worn away. Thus, it seems quite reasonable and interesting to revisit the question of how much legitimacy the Supreme Court has today. More specifically, have divisions over policy issues spilled over to undermine the Court's legitimacy?

In addition to answering that important factual question, however, we need to re-examine the sources of the institution's legitimacy. Has support for the Court become dependent upon partisanship and ideology, and even policy agreement with the institution? To what degree has the etiology of institutional support changed over time? To the extent that the bases of legitimacy have become more fragile, Legitimacy Theory itself may require rethinking and reconsidering. Based on our nationally representative face-to-face survey conducted in 2005, we attempt in this chapter to answer these questions in a rigorous and comprehensive fashion.

Theories of Institutional Legitimacy

Considerable agreement exists among political scientists on most of the major contours of Legitimacy Theory.[7] For instance, most agree that legitimacy is a normative concept, having something to do with the right (moral and legal) to make decisions. "Authority" is sometimes used as a synonym for legitimacy. Institutions perceived to be legitimate are those with a widely accepted mandate to render judgments for a political community; those without legitimacy find their authority contested. "Basically, when people say that laws are 'legitimate,' they mean that there is something rightful about the way the laws came about. . . . [T]he legitimacy of law rests on the way it comes to be: if that is legitimate, then so are the results, at least most of the time" (Friedman 1998, 256).

[6] On the other hand, Kritzer (2005, 173) analyzes multiple opinion surveys and concludes: "What is perhaps most striking about the analysis presented above is that one is likely to draw different conclusions about trends in support for the Supreme Court depending upon which survey series one looks at."

[7] For a most useful recent review of Legitimacy Theory, see Tyler 2006. For a superb collection of essays on legitimacy, mostly from psychologists, among whom the theory has recently received great currency, see Jost and Major 2001.

Legitimacy becomes especially relevant when people disagree about public policy. When a court, for instance, makes a decision pleasing to all, discussions of legitimacy are rarely relevant or necessary and do not emerge. When there is conflict over policy, then some may ask whether the institution has the authority, the "right," to make the decision. Legitimate institutions are those recognized as appropriate decision-making bodies *even when* one disagrees with the outputs of the institution. Thus, legitimacy takes on its primary relevance in the presence of an *objection precondition.* As Friedman (1977, 141) rightly noted long ago: "We do not need a theory of legitimacy to explain why people obey a person with a gun, or adhere to an order that brings them personal honor or gain, or obey their religions or their moral codes."[8] Policy disagreements—even very strong ones—may have few lasting systemic consequences if the basic legitimacy of the key political institutions remains intact.

But what exactly are the indicia of institutional legitimacy? Empirically oriented scholars have been unhappy with the amorphous nature of the concept of legitimacy. Under the influence of David Easton (1965, 1975), researchers have instead been attracted to the notion of institutional "support,"[9] with a distinction often being made between "diffuse" and "specific" support. Although a few important scholars doubt that the two types of support can be differentiated empirically (e.g., Mishler and Rose 1994), most recognize a difference, at least at the theoretical level, between approval of policy outputs in the short term and a more fundamental loyalty to an institution over the long term.

Diffuse support therefore refers to "a reservoir of favorable attitudes or good will that helps members to accept or tolerate outputs to which they are opposed or the effects of which they see as damaging to their wants" (Easton 1965, 273). Diffuse support is institutional *loyalty*; it is support that is *not* contingent upon satisfaction with the immediate outputs of the institution. Easton's apt phrase—a "reservoir of goodwill"—captures the idea that people have confidence in institutions to make, in the long run, desirable public policy. Speaking of parliaments, Loewenberg and Patterson (1979, 285) claim:

[8] Moreover, the literature on distributive and procedural justice (e.g., Lind and Tyler 1988; Tyler 1990) teaches us that those who lose on distributive issues often find losing palatable if the procedures leading to the decision are perceived to be fair (e.g., Baird 2001). Controversy exists, however, in the literature on the causal relationships among perceived fairness, legitimacy, and compliance (see Gibson 1989; Tyler and Rasinksi 1991; Gibson 1991; see also Mondak 1993; Scherer and Curry 2006).

[9] Research on legitimacy sometimes addresses the legitimacy of regimes and states but at other times focuses on the legitimacy of specific institutions. This chapter addresses the latter. For a useful discussion of the objects of support, see Norris 1999.

> Although public attitudes toward legislatures vary depending on short-term public satisfaction with their performance, some part of the public attitude toward the institution is unrelated to its performance but reflects long-term influences. . . . This more enduring attitude, based on cumulative experience with the institution or with political authority over a lifetime, has been called diffuse support, to indicate that it is general, that is, unrelated to specific experiences. This part of the attitude toward legislatures is theoretically of great significance, since it can be a source of public commitment to the institution through good times and bad and a basis for public compliance with the enactments of the legislature whether they are liked or not.

Institutions without this reservoir of goodwill may be emasculated and therefore limited in their ability to go against the preferences of determined majorities.[10]

Although there are many ways to conceptualize the orientations ordinary citizens hold toward institutions like the Supreme Court, we contend that the most politically significant attitudes are best thought of as a form of institutional loyalty. "Loyalty" represents the idea that failure to make policy that is pleasing in the short term does not necessarily undermine basic commitments to support the institution. Institutions such as courts need the leeway to be able to go against public opinion (as for instance in protecting unpopular political minorities). Thus, a crucial aspect of the political capital of institutions is the degree to which they enjoy the loyalty, not just approval, of their constituents.[11]

The Consequences of Institutional Legitimacy

At this point in the theory, an important disagreement over definitions exists. Some scholars *equate* legitimacy with compliance. For instance,

[10] Consequently, Legitimacy Theory is closely tied to—and often debated within—more general democratic theories concerning majorities and minorities. For a recent useful overview of this body of literature, see Fallon 2005. Moreover, Comparativists (e.g., Tsebelis 2000; Alivizatos 1995) have focused on courts as "veto players" and have acknowledged that legitimacy is a necessary resource if courts are to play this role. See also Gibson and Caldeira 2003; Walker 2006.

[11] Within the context of a formal model of relations between legislatures and constitutional courts, Vanberg (2001) places great emphasis on the degree of support enjoyed by constitutional courts. The logic goes as follows: courts enjoying high support also enjoy a presumption that their decisions ought to be complied with by the legislature. To the extent that the legislature seeks to evade compliance with a court decision, a backlash will likely result. "The fear of such a backlash can be a powerful inducement for legislative majorities to respect judicial decisions as well as the institutional integrity of a court" (Vanberg 2001, 347).

Yoo (2001, 225) uses the following definition: "We can think of institutional 'legitimacy' as the belief in the binding nature of an institution's decisions, even when one disagrees with them." By "binding," he means an obligation to obey. Others treat legitimacy as one of many possible causes of compliance. We take this alternative tack, theorizing that the decision to obey or not obey a law is *conceptually* independent of whether an institution is judged to have the authority to make a decision, and contending that people obey laws for many reasons, not just due to legitimacy. The degree to which legitimacy and compliance are related must be treated as an empirical question (as it is, for example, in Gibson, Caldeira, and Spence 2005). To do otherwise makes tautological the relationship between perceived legitimacy and compliance, and precludes consideration of determinants of compliance that are not grounded in legitimacy.[12]

Indeed, one of the most interesting unresolved questions in this literature has to do with the "legitimacy-conferring" powers of courts. First clearly articulated by Dahl (1957), this theory asserts that a court ruling can induce people to accept the decision of other political institutions because the court has ratified and sanctioned the decision. Since courts rarely challenge the ruling coalition in the United States (Dahl 1957), the American judiciary essentially places its imprimatur on policies, thereby encouraging citizens to accept outcomes with which they disagree (see Clawson, Kegler, and Waltenburg 2001). Mondak and others (e.g., Choper 1980) refer to this as the "political capital"of courts, and note that institutions must husband this capital and spend it wisely if they are to be effective. As Mondak (1992, 461) notes, "[S]ponsoring a policy is a type of gamble; the possibility of [a] negative reaction endangers the institution's lifeblood, institutional legitimacy." Exactly this theory was cited when scholars asserted that the Court "wounded" itself by its decision in *Bush v. Gore*. The Supreme Court decision, even though badly divided, effectively ended the election dispute. The Court ruling eroded Gore's support, making it difficult if not impossible to continue his challenge to the election outcome. On its face, the election controversy seems to provide compelling evidence in support of legitimacy theory.[13] To the extent that courts are perceived as legitimate, citizens tend to acquiesce to unpopular judicial rulings, even ones with which they strongly

[12] For example, Tyler (1990, 4) makes this distinction: "Normative commitment through personal morality means obeying a law because one feels the law is just; normative commitment through legitimacy means obeying a law because one feels that the authority enforcing the law has the right to dictate behavior."

[13] For an empirical analysis of the effect of this decision on the Court's legitimacy, see Gibson, Caldeira, and Spence 2003a (see appendix C). See also Yates and Whitford 2002; Kritzer 2001; Gillman 2001; Kritzer 2005.

disagree. Thus, to lose this legitimacy-conferring capacity—especially in the context of deep political divisions in American politics—would deal a serious blow to the function of the Supreme Court in the American political system and to the ability of the Court to contain and manage political conflict.

Extant Research on the Legitimacy of the United States Supreme Court

Much of what we know about recent public attitudes toward the United States Supreme Court comes from the nationally representative surveys conducted by us in 1987, 1995, and 2001. Relying on the widely accepted conceptualization of diffuse support provided by Easton (1965, 1975),[14] this research documents several important findings. First, the United States Supreme Court is in general regarded as a quite legitimate institution (e.g., Gibson, Caldeira, and Baird 1998). Second, the legitimacy of the Court has waxed and waned little over time, although the number of available surveys of institutional legitimacy is small. Even controversial decisions like that in *Bush v. Gore* seem not to have undermined the Court's legitimacy (Gibson, Caldeira, and Spence 2003a; see appendix C). Among some groups, however, legitimacy has in fact declined, as in the rather distinct (but not necessarily abrupt) "about-face" of African American attitudes toward the Court (e.g., Gibson and Caldeira 1992). Finally, support for the Court has important implications for willingness to accept even disagreeable judicial decisions (Gibson, Caldeira, and Spence 2005). We should reiterate, however, that all of these conclusions are drawn from a period in American history that predates the current era of strong partisan and ideological divisions.

[14] A considerable body of research has evolved based on national surveys asking a question about confidence in the leaders of the United States Supreme Court. It is unclear to us, however, what exactly this question is measuring: For instance, is "confidence" the same as predictability, or is it instead equivalent to confidence that the leaders will do what is right, and if the latter, right for the country, me, my group, or my ideological preferences? And who are the leaders of the United States Supreme Court? Does the question refer to the chief justice, the most senior member of the Court, or whom? It seems easy to imagine the following sort of citizen: one who is liberal, is completely confident that the right-wing leadership of the Court will make right-wing decisions, of which the citizen strongly disapproves, but who nonetheless does not seek to emasculate the Court since either: a) liberals may one day again control the Court; and/or b) whatever the Court may be doing at the moment, the institution plays a vital role in American politics and therefore must be respected, protected, and obeyed. We are certain there is at least one such citizen in the United States, and strongly suspect that there are more. Gibson, Caldeira, and Spence (2003b) provide more rigorous evidence that this survey item measuring confidence is not a very useful measure of institutional loyalty.

Earlier research has also provided reasonable explanations of the variability in attitudes toward the Supreme Court, with extant research identifying four important sources of support: (1) ideology, partisanship, and policy agreement; (2) knowledge of the institution and its role in American politics; (3) support for democratic institutions and processes; and (4) race. We will briefly consider each.

Although clouded by causal ambiguity, a relationship between approval of performance and policy outputs (specific support) and institutional loyalty is typically found in research on public attitudes (e.g., Caldeira and Gibson 1992). The relationship varies over time (as different segments of the population are pleased or displeased with Court outputs), and the relationship often implicates partisanship and ideology since they help structure evaluations of Court decisions. To the extent, however, that these relationships are very strong, they undermine the validity of measures of diffuse support. Whether this is a causal relationship remains unclear (and indeed, perhaps diffuse support creates specific support via processes of framing—see Gibson and Caldeira 2006; Baird and Gangl 2006).

Race may be a surrogate for policy disagreement with the Court. Several studies have documented that African Americans exhibit less support for the Supreme Court than whites (e.g., Gibson and Caldeira 1992). This research is also important because it reveals something about the processes by which legitimacy deteriorates. As a "reservoir of goodwill," legitimacy is not easily shaken in the short term by policy disagreements. But over the long haul, the repeated failure of an institution to meet policy expectations can weaken and even destroy that institution's legitimacy in the eyes of disaffected groups. This seems to be exactly what happened with African Americans: as the Court changed its policy orientation, so too did African Americans' opinions of the Court change.

Although early socialization processes are thought by many to be influential in creating support for the judiciary, perhaps more important are the basic political values to which people subscribe. Those with commitments to individual freedom and other democratic values (perhaps grounded in individualism) are more likely to support minoritarian institutions like courts (Caldeira and Gibson 1992, 1995). This finding is important because it implies that support for the Supreme Court will change only slowly over time (since values themselves change only slowly). Perhaps the most important contribution of this body of work on the etiology of Court support is the evidence that the Supreme Court gets much of its legitimacy from its role in the American democratic process, and, apparently, Americans' understanding of that role.

Extant research has also consistently shown that those who know more about courts are more likely to support them (e.g., Gibson, Caldeira, and

Baird 1998). Above, we explicated this finding within the context of the theory of positivity bias. As people become attentive to courts in the context of policy controversies or events like confirmation hearings, judicial symbols proliferate so it is impossible for attentive citizens to avoid exposure to them. Exposure to legitimizing judicial symbols reinforces the message that "courts are different," and owing to such difference, courts are worthy of more respect, deference, and obedience—in short, legitimacy. Thus, paying attention to courts is typically associated with extending more legitimacy to the judiciary.

Thus, a tension exists in the literature on support for the Supreme Court. On the one hand, support is to some degree related to approval or disapproval of the performance of the institution. Why did support for the Supreme Court decline precipitously within the black community in the United States? The simple answer is that the Court reversed policy courses, with the result that the long-standing support African Americans had extended to the Supreme Court withered. From this perspective, Court support can change fairly quickly over time; from this perspective, the deep disagreements existing in the United States today may have a strongly corrosive impact on institutional support.

Support may instead reflect processes of political socialization, the creation of political values, and the reinforcement of such values through highly potent judicial symbols. Loyalty to institutions like the Supreme Court is therefore a natural extension of broader support for democratic institutions and processes. If this latter process is dominant, then one would not expect much change in the short term, since values change slowly, and since legitimizing symbols are so widely available to reinforce support. Under this process, it is unlikely that the current divisions over public policy will spill over and affect the legitimacy of the Supreme Court. It is these alternative possibilities that this chapter investigates.

Measuring Institutional Legitimacy

Our thinking about operationalizing institutional loyalty follows a considerable body of research on theorizing about and measuring mass perceptions of high courts (see Caldeira and Gibson 1992, 1995; Gibson, Caldeira, and Baird 1998; Gibson and Caldeira 1995, 1998, 2003; Gibson 2007a). That research conceptualizes loyalty as opposition to making fundamental structural and functional changes in the institution (see Boynton and Loewenberg 1973), and is grounded in the history of attacks by politicians against courts in the United States (see Caldeira 1987) and elsewhere (e.g., manipulation of their jurisdiction).[15] As Caldeira and Gibson describe it (1992, 638), those who have little or no loyalty toward the U.S. Supreme Court are willing "to accept, make, or countenance major changes in the fundamental attributes of how the High Bench functions or fits into the U.S. constitutional system" (see also Loewenberg 1971). Loyalty is also characterized by a generalized trust that the institution will perform acceptably in the future. To the extent people support fundamental structural changes in an institution, are willing to punish the institution for its policy outputs, and generally distrust it, they are extending little legitimacy to that institution. Conceptually, loyalty thus ranges from complete unwillingness to support the continued existence of the institution to staunch institutional fealty.

Consequently, our measure of the legitimacy of the Supreme Court is derived from that used by Gibson, Caldeira, and Spence (2003a). In the 2005 survey, four statements were put to the respondents, with the request that they indicate their degree of agreement or disagreement with the statement. Table 3.1 reports the 2005 findings, along with the findings from the 2001 national survey by Gibson, Caldeira, and Spence. Since similar questions were asked in national surveys in the United States in 1987 and 1995, those results are reported as well. The table is structured so that the third data column (labeled "Supportive of the Institution") reports the percentage of respondents giving a favorable answer to the statement, irrespective of whether the answer is "agree" or "disagree." For instance, in 2005, 68.9 percent of Americans disagreed with the statement, "If the U.S. Supreme Court started making a lot of decisions that most people disagree with, it might be better to do away with the Supreme Court altogether." We deem a disagree response to represent loyalty toward the institution, and therefore the level of support for the Court is 68.9 percent.

The first conclusion to be drawn from table 3.1 is that, in 2005, the Supreme Court seemed to have a fairly broad base of support within the American mass public. At one extreme, only a very small proportion (18.2 percent) favored doing away with the Court, even if a plurality (44.4 percent) believed that the Court gets too mixed up in politics. A substantial majority (65.5 percent) believed the Court can generally be trusted, and a slim majority did not want the jurisdiction of the institution altered. Counting across all four statements, the average number of supportive

[15] For instance, during apartheid, the independence of South Africa's Appellate Division of the Supreme Court was often under attack. For excellent histories of that court, see Ellmann 1992 and Forsyth 1985. For a more recent analysis, see Haynie 2003. For European examples, see Schwartz 2000. For a discussion of court-curbing efforts in the American case, see Friedman 2005, 314–15.

Table 3.1.
Loyalty toward the United States Supreme Court, 1987–2005

		Level of Diffuse Support for the Supreme Court					
		Percentage					
Item	*Year*	*Not Supportive*	*Undecided*	*Supportive*	*Mean*	*Std. Dev.*	*N*
Do away with the Court							
	1987	9.4	12.9	77.7	3.9	0.9	1218
	1995	16.8	7.2	76.0	3.8	1.0	803
	2001	12.9	4.4	82.7	4.2	1.2	1418
	2005	18.2	12.9	68.9	3.7	1.0	995
Limit the Court's jurisdiction							
	1987	28.4	24.4	47.2	3.3	1.0	1216
	1995	35.5	11.7	52.8	3.2	1.1	803
	2001	28.3	11.0	60.7	3.6	1.3	1418
	2005	32.4	16.2	51.4	3.2	1.1	996
Court can be trusted							
	1987	not asked	—	—	—	—	—
	1995	25.1	9.6	65.3	3.4	1.0	804
	2001	17.0	5.1	77.8	3.9	1.2	1418
	2005	18.7	15.8	65.5	3.5	0.9	996
Court gets too mixed up in politics							
	1987	not asked	—	—	—	—	—
	1995	not asked	—	—	—	—	—
	2001	40.8	15.9	43.3	3.1	1.4	1418
	2005	44.4	18.4	37.2	2.9	1.1	997

Source: 1995—Gibson, Caldeira, and Baird 1998, 350–351, table 4.

Note: The percentages are calculated on the basis of collapsing the five-point Likert response set (e.g., "agree strongly" and "agree" responses are combined). The means and standard deviations are calculated on the uncollapsed distributions. Higher mean scores indicate more institutional loyalty.

The propositions are:

Do away with the Court:

1987: If the Supreme Court continually makes decisions that the people disagree with, it might be better to do away with the Court altogether.

1995/2001/2005: If the US Supreme Court started making a lot of decisions that most people disagree with, it might be better to do away with the Supreme Court altogether.

Limit the Court's jurisdiction:

1987: The right of the Supreme Court to decide certain types of controversial issues should be limited by the Congress.

1995/2001/2005: The right of the Supreme Court to decide certain types of controversial issues should be reduced.

Court can be trusted:

1995/2001/2005: The Supreme Court can usually be trusted to make decisions that are right for the country as a whole.

Court gets too mixed up in politics:

2001/2005: The U.S. Supreme Court gets too mixed up in politics.

replies is 2.2, with only 12.8 percent of the respondents expressing no support at all for the Court, and 20.3 percent issuing supportive replies to all four statements.

The data in table 3.1 also allow some conclusions about change in attitudes toward the Supreme Court. Interestingly enough, the apogee of support for the Court was reached right in the midst of the struggle over the 2000 presidential election and the Court's highly controversial decision in *Bush v. Gore*. Consider the results on the "Court can be trusted" statement. In 1995, 65.3 percent of the respondents agreed. This figure rose significantly in 2001 to nearly 78 percent, before declining in 2005 to almost exactly the same level as was observed a decade earlier. Roughly similar patterns characterize the jurisdiction item and even the measure of institutional commitment. From these data, it seems obvious that the effect of the presidential dispute in 2000 was to *elevate* the perceived legitimacy of the Court (see Gibson, Caldeira, and Spence 2003a; see appendix C), even if only temporarily.

More important, we see in these data *no evidence that the current political climate has tainted the legitimacy of the Supreme Court.* Support for the Court has declined in the last few years, but its decline seems to be a retreat from the unusually high levels of loyalty it enjoyed around the time of the 2000 presidential election dispute, and a return to a level predating that dispute. Although at this point in our analysis the data are not dispositive—partisan and ideological divisions may explain the decline since 2001—the most reasonable tentative conclusion is that 2001, not 2005, was somewhat unusual.

One other basis of comparison is available. Based on the data reported by Gibson, Caldeira, and Baird (1998), supplemented with research conducted since then in Canada (Fletcher and Howe 2000) and South Africa (Gibson 2008b), it is possible to compare the legitimacy of the United States Supreme Court with that of other high courts throughout the world. Figure 3.1 reports data on the summary indicator of support for the high courts in about twenty countries. The item used refers to "doing away with" the court if it continually makes decisions with which many people disagree. This summary of institutional loyalty provides a useful basis for cross-national comparison.

These data support several conclusions (including the conclusion that enormous variability exists in the legitimacy of these constitutional courts). Most important, in comparison to other national high courts, the United States Supreme Court enjoys an extraordinarily wide and deep "reservoir of goodwill"—only a handful of institutions has support percentages approaching those of the American Court. Thus, in comparison to the past and to other national high courts, the Supreme Court today enjoys widespread institutional legitimacy.

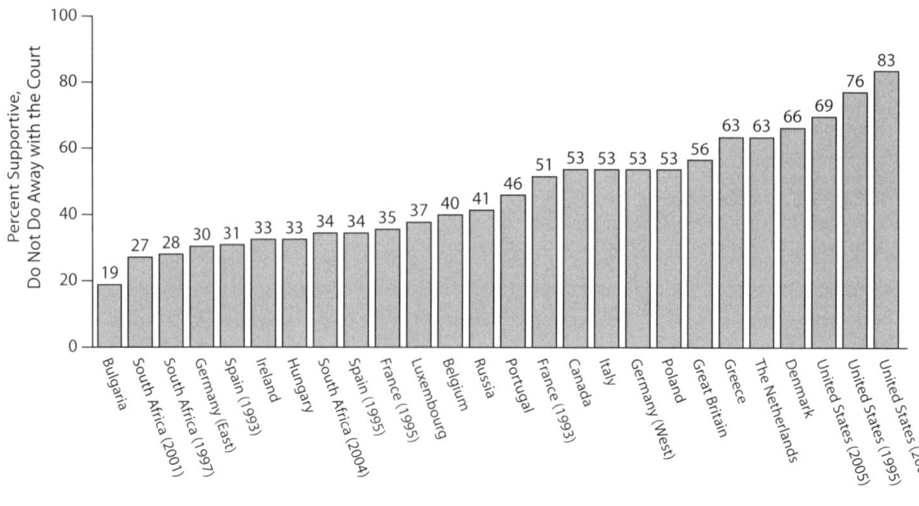

Figure 3.1. Cross-National Variability in Support for Constitutional Courts: Do Not Do Away with the Institution

Note: Most of these data are taken from Gibson, Caldeira, and Baird 1998, Table 4, p. 340. When not otherwise indicated, the data are taken from surveys conducted in the period 1993–1995. For a few countries, more than a single survey is available; for these, the year of the survey is indicated in the country caption. The Canadian data are taken from Fletcher and Howe 2000; the South African data are from Gibson 2008b.

In order to assess more rigorously the hypotheses concerning the etiology of Court support, we require a summary index of loyalty toward the institution. Our analysis reveals that these 2005 measures of legitimacy are reasonably reliable, with a Cronbach's alpha of .64. The average inter-item correlation is .31, which is moderately strong given categorical data that only approximate an interval-level scale, and given some degree of degenerate variance in some of the items. In terms of validity, the item set is clearly unidimensional, with Common Factor Analysis extracting a single dominant factor (eigenvalue_1 = 1.94; the eigenvalue of the second extracted factor is .85). The two most valid indicators of institutional loyalty are the statement about the Court's jurisdiction (factor loading = .78), and the statement about doing away with the Court (loading = .63). The assertion that the Court gets too mixed up in politics has an acceptable loading (.48), although the general statement about trusting the Court has a relatively low correlation with the latent factor (.35).[16] The

[16] Cronbach's alpha does not improve with the deletion of this item from the set of measures, and the correlation between the four-item and three-item indices is .95. Consequently, we use the four-item index in the remainder of this analysis.

factor score (from the first unrotated factor) and a simple summated index of the responses to the four items are correlated at .96. For purposes of analyzing inter-individual variability in support for the Court, we therefore use the summated index as the indicator of institutional loyalty.

Summary

The data produced to this point strongly suggest that the legitimacy of the Supreme Court has not been undermined within this most recent period of strong partisanship and deep ideological divisions. Indeed, the Court seems as widely trusted today as it was a decade ago. Large majorities of the American people express loyalty toward the institution. However much Americans may dislike those of opposing ideologies and partisan attachments, they seem to be reasonably united in their commitment to the Supreme Court.

Accounting for Individual-Level Variability in Institutional Loyalty

Data on the univariate frequency distributions of these items are, however, obviously not definitive on the issue of whether loyalty toward the Court is grounded in ideology and partisanship. To answer that question more rigorously requires that the origins of institutional support be more thoroughly investigated.

Partisanship and Ideology

The first hypothesis requiring consideration is relatively simple and straightforward. We hypothesize that citizens in ideological and/or partisan disagreement with the Supreme Court will express less support for the institution. We therefore hypothesize that Democrats support the Court less than Republicans, just as liberals are expected to extend less legitimacy to the institution than conservatives.

The data reveal that attitudes toward the Supreme Court are *not* strongly influenced by the ideological predispositions of the respondents. For instance, the correlation between loyalty and the respondent's self-identification on a liberalism-conservatism scale does not even achieve statistical significance (with nearly 1,000 cases). A slightly stronger relationship exists between simple affect toward conservatives and institutional loyalty ($r = .10$), but there is also a similar relationship between feeling *positively* toward liberals and loyalty toward the court ($r = .09$). The relationship between relative affect toward liberals and conservatives and loyalty is absolutely trivial. Finally, there is only the slightest tendency for individual ideological polarization (here defined as the square of the difference between affect toward liberals and affect toward conservatives) and support for the Court, with those adopting more polarized views expressing *more* support for the Court. Thus, the most appropriate conclusion from this portion of the analysis is that *loyalty toward the Supreme Court has very little to do with the ideological orientations of citizens.*

The relationship between attitudes toward the Court and party identification is similarly tepid. There is little tendency for Republicans or Democrats to express more support for the Court, although there is some tendency for those adopting a strong party attachment (Republican *or* Democratic) to be *more* supportive. If we take the conventional tack of collapsing strong partisans, weak partisans, and those claiming to lean toward a party, we find that 49.2 percent of the Republicans express relatively high support for the Court (support the Court on at least three of the four propositions), while 42.6 percent of the Democrats are similarly opinionated. Those without a party attachment (independent independents) are slightly less likely to support the Court (39.8 percent), in part because this category (as usual) includes the most poorly informed citizens. As we have noted, Republicans are slightly more supportive of the Court than Democrats, but the differences are so small that one would be hard pressed to term these differences "partisan polarization."

By way of comparison, we can consider the relationship between ideology and partisanship and policy preferences on a variety of legally relevant issues. We focus on four areas of public policy: (1) the right of a woman to chose whether to have an abortion, (2) affirmative action, (3) the rights of gay people, and (4) invasions of citizen privacy by the government. According to Gibson and Caldeira (2006), these four issues represent the most important policy concerns for roughly 75 percent of the American people. Table 3.2 reports the bivariate relations between ideology and partisanship and each issue variable, as well as the amount of variance jointly explained by these factors. For comparison, we also include in that table comparable analysis of institutional loyalty.

With one exception, all of the policy preferences represented by these variables are moderately to strongly predicted by the respondent's partisan and ideological identification. Liberals and Democrats tend to favor extending the right to choose whether to have an abortion to women, affirmative action, and gay rights. In general, the relationships are stronger with ideology than they are with partisanship. Consider abortion attitudes: the percentages of respondents who would grant considerable rights of choice to women with respect to abortions range from 35.0 percent to 71.7 percent across the seven categories of party identification, and for the eleven categories of ideological self-identification, abortion permissiveness ranges from 37.0 percent to 81.8 percent. These are rea-

TABLE 3.2.
Partisan and Ideological Divisions on Public Policy Issues

	Bivariate Correlation		
Policy	*Partisanship*	*Ideology*	*R*
Abortion	.20 ***	.29 ***	.30 ***
Affirmative $Action_1$	.16 ***	.24 ***	.25 ***
Affirmative $Action_2$	.16 ***	.29 ***	.29 ***
Gay Freedom	.15 ***	.33 ***	.33 ***
Gay Marriage	.22 ***	.38 ***	.39 ***
Civil Liberties	.09 **	.06 *	.10 **
Supreme Court Loyalty	–.05 *	.03	.08

*** $p < .001$ ** $p < .01$ * $p < .05$

Note: All policy variables are scored such that high values indicate liberal responses. For Supreme Court loyalty, high scores indicate greater loyalty. R is the multiple correlation coefficient.

Measures of policy preferences:

Which one of the opinions on this page best agrees with your view on the abortion issue? You can just tell me the number of the opinion you choose.

1 By law, abortion should never be permitted.

2 The law should permit abortion only in case of rape, incest, or when the woman's life is in danger.

3 The law should permit abortion for reasons other than rape, incest, or danger to the woman's life, but only after the need for the abortion has been clearly established.

4 By law, a woman should always be able to obtain an abortion as a matter of personal choice.

Equal opportunity for blacks and whites is very important but it's not really the government's job to guarantee it. (Likert response set)

Irish, Italian, Jewish, and many other minorities overcame prejudice and worked their way up. Blacks should do the same without any special favors. (Likert response set)

Gay men and lesbians should be free to live their own lives as they wish. (Likert response set)

There has been much talk recently about whether gays and lesbians should have the legal right to marry someone of the same sex. Which of the following comes closest to your position on this issue? Do you support full marriage rights for gay and lesbian couples; do you support gay civil unions or partnerships, but not gay marriage; or, do you oppose any legal recognition for gay and lesbian couples?

1 Full Marriage Rights
2 Civil Unions/Partnerships but not full marriage rights
3 No Legal Recognition

In order to curb terrorism in this country, it will be necessary to give up some civil liberties OR We should preserve our freedoms above all, because otherwise the terrorists will win.

1 First
2 More first than second
3 Can't say
4 More second than first
5 Second

sonably strong relationships. The single exception has to do with the civil liberties measure, on which liberals and Democrats tend to favor individual liberty over security, but only slightly so.[17]

The most important contrast in this table is of course with the failure of ideological and partisan identification to predict loyalty toward the Supreme Court. Americans may be divided, even sharply so, on many of the policy issues on which the Supreme Court rules, but with regard to the institution itself, similar divisions are not manifest. Indeed, when institutional loyalty is regressed on the measures of ideological and partisan self-identification, the resultant variance explained is a mere 0.6 percent.

These data do not indicate that support for the Court suffers from partisan polarization, as so many other aspects of American politics seem to. This is not to say that partisanship and ideology do not shape reactions to individual court decisions or to the issues that underlay them.[18] But attitudes toward the institution itself are not at all determined by partisanship or ideology. We must look elsewhere for an explanation of the variability in institutional support.

Knowledge of the Court and Support for It

In general, an important subtext of the findings to this point is that lack of support for the Court is concentrated among people with so little political information that they have difficulty placing themselves on a scale of ideology or partisanship. It is therefore worth considering more completely the relationship between information levels and attitudes toward the Supreme Court.

To what degree does loyalty toward the Supreme Court reflect knowledge of the institution? Fortunately, this important question can be answered since a three-item set of knowledge items was included on the survey (see chapter 2, above). The respondents were asked:

- Some judges in the United States are elected; others are appointed to the bench. Do you happen to know if the justices of the U.S. Supreme Court are elected or appointed to the bench? (65.4 percent correct)

[17] This lack of relationship may be due to the fact that only one-third of the respondents were willing to give up some of their civil liberties in order to fight against terrorism.

[18] Caldeira and Gibson (1992) found that individual policy agreement and disagreement exerted little independent influence on support for the Supreme Court. The same is true in the 2005 data, at least insofar as these four areas of policy attitudes are concerned. Regressing institutional loyalty on the policy measures shown in table 3.2 results in an R^2 of .013, with none of the indicators being significantly related to Court loyalty. For example, the bivariate correlation between attitudes on how much abortion policy should restrict the choices of women and attitudes toward the Court is a trivial .03.

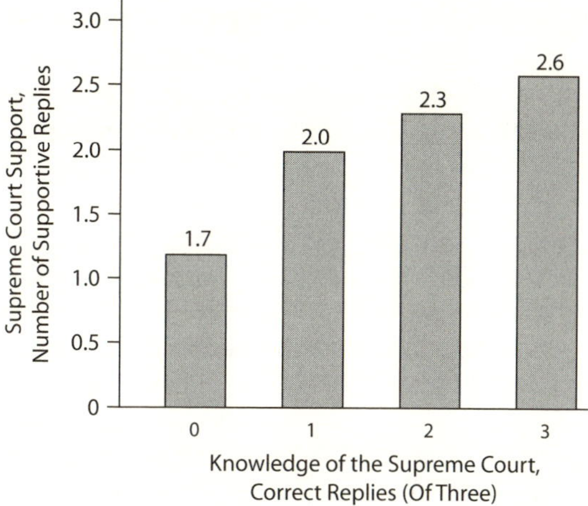

Figure 3.2. The Relationship between Political Knowledge and Institutional Support

- Some judges in the United States serve for a set number of years; others serve a life term. Do you happen to know whether the justices of the U.S. Supreme Court serve for a set number of years or whether they serve a life term? (60.5 percent correct)
- Do you happen to know who has the last say when there is a conflict over the meaning of the Constitution—the U.S. Supreme Court, the U.S. Congress, or the president? (57.2 percent correct)

The hypothesis is that those who are more knowledgeable about the Court will be more supportive of it.[19]

Figure 3.2 reports the mean level of support for the Supreme Court (here indicated, to simplify interpretation, by the number of supportive replies, out of four questions) by levels of knowledge about the institution.[20] The data clearly demonstrate that as knowledge of the Supreme Court increases, so too does loyalty toward the institution. The relationship is at least moderate ($r = .27$). To know more about the Court is indeed to be more favorably predisposed toward the institution.

This finding confirms a considerable body of earlier research on the legitimacy of courts throughout the world (e.g., Gibson, Caldeira, and Baird 1998). We presume that the relationship is based on the following causal chain: attentiveness to the institution is associated with knowledge

[19] This set of indicators is quite reliable, with a Cronbach's alpha of .75.

[20] As we noted in chapter 2, above, the level of knowledge we discovered in this survey is quite high. For a review of the literature on knowledge of the judiciary see Caldeira and McGuire 2005.

of its structure and function, but also with exposure to the legitimizing symbols of the judiciary. Consequently, as citizens are learning about the institution, they are also learning about its special, nonpolitical methods of policy making. In short, they are learning to accept the legitimacy of the institution.

Finally, we have considered the possibility of an interaction between ideology and levels of information about the court, under the hypothesis that support for the Court is more closely connected to ideology among the most informed Americans. In fact, there is some slight evidence of such an effect, with the addition of the ideology interaction producing a statistically significant increase in the explained variance in Court support. (No meaningful interaction exists between partisan identification and knowledge of the Court.) The standardized regression coefficients indicating the connection between ideology and support are: −.09, −.02, −.01, and .14, ranging from the lowest level of knowledge to the highest. Thus, among all respondents who scored less than the highest score on the knowledge index (a score of 3), support for the Court varies independently of one's ideology (the three negative coefficients are not distinguishable from zero). Among the most informed Americans, those who are more *liberal* tend slightly to support the Court more. Since it is doubtful that liberals are supporting the current Supreme Court out of satisfaction with the Court's policy outputs, we interpret this relationship as reflecting the commitment of liberals to institutions generally associated with advancing individual rights, and therefore more akin to diffuse support than specific support. Since no relationship exists between ideology and Court support for most Americans, and since the weak tendency of liberals to support the Court more runs counter to the polarization hypothesis, we will not consider this interactive relationship any further in this analysis.

Democratic Values and Court Support

Caldeira and Gibson found in earlier research (1992) that support for the Supreme Court is fairly strongly grounded in more general commitments to democratic institutions and processes. Those committed to democracy tend to express stronger support for the Supreme Court. We test that hypothesis here, with a more extensive (and perhaps more valid) set of measures of support for democratic institutions and processes.

We have measured support for democratic institutions and processes as a multidimensional metaconcept composed of four distinct subdimensions: (1) political tolerance, (2) the relative value attached to social order versus individual liberty, (3) support for the rule of law, and (4) support

TABLE 3.3.
Support for Democratic Institutions and Processes

	Factors			
Item	*1. Political Tolerance*	*2. Multi-party System*	*3. Order v. Liberty*	*4. Rule of Law*
$Tolerance_1$	.87			
$Tolerance_2$	.85			
$Tolerance_3$	.82			
$Tolerance_4$	.82			
$Tolerance_5$	.54			
$Tolerance_6$	.51			
$Party_1$		.77		
$Party_2$		.60		
$Party_3$		.56		
$Order_1$			.66	
$Order_2$			.57	
$Order_3$			.50	
$Order_4$			.39	
$Order_5$			[.29]	
Rule of Law_1				.67
Rule of Law_2				.61
Rule of Law_3				.41
Rule of Law_4				[.22]

Notes continued on following page.

for a multiparty system. Table 3.3 reports the factor structure resulting from a Common Factor Analysis with oblique (biquartimin) rotation.

As hypothesized, a four-dimensional solution emerged from the factor analysis. With only two somewhat minor exceptions, each item strongly loaded on the factor on which it was expected to load. In the two exceptions (a rule-of-law item and a newly created measure of support for individual liberty), the highest loading of the variable is on the hypothesized factor, even if the loading is less than .30. We have not excluded these items from the factor analysis, but, given their factor loadings, their contribution to the measurement of the construct is small.

The factors are themselves intercorrelated (as they should be). One consequence of this, however, is that multicollinearity exists. The correlation

TABLE 3.3. (*continued*)

Note: Entries shown are factor loadings from the pattern matrix. All loadings greater than or equal to .30 are shown. When the loading of a variable on its hypothesized factor is less than .30, the coefficient is reported in brackets.

The items are:

Tolerance_1: Members of the [GROUP X] should be allowed to a make a speech in our community.
Tolerance_2 Members of the [GROUP X] should be allowed to hold public rallies and demonstrations in our community.
Tolerance_3: Members of the [GROUP Y] should be allowed to a make a speech in our community.
Tolerance_4: Members of the [GROUP Y] should be allowed to hold public rallies and demonstrations in our community.
Tolerance_5: Members of the [GROUP X] should be banned from running for public office.
$\text{Tolerance}_{6:}$ Members of the [GROUP Y] should be banned from running for public office.

Party_1: What our country needs is one political party which will rule the country.
Party_2: The party that gets the support of the majority ought not to have to share political power with the political minority.
Party_3: Our country would be better off if we just outlaw all political parties.

Order_1: It is better to live in an orderly society than to allow people so much freedom that they can become disruptive.
Order_2: Society shouldn't have to put up with those who have political ideas that are extremely different from the majority.
Order_3: When America is at war, people should not criticize the government.
Order_4: Free speech is just not worth it if it means that we have to put up with the danger to society of extremist political views.
Order_5: We are all better off if everyone is free to speak their mind in politics, even if some of things people say are obnoxious and offensive.

Rule of Law_1: It is not necessary to obey a law you consider unjust.
Rule of Law_2: Sometimes it might be better to ignore the law and solve problems immediately rather than wait for a legal solution.
Rule of Law_3: It is not necessary to obey the laws of a government that I did not vote for.
Rule of Law_4: The government should have some ability to bend the law in order to solve pressing social and political problems.

between political tolerance and support for individual liberty is .54; support for a multiparty system is correlated with individual liberty at .56. We have resisted the temptation to reduce this four-dimensional structure to a single measure of support for democratic institutions and processes because one of the most important subscales we wish to analyze is support for the rule of law, and this factor is only weakly correlated with political tolerance and support for individual liberty (although it is strongly correlated with support for a multiparty system). Therefore, in the analysis of this chapter, we incorporate measures of each of these subdimensions of support for democratic institutions and processes within the equations predicting institutional loyalty. Table 3.4 reports the results.

TABLE 3.4.
Democratic Values as Predictors of Loyalty to the Supreme Court

Predictor	*r*	*b*	*s.e.*	*β*
Support for the Rule of Law	.31	.21	.03	.24 ***
Support for a Multiparty System	.33	.14	.03	.17 ***
Political Tolerance	.18	.11	.03	.15 ***
Support for Liberty over Order	.23	.02	.04	.02
Equation				
Intercept		3.34	.02	
Standard Deviation—Dependent Variable		.70		
Standard Error of Estimate		.64		
R^2				.16 ***
N		922		

Note: Significance of standardized regression coefficients (β):
*** $p < .001$ ** $p < .01$ * $p < .05$

We observe a fairly strong relationship between support for democratic institutions and processes and loyalty toward the Supreme Court. The equation with the four predictors is able to explain 16 percent of the variance in loyalty toward the Court. The single best predictor (as indicated by the multivariate regression coefficient) is support for the rule of law, although the high multicollinearity between tolerance and individual liberty dilutes the regression coefficient of each. (For purposes of this analysis, whether one democratic value or the other is the most influential is of modest substantive consequence.) Thus, like the evidence from an earlier, less divisive era, these data demonstrate that attitudes toward the Supreme Court are closely connected to more general orientations toward democratic institutions and processes.

Why do those who support democratic institutions and processes support the Supreme Court more? It seems likely that there are two driving forces in this relationship. First is the rule of law. The Court is obviously a preeminent rule-of-law institution; indeed, the Court is in some sense the principal guardian of the rule of law. Those with great respect for the law tend to favor the Court. Second, the democratic values we measure have much to do with individualism and individual liberty (e.g., tolerance). The Supreme Court is the quintessential minoritarian institution in the American system of government; indeed, it is the primary institution designed and empowered to protect minorities against abuse by the majority. Thus, it is not surprising that loyalty toward the Court is so firmly embedded within the democratic values belief system.[21]

Multivariate Analysis

To this point we have established several possible causes of variability in loyalty toward the Supreme Court. It remains to consider these variables within the context of an overall multivariate equation. We considered including in that equation a variety of additional control variables, following primarily the earlier work of Caldeira and Gibson (1992). Trivial bivariate correlations were, however, found between Court attitudes and gender and age, so these variables were excluded from further consideration. In addition, from the analysis above, the following variables have no connection whatsoever with support for the Court,[22] and therefore have been dropped from the equation: party identification, ideological self-identification, and attitudes toward a woman's right to choose on the issue of abortion.[23] On the other hand, also following Caldeira and Gibson (1992), we added a measure of the respondent's political efficacy,[24] as well as dummy variables for the three racial minorities included in our sample. Table 3.5 reports the results.

[21] These beliefs about democracy are not, however, necessarily grounded in direct individual self-interests. For instance, we asked the respondents whether they would describe themselves "as being a member of a group that is discriminated against in this country." Nearly one-fourth of the respondents (23.2 percent) said yes. The most common basis of claimed discrimination is race (11.7 percent), followed by gender (6.6 percent), age (5.2 percent), ethnicity (4.6 percent), and a variety of other attributes. Those who believe they are victims of discrimination are *not* any more likely to support the Supreme Court than those who perceive no discrimination. Support seems not to be contingent upon having been victimized by the majority. Instead, it seems to be predicated on more general and abstract commitments to individual rights and minoritarianism. This finding is not surprising insofar as sociotropic factors typically are more influential than egocentric factors in shaping political and legal opinions (see, for example, Gibson and Gouws 2003).

[22] Although this decision has no consequence whatsoever for the statistical results, we have excluded these variables in order not to mis-specify the equation. Mis-specification is typically understood as the failure to include relevant predictors, but the concept also refers to the inclusion of irrelevant variables. But as we note, the statistical results are virtually identical when these variables are added to the equation.

[23] Although ideology does not have a direct effect on support for the Court, we do find that conservatives seem to form their views of the Court based on their general commitments to the rule of law, while liberals' support for the Court is more firmly grounded in attitudes toward the party system and political tolerance and much less on support for the rule of law. These findings suggest to us that conservatives may be judging the Court more on majoritarian criteria, while liberals are basing their support on more minoritarian factors. Our data, however, are insufficient to pursue this possibility further.

[24] The measure is a simple index of efficacy derived from responses to four conventional indicators of internal and external political efficacy.

TABLE 3.5.
Multiple Predictors of Loyalty to the Supreme Court

Predictor	*r*	*b*	*s.e.*	*β*
Support for the Rule of Law	.31	.18	.03	.21 ***
Support for a Multiparty System	.33	.12	.03	.15 ***
Political Tolerance	.18	.08	.03	.11 **
Support for Liberty over Order	.23	.00	.04	.01
Court Knowledge	.22	.02	.02	.03
Level of Education	.20	.03	.01	.07
Political Efficacy	.17	.14	.04	.12 ***
African American	–.14	–.22	.07	–.10 ***
Hispanic	–.09	–.11	.07	–.05
Asian	–.06	–.24	.11	–.07 *
Equation				
Intercept		2.94	.10	
Standard Deviation—Dependent Variable		.70		
Standard Error of Estimate		.63		
R^2				.20 ***
N		919		

Note: Significance of standardized regression coefficients (β):
*** $p < .001$ ** $p < .01$ * $p < .05$

First, we note that a considerable amount of variance in institutional loyalty is explained by this simple equation: $R^2 = .20$. Second, despite significant bivariate relationships, three predictors are entirely insignificant in the full equation: knowledge of the judiciary, the respondent's level of education, and the relative value the respondent attaches to liberty and order. The latter is largely a function of multicollinearity (with political tolerance and support for a multiparty system). In addition, the direct impact of knowledge in the multivariate equation vanishes owing to its strong relationships with support for democratic institutions and processes, and via its moderate bivariate relationship with level of education.[25] Third, the most powerful predictors of Court attitudes are two of the measures of democratic values: support for the rule of law and support

[25] When knowledge is regressed on the four measures of democratic attitudes, 20 percent of its variance can be accounted for. The addition of education to that equation adds another 6 percent to R^2.

for a multiparty system. Loyalty toward the Supreme Court is very much a function of broader support for democratic institutions and processes.[26] Finally, as in earlier analyses, we find that African Americans are significantly less supportive of the Court. To a lesser degree, Asian Americans are as well. The coefficient for Hispanics, while negative, does not achieve statistical significance. Care must be taken with these conclusions regarding race and loyalty, however, since relatively small numbers of blacks, Hispanics, and Asians are included in the sample.[27]

If we are allowed to take some liberties in moving away slightly from the data, the causal process involved here seems relatively clear. Citizens who are better educated learn more about the Supreme Court and the democratic theory in which the Court is embedded and sustained. We suspect that the primary content of the learning is to stress that "courts are different." They are relatively nonpolitical, and judges make decisions on the basis of principled criteria—impartiality, for instance—without regard to self-interest (even the self-interest of being re-elected or reappointed). This knowledge predisposes people to accept the viewpoint that courts have a distinctive role in democracy and that that role is not necessarily to mollify the preferences of the majority. The reason why democratic values and court support are so closely connected is that supporting a court—an institution that often tells the majority that it cannot do that which it very much wants to do—requires a relatively sophisticated understanding of democratic theory. For instance, we suspect that the strong correlation between attitudes toward the party system and court support actually has little to do with political parties per se. Those who support a multiparty system are rejecting the sort of knee-jerk antiparty reaction that is common in American society. To support parties in the current

[26] We tested for an interactive effect between political knowledge and democratic values, under the hypothesis that Court support is more strongly grounded in democratic values among those high in political knowledge (see Mondak et al. 2007 for a similar hypothesis regarding attitudes toward Congress). No such effect was found. For instance, the R^2 between Court support and the four measures of political values is .16 for those with the lowest level of information; for those with the highest level of information, the coefficient is .15. Moreover, the analysis reveals no consistent differences in the association between particular democratic values and Court support (e.g., the regression coefficient connecting rule-of-law attitudes with support is .29 for those with the lowest level of knowledge and .24 for those with the highest level of knowledge). Perhaps the difference between these findings on the Supreme Court and those of Mondak et al. on Congress have to do with the remarkably high level of information people have about Congress (2007, 38), although rigorous comparison between the two studies is limited by the use of different measures of institutional attitudes.

[27] Note that Caldeira and Gibson (1992) had a bona fide oversample of African Americans and therefore could give this group much more substantive attention than is possible with the 2005 sample.

context in the United States requires at least the implicit understanding that "modern democracy is unthinkable save in terms of political parties (Schattschneider 1942, 1). As it turns out, a reasonable number of Americans understand this, and therefore support for the Court is quite high.[28]

Discussion

An important finding of this research is that the United States Supreme Court is widely supported by the American people, and that support has little to do with ideology or partisanship. Instead, loyalty toward the institution is grounded in broader commitments to democratic institutions and processes, and more generally in knowledge of the role of the judiciary in the American democratic system.

These findings thus reinforce rather than challenge existing research on public attitudes toward the Court. That this is so is the most important finding of this research, given strong reasons for expecting otherwise. Although the American people are severely divided on many important issues of public policy, when it comes to the institution itself, support for the Court has little if anything to do with ideology and partisanship. Liberals trust the Court at roughly the same level as conservatives; Democrats and Republicans hold the Supreme Court in similar regard. We do not argue that different people do not have different expectations and evaluations of Court-made policy: Liberals and conservatives unquestionably differ in their preferences for how the Supreme Court should decide important issues of public policy. But, as yet, the legitimacy of the Court has not been threatened by the divisions over public policy. Even the most contentious of issues—such as those decided in *Bush v. Gore* or abortion rights—seem not to have undermined public confidence in the Supreme Court as an institution.

From the analysis presented here, it appears that the Supreme Court has sufficient institutional legitimacy to be able to continue to perform

[28] In an earlier analysis of data from 1987, Caldeira and Gibson (1992) discovered significant differences in how opinion leaders formed their attitudes toward the Supreme Court. In particular, their support for the Court seemed to be more highly conditional upon policy agreement. We have explored this issue in these data, but, with fewer than seventy-five respondents claiming to be opinion leaders, the analysis is not stable enough to warrant much attention. Nonetheless, in these limited data it appears that the views of opinion leaders toward the Supreme Court are *not* more closely connected to policy views than they are among the mass public as a whole. Nor are partisan and ideological identifications in any way connected to loyalty toward the Court. If anything, the views of opinion leaders are more solidly grounded in their attitudes toward democratic institutions and processes. As we note, these results must be treated as highly tentative in light of the relatively small number of opinion leaders included in the sample.

its assigned role within the American democratic scheme, even within the context of deep substantive divisions among the American mass public. Whether this will remain so is unclear, especially if the Supreme Court takes a dramatically rightward shift in its policy outputs (as many expect it will). As African Americans have shown us, even obdurate loyalty toward an institution can indeed wither away. But, at present, for those who worry about the systemic consequences of sharp ideological divisions in American politics, the findings of this analysis will surely provide some solace.

CHAPTER FOUR

Institutional Loyalty, Positivity Bias, and the Alito Nomination

On January 31, 2006, Judge Samuel Alito was confirmed as the 115th justice of the United States Supreme Court. The vote in the Senate was 58 in favor, 42 opposed, which makes the Alito confirmation one of the more controversial and divisive in recent times.[1] Judge Alito is expected, and so far has proven, to be among the most conservative justices to sit on the Supreme Court in the modern era. With the country closely divided on so many ideological and partisan dimensions, the confirmation of Alito to a seat on the High Court may have vast and lasting political consequences.

One plausible explanation for the success of President Bush's nomination is that the mass public in the United States was convinced that Judge Alito was neither too extreme nor intemperate to sit on the country's most prestigious court. If indeed Americans came to view Judge Alito as sufficiently moderate and temperate, it is not due to lack of effort on the part of the Democrats and liberal interest groups. For instance, all told, liberal interest groups spent $1,365,857 on advertising in trying to convince the American people that Alito should not be confirmed (and conservatives spent $1,041,535 in favor of his confirmation), making this one of the more expensive confirmation fights ever.[2] As a result of the Republicans' successful campaign, the charge that Judge Alito was outside the ideological mainstream seemed to resonate with only a minority of Americans.

Thus, at least from casual observation, it appears that the American public may have formed its preferences on the nomination on the basis of two types of considerations. People either (1) decided to evaluate Alito on relatively nonpartisan grounds, asking only whether he possessed the legal and technical qualifications necessary to be a good judge, or (2) decided that the judge's ideology was indeed relevant to making a decision

[1] For a record of Supreme Court confirmations, see Epstein et al. 2003, 352–58.

[2] Data compiled by the Brennan Center. See http://www.brennancenter.org/programs/scnominations/Alitopercent20statepercent20chartpercent20.pdf (accessed 4/12/2006). According to these data, spending by "progressive groups" exceeded spending by "conservative" groups.

on his confirmation, but that his ideological position, although conservative, sits squarely within the mainstream of American politics. Indeed, perhaps these two decision-making processes are not independent but are instead crucially interrelated: if judicial qualifications are clear, ideological questions are muted; if the nominee's qualifications are called into doubt, then a second-stage dimension—defined by ideology, policy, and partisanship—becomes relevant. It seems that, for most Americans, Alito possessed the appropriate judicial skill and temperament and therefore questions of ideology became less relevant. And for those who questioned Alito's qualifications, scrutiny of his ideology led many to the conclusion that the judge is not an extremist.

Of course, this view of how ordinary people form their preferences is highly speculative. In fact, we know precious little about how ordinary citizens evaluate Supreme Court nominees. The public opinion industry deems citizens' views important in confirmation fights and therefore pays some attention to their opinions toward nominees (e.g., Pew Research Center 2005), but in-depth analyses are practically nonexistent. Academic research on citizen preference-formation in confirmation fights is also relatively rare, in part owing to the difficulty of mounting and executing major academic surveys within the confines of the relatively short period between a vacancy on the Court and a Senate vote on a successor. Consequently, although we know something about how familiar demographic variables and partisanship/ideology relate to confirmation preferences, we understand virtually nothing about how ordinary citizens view the process and form their opinions.

A recently developed theory—the theory of positivity bias—may provide a useful framework for analyzing mass opinion-formation. This theory was created in part to account for the U.S. Supreme Court's unexpected success at protecting its institutional legitimacy even while awarding the presidency to George Bush in a bold and highly controversial 5-4 decision, on which the justices divided by partisanship (*Bush v. Gore*). According to Gibson, Caldeira, and Spence (2003a; see appendix C), when ordinary citizens become motivated to pay attention to the U.S. Supreme Court—when their attitudes come out of hibernation—they approach the context with preexisting beliefs about law and politics. Some have in the past developed strong loyalty to judicial institutions, a loyalty that makes them particularly receptive to the legitimizing judicial symbols that envelope any judicial events or controversies attracting the attention of the mass media. These citizens may initially pay attention to the Court out of dissatisfaction and displeasure. Yet, because they are susceptible to (predisposed to) the influence of strong legitimizing legal symbols, they tend to wind up accepting the argument that courts are different from other political institutions and that "politics" plays a limited role in the judicial process. Suspicions about partisan and ideological influences on legal processes are dispelled, owing to the frame created by standing commitments to the Court. In this bias we see the powerful influence of institutional legitimacy: to the extent that an institution has built a loyal constituency, it possesses a "reservoir of goodwill" that allows it to "get away with" unpopular decisions. This is precisely what Gibson, Caldeira, and Spence (2003a; see appendix C) argue happened in the fabled case of *Bush v. Gore*.

Are confirmation processes analogous to highly salient and controversial court decisions? Yes. In the typical confirmation controversy, one side alleges that the nominee lacks the qualities of a good judge. Opponents may ground this contention in any of several factual contexts: the nominee is prejudiced, has associated with biased or extremist groups (e.g., memberships in discriminatory clubs), is dogmatic, and/or is outside the broad ideological consensus in the country. Proponents of the nominee seek to emphasize the "judiciousness" of the candidate, arguing in terms of judicial qualifications, temperament, and role orientations (e.g., judicial restraintism), typically making extensive use of the potent symbols of judicial legitimacy.[3] Thus, in a contentious confirmation, the American people confront two competing *frames* for evaluating nominees: the frames of judiciousness and of ideology and partisanship. Understanding which frame comes to dominate in the minds of ordinary Americans in any particular confirmation fight is an issue of considerable theoretical and practical importance.

The purpose of this chapter is therefore to investigate the nature of the confirmation decisions made by the American public in the Alito confirmation. Based on a nationally representative panel survey, initiated in 2005 and followed with extensive re-interviews conducted during the heat of the Alito controversy, we explore the hypothesis that the framing of positivity bias accounts for public preferences on Alito's confirmation. We begin by recounting the highlights of the Alito confirmation fight. We next argue that the theory of positivity bias is relevant to the dispute, and we derive hypotheses from that theory. In the empirical portion of the

[3] During the confirmation hearings for Judge Alito, Professor Anthony Kronman (former dean of the Yale Law School) provided a useful understanding of "judiciousness" (D.C.H e-Media 2006):

> The temperament of the judge, as we see it, is marked by modesty, by caution, by deference to others, in different roles with different responsibilities, by an acute appreciation of the limitations of his own office, and by a deep and abiding respect for the past. There is a name that we give to all of these qualities taken together. We call them judiciousness. And in calling them that, we recognize that they are the special virtues of a judge.

chapter, we contrast two models of confirmation preferences: one based on ideological, policy, and partisan considerations; the other, on what we term "judiciousness"—the satisfaction of legalistic expectations citizens hold of judges. Our initial analysis reveals that both models are useful predictors of preferences. We next test the crucial conditional hypothesis: preexisting institutional loyalty structures the decision-making processes citizens use in evaluating confirmation controversies. In line with the theory of positivity bias, those with strong loyalty to the Supreme Court weigh judiciousness much more heavily in their calculus, even if they are similar to those with less loyalty in their use of ideological and partisan considerations in forming their opinions.

We conclude the chapter by reconnecting the findings to the theory. Institutional loyalty provides a frame through which people perceive and judge events. In the case of the U.S. Supreme Court, that frame centers on law, not politics. The Court has a large constituency in the United States that is prepared to accept the argument that "courts are different," that courts are not ordinary political institutions. So long as a controversy is associated with sufficient reinforcing stimuli—emphasizing the powerful and persuasive symbols of the judiciary— opponents will find it difficult to substitute an alternative frame centered on ideology and partisanship. In terms of future nominations to the Court, we predict that this theory is so well understood (de facto) by the central actors in the confirmation process that, other things being equal (e.g., control of the Senate), it will be difficult indeed for even a determined minority to succeed in blocking a president's nomination—that is, so long as the U.S. Supreme Court is able to maintain its extraordinary store of institutional legitimacy within the American mass public.

The Confirmation of Samuel Alito to the Supreme Court

For the Supreme Court, 2005 was a year of great speculation and anticipation—about retirements and resignations, Chief Justice Rehnquist's health, potential battles royale over nominees, and of course long lists of aspiring candidates. Public interest picked up markedly when, in August of 2004, Chief Justice Rehnquist announced that he had cancer and was undergoing treatment; this information naturally brought about a drum beat of stories. As if to dramatize the possibilities of massive change on the Supreme Court, the frail chief justice administered the oath to President Bush in mid-January of 2005 and quickly left the stands, thereby fueling comment on how long he would remain on the Court. To the surprise of most, the chief justice was not the first departure. Justice

O'Connor announced her retirement in early June of 2005. In July, President Bush sent up Judge John Roberts to the Senate as her replacement. Judge Roberts's nomination proceeded smoothly through the summer and seemed to be well-poised for the Judiciary Committee's hearings in September. Then, in early September, the chief justice died. After an interval, the president switched Roberts's nomination to the chief justiceship, and, a month later, to the shock of most observers, named his chief of staff, Harriet Miers, to replace O'Connor. This nomination, as is well known, was ill-starred from the outset and, in a rare move for a president, was withdrawn after three weeks, largely on the basis of conflict within the Republican coalition. Judge Alito, who had been on the short list for each previous opening, received the nomination from the president on October 31, 2005.

Organized interests on the left and right prepared long before Alito's nomination, amassing war chests in the millions of dollars. Prior to the Roberts nomination, in July of 2005, each side threatened to spend more than $10 million, if need be, on advertising on the radio, television, and newspapers, polling, grassroots lobbying, direct lobbying, and research. From a Brennan Center study, we know that liberals spent $1,365,857, conservatives $1,041,535, for advertising relating to the Alito nomination. How much the opposing coalitions spent on other facets of the campaign (e.g., private polling), presumably much more than the figures recorded for television advertising, we of course cannot tell. Many organized interests on both sides took positions on Alito immediately or in the early days after President Bush announced his nomination; several released detailed studies of Alito's record with breathtaking speed, all of which indicated the intensity of feeling about the Court and how much preparation organized interests had done in anticipation of this nomination.

Opponents of Judge Alito sought to portray him as an extremist, a far-right conservative, in the mode of Judges Bork and Scalia; an eager and early Reaganite and follower of Attorney General Meese; unsympathetic to underdogs of all sorts; an antagonist to civil rights and freedom of speech; a hard-core opponent of the right to privacy and reproductive freedom, and thus a very likely vote against *Roe v. Wade*; an abject supporter of executive power over legislative authority and individual freedom; tepid on voting rights (as exhibited by his youthful criticisms of the reapportionment decisions); and much too willing to countenance breaches of the separation of church and state.

Proponents in turn pointed to Judge Alito's long record of professional distinction, as a top graduate of Princeton and Yale Law; on the staffs of the Department of Justice and the Solicitor General; as U.S. attorney for the District of New Jersey; and fifteen years as judge on the U.S. Court of Appeals for the Third Circuit; plaudits from fellow students, lawyers, and judges, including the extraordinary appearance of many of his colleagues from the Third Circuit in his support at the Senate hearings; the ABA's seal of approval of his nomination to the Court of Appeals in 1990; and, later, on his nomination to the Court, the ABA's evaluation of him as "highly qualified."

Supporters on the right and the White House and opponents on the left targeted the same senators and states, a small set of senators in the ideological middle, who in the past had demonstrated a willingness to cross party lines on judicial nominations, including in particular the Gang of Fourteen and swing or battleground states.[4] The states targeted for paid advertising and grassroots lobbying included Nebraska, North Dakota, South Dakota, Louisiana, Arkansas, Maine, Rhode Island, Montana, Ohio, Washington, and West Virginia. Fence-sitting senators, as befitting their position, by and large delayed making public announcements on Alito until after the first of the year.

On the Alito nomination, in contrast to controversial nominations of the past, the nominee drew surprisingly little criticism from the legal academy, lawyers, or fellow judges. The silence of the stars of the legal academy's firmament to sound off on Judge Alito was deafening; no letters, public statements, or pronouncements came from such voluble law professors as Lawrence Tribe, Cass Sunstein, Jack Balkin, and their ilk. To be sure, several hundred legal academics did sign a letter of opposition against Alito and conveyed it to the Senate Judiciary Committee, but the cast of characters, with the exception of a few, did not come from the "A list" of law professors.

[4] In May 2005, with numerous controversial judicial nominations stalled and Senate Majority Leader Bill Frist threatening to utilize the "nuclear option" to override the filibuster, a group of fourteen moderate Senators reached an agreement that would save the filibuster and force a vote on a number of nominees (see, e.g., Law and Solum 2005). Calling themselves the "Gang of Fourteen" and led by Senators McCain and Nelson, these seven Republican and seven Democratic Senators issued a "Memorandum of Understanding on Judicial Nominations." In that memo, the "Gang of Fourteen" agreed to invoke cloture on three of the pending nominations. They also committed that in the future "nominees should only be filibustered under extraordinary circumstances." Finally, the "Gang" agreed to oppose any rule changes in the 109th Congress that would eliminate the power of the filibuster. With the support of these fourteen Senators, there were over sixty votes to invoke cloture and end a filibuster under the Senate's Rule 22 on the nominations of Janice Rogers Brown, Priscilla Owen, and William Pryor. Because, however, these fourteen Senators also opposed the "nuclear option" (eliminating the filibuster), Senator Frist lacked the simple majority of votes required to change the Senate's rules regarding the filibuster. Thus, by so acting, these fourteen Senators advanced Senate business (by mandating an "up or down" vote on a few nominees), developed a precedent of filibustering judicial nominees only in times of "extraordinary circumstances," and saved the filibuster from demise.

During the Senate Judiciary Committee's hearings, in January of 2006, proponents and opponents attempted to gather evidence consistent with the claims they had staked out at the beginning of the nomination: Alito as a mainstream conservative, restrained in his view of the law, a judge who would interpret the law rather than make it and who would respect precedent and other sources of law, versus Alito as an extreme conservative, a conservative activist, ready to overturn long-established precedents. Alito's opponents on the committee tried to draw him in to taking clear positions on issues before the Court or in the immediate past; for the most part, Alito refused to commit himself and tried to reassure skeptics by saying that he supported a number of superprecedents or "established law," such as *Griswold v. Connecticut*. Democrats on and off the committee seemed, in the view of most observers, not to have made much headway in portraying Judge Alito as out of the mainstream of American judicial thinking.

Despite a last-minute effort by Senate liberals to mount a filibuster against Judge Alito, and great exertions by liberal interest groups, the Senate confirmed him at the end of January on a vote of 58-42. In the end, it appeared that most Americans concluded that President Bush should not be denied the judge he wanted to place on the Supreme Court. Indeed, Judge Alito seemed to be successful in gaining the fairly robust support of the American people, including most Democrats. Those who managed the campaign, including in particular Alito's testimony before the Senate Judiciary Committee, executed a nearly perfect, textbook example of how to get a president's nominee confirmed (on presidential public relations efforts, see Maltese 1995). A significant part of this victory had to do with effectiveness in portraying Alito as conservative, but as a mainstream conservative, certainly not an extremist. Perhaps more important was their success at focusing the debate, not on ideology, but instead on Alito's professional accomplishments and judicial qualifications.

The Positivity Theory Hypotheses

Yet, another large part of the confirmation story has to do with preexisting attitudes toward the Supreme Court. As it has been developed, the theory of institutional loyalty and positivity bias suggests that standing commitments to an institution generate a bias in expectations and perceptions of confirmation struggles that predisposes people to emphasize certain criteria and ultimately to accept judicial nominees.

As we noted in the introductory chapter to this book, positivity bias can be understood as a frame through which events are perceived and evaluated (on framing, see Druckman 2004). Framing is a process by which the salience or accessibility of different criteria or dimensions by which an event or case might be judged varies according to established characteristics of the individual. In events like confirmation hearings, different parties seek to activate preexisting frames in the minds of ordinary citizens in the hopes that the frame will influence how the event is perceived and judged. From one camp—typically by proponents of the nominee—the frame of legality is advanced, under the argument that the nominee ought to be judged primarily (if not exclusively) on legalistic criteria like judiciousness. On occasion, the opponents will take issue with the nominee's judiciousness, but it is more likely that they will attempt to substitute a frame defined by ideology, partisanship, and policy. Which frame comes to dominate depends in part on the nominee and the elements of the specific context, but also in part on whether citizens have preexisting commitments (loyalty) to the institution that can be activated by the various groups and interests involved in the nomination controversy. In the case of the Supreme Court, the outcome of a confirmation controversy depends in significant part on the degree to which citizens subscribe to the myth of legality, which is of course a central element of positivity bias. Thus, competing frames are typically available in the political marketplace, and the battle for public support of the nominee is often, if not typically, a battle of one frame against another.

Thus, the central hypothesis emerging from the theory of positivity frames is that preexisting institutional loyalty plays a crucial role in how people perceive and judge confirmation processes. Of course, facts and contexts are not unimportant; how people perceive the details of confirmation fights is crucial to the formation of their preferences. But we hypothesize that institutional loyalty interacts with events surrounding the confirmation, leading citizens with a sense of loyalty toward the Court to rely primarily upon criteria of judiciousness in judging the nominee. In contrast, those without a sense of institutional loyalty are likely to judge the confirmation process largely in terms of ordinary political criteria.

In sum, our view of citizen preference-formation in the confirmation process is as follows:

- Those holding strong institutional commitments to the U.S. Supreme Court tend toward accepting the myth of legality, rejecting the view that courts are ordinary political institutions.
- Both institutional loyalty and belief in the myth of legality generate a particular set of expectations about the desirable qualities of a Supreme Court nominee and how the confirmation process ought to unfold. The central element of these expectations is that judges and

courts are different from ordinary politics. We refer to this package of expectations as "judiciousness."

- Intelligent confirmation strategies exploit predispositions to perceive nominees as judicious and not political. With prominent exceptions, the opposition tends not to directly challenge the judiciousness of the candidate, focusing instead on trying to exploit the political dimension. But predispositions to see nominees in nonpolitical frames are strong and difficult to overcome.
- Our most important general hypothesis is thus that institutional loyalty tends to shield candidates from ideological scrutiny (and therefore we posit a conditional/interactive relationship).

Assessments of the Confirmation Process

Like other nominations to the Supreme Court, the Alito case was quite salient to the American people. One-half (51.9 percent) of our respondents claimed to have followed the events either very or somewhat closely, with 22.2 percent admitting that they paid relatively little attention to the process ("not at all closely"). Perhaps more telling, 62.5 percent of the respondents said that they had in fact seen or heard an advertisement on TV, radio, or in the newspapers concerning whether Alito should be confirmed. Earlier research has shown that confirmation hearings can be quite visible to the American people. For instance, 95 percent of Americans held an opinion about whether Clarence Thomas should be confirmed to the U.S. Supreme Court (see Gimpel and Wolpert 1996; Wolpert and Gimpel 1997; see also Hutchings 2001).

What were the preferences of the American people regarding Judge Alito: should he have been confirmed? We asked the respondents their views on this question and the evidence is unequivocal: a substantial majority of Americans (62 percent) supported Alito's confirmation.[5] Only 26 percent felt the nominee should not be confirmed. Perhaps somewhat surprisingly, only 12 percent of the respondents had no opinion about Judge Alito. In a follow-up question asking how important it is to the respondents that their senator vote their preferred way on the nomination, nearly one-third (32 percent) thought the senator's vote very important and another 45 percent rated it somewhat important, while only

[5] Most public opinion polls agree with our findings that a majority of Americans supported the confirmation. Specific poll results varied considerably, however, in large part (we believe) owing to the time period during which they were conducted, differences in how "don't know" or "uncertain" replies were managed, and also whether the respondents were qualified as registered or likely voters. Our findings match very closely the results of a Democracy Corps Poll conducted January 22–25, 2006.

4 percent judged how their senator voted on the nomination as not important at all (for earlier research on the effects of confirmation battles on the votes of the constituents of U.S. Senators, see Overby et al. 1992). In general, the Alito nomination was salient and significant to the American people, and a sizeable majority favored the ascension of Alito to the High Bench.

But do Americans view the confirmation process as having been fair? We also asked our respondents to rate "the overall fairness of the [confirmation] process." By far, the modal reply was that the process was "somewhat fair" (60.3 percent). Only one-fourth of the respondents thought the process "not very" or "not at all" fair (25.8 percent). In general, most Americans voiced few complaints about the overall fairness of the confirmation process.

For the purposes of this analysis, the dependent variable under scrutiny is preferences on whether Judge Alito should be confirmed to the U.S. Supreme Court. The specific measure we analyze in this chapter is an index that combines the responses to the question about whether Judge Alito ought to be confirmed with the replies to a query about the importance of the issue to the respondent (using the importance of the votes of the respondent's senators on the confirmation). This measure is a continuous variable, which we rescaled to range from zero to one. The mean of the index is .61, and it is correlated with the five-point Alito preference measure at .99, and with a preference trichotomy (favor, don't know, oppose) at .94. Thus, this measure captures the intensity of support or opposition to Alito's nomination and therefore can serve as a useful dependent variable for the analysis that follows.[6]

The Models

Our analysis focuses on two major classes of explanations of preferences on the confirmation process. The first we term the Model of Judiciousness; the second, a Policy Agreement Model.

The Policy Agreement Model

The simplest way to think about how confirmation preferences are formed is to focus on policy and ideological agreement. We hypothesize that those who perceive the nominee's policy and ideological positions as congruent with their own will support the nominee's confirmation.

[6] Note that we have replicated all of the analysis that follows using the simple five-point preference indicator as the dependent variable and the differences in the resulting coefficients are minuscule.

The greater the policy distance between the respondent and the perceived location of the nominee, the less likely will the respondent be to support the confirmation.

We measured congruence along two dimensions. The first is broad ideological agreement. Using a scale ranging from (0) extremely liberal to (10) extremely conservative, we asked the respondents to locate themselves, President Bush, and Judge Alito in ideological space. The results are reported in figure 4.1.

The results indicate that the opponents of Judge Alito failed in their efforts to paint the nominee as an extreme conservative. With the center point on this 11-point scale at 5.5, the average American places herself/himself very near the middle of the continuum (5.8); Bush is only somewhat to the right (6.3); and Alito is only very slightly to the right of Bush (6.5).[7] On average, the American people viewed Judge Alito as 0.7 points more conservative than themselves, based on an 11-point scale. It is perhaps a bit unexpected to observe that Bush is not seen as a quite conservative president, but, most important for this analysis, Alito is *clearly not* perceived as an extreme conservative. Only 9.8 percent of the respondents placed Alito at the most extreme point (10) on the liberalism–conservatism continuum. Were we to treat scores of 8 through 10 as indicative of being quite conservative, only 35.2 percent of our respondents rated Alito as quite conservative.[8] The data seem to indicate that Americans see Alito as conservative, but not as excessively or unacceptably so.

[7] Perhaps some will find it surprising that fully 92 percent of the respondents were able to assign Judge Alito a position on this continuum.

[8] For our purposes, we can remain agnostic about Alito's true ideological location. Segal and Cover (1989), however, have developed a methodology to measure the ideological positions of Supreme Court nominees. The method analyzes the editorials written about a nominee (from when he was nominated to when the Senate first votes on that nomination) in four newspapers, with each of the paragraphs of these editorials coded as liberal, moderate, or conservative. A final score for each nominee's ideology is computed based on the subtraction of the fraction of paragraphs coded as conservative from the fraction that are coded as liberal and then dividing by the total number of coded paragraphs. The resulting scores range from 0 (most conservative) to 1 (most liberal) (see Segal and Cover 1989; Epstein and Segal 2005). According to this perceived ideology indicator, Alito scores at .10 (Segal 2006). In comparison, Justice Scalia has a score of 0 and Justice Thomas has a score of .16, both of whom are commonly perceived to be extremely conservative members of the Court. Although Segal-Cover ideology scores will on occasion inaccurately represent the ideological position of a justice once he or she begins service on the bench (as in, for example, Justice Stevens, who has a moderate Segal-Cover ideology score but has been a consistently center-left justice), most of the scores are remarkably accurate in capturing the ideological preferences of future justices on the Court, particularly in the context of civil liberties and civil rights (Epstein and Mershon 1996). Thus, it appears that Justice Alito could very well become one of the most consistently conservative of the justices now serving on the Supreme Court (and Alito's votes to date bear out this conjecture).

Ideological Position of	Mean	Std. Dev.	N
Me (The Respondent)	5.8	2.3	327
President Bush	6.3	3.1	325
Nominee Alito	6.5	2.3	307

Perceptions of ideological location: 0 = extremely liberal 10 = extremely conservative

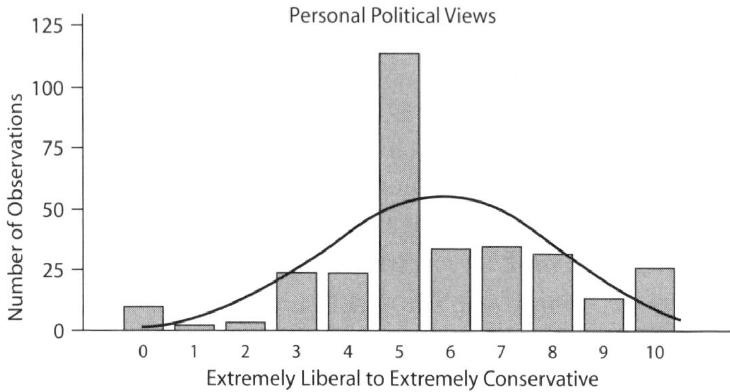

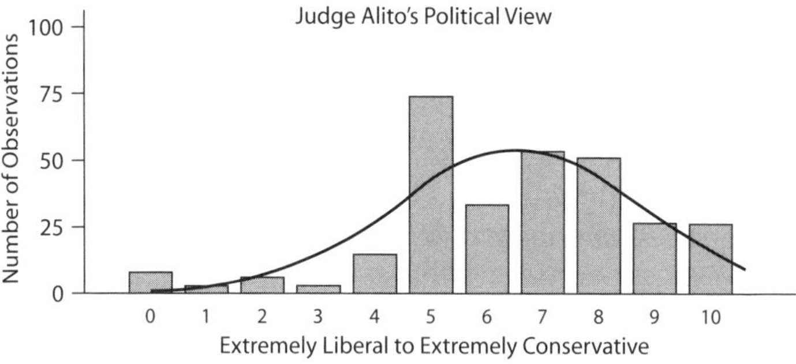

Figure 4.1. Ideological Placements and Perceptions

Another way to parse these data is to compare the respondent's own position to her/his perception of Bush and Alito. The data in table 4.1 show whether Bush and Alito are seen as more liberal than the respondent, more conservative, or about the same. The latter category is defined as being within plus or minus two points from the respondent's own position on the 11-point scale. Thus, if the respondent places herself at 6 on the continuum, then scores from 4 through 8 are categorized as "about the same."

TABLE 4.1.
Relative Ideological Positions

	More Liberal	*About the Same*	*More Conservative*	*Total*
Alito compared to me (N = 304)	13.3	60.9	25.8	100 %
Alito compared to Bush (N = 302)	12.3	70.7	17.0	100 %
Bush compared to me (N = 321)	22.1	45.6	32.3	100 %

Note: Rows total to 100 % (except for rounding error).
"About the Same" = ± 2 points away.

The compelling finding in table 4.1 is of course the 60.9 percent of the respondents who see Alito as being relatively close to their own ideological position. That figure strikes us as emblematic of the opposition's abject failure at portraying Alito as excessively and illegitimately conservative.[9] By an almost two-to-one margin, the respondents who do not share Alito's ideology see him as more conservative, but this is within the context of six out of ten Americans perceiving themselves to hold roughly the same ideological position as the judge. Moreover, the average of the absolute values of the distance between the respondent and Judge Alito is 2.4 (standard deviation = 2.3). When the differences are collapsed, we find that 28 percent of the respondents saw Alito as more liberal than themselves, 50 percent saw him as more conservative, and 22 percent (the mode of the uncollapsed distribution) rated him as having exactly the same score on the ideological continuum. The respective figures for the differences between the respondents and President Bush are 32 percent, 52 percent, and 16 percent. If we narrow the measure of the ideological distance between the respondent and Judge Alito to only a single point (plus or minus) on the 11-point scale, we find that 43 percent of the respondents differ little from their perceptions of the ideological position of the judge.[10]

[9] Although we know of no surveys that have measured public perceptions of the ideological location of Supreme Court nominees, we believe that the failure of the Bork nomination was to a considerable degree due to his opponents' success at painting him as an extremist. For a review of the public opinion evidence on this score, see Vieira and Gross 1998, chap. 14, 151–59.

[10] Owing to space limitations, the survey did not ask any questions about other sitting justices. Note that in the statistical analysis that follows we of course use the uncollapsed measure of ideological distance. The categorical variables we discuss here are presented for illustrative purposes only.

So the evidence from this survey is that Bush was perceived to have nominated someone of roughly his own ideological position to the Court. This seems to fit with the oft-heard argument that "Bush won the election, therefore he gets to pick the judges," so long as they are not too extreme. Clearly, Alito was not perceived by most as an extremist. It is therefore not very surprising that a majority of Americans supported Alito's confirmation and that the Senate vote turned out the way it did.

Our survey also posed several questions about policy preferences, beginning by asking the respondent to rate six policy areas on their importance to her or him.[11] The issues were: (1) abortion, (2) affirmative action, (3) issues related to homosexuality, (4) the amount of money courts can award in personal-injury lawsuits, (5) whether to allow religious displays on government property, and (6) whether the government has the right to record the telephone calls and monitor the e-mail of private U.S. citizens in order to prevent people from planning terrorist or criminal acts. Next, we asked the respondent to identify the most important issue of this group. The results are reported in table 4.2.

The most important court-related issue to these respondents is the government's right to circumvent the privacy of citizens in order to deal with terrorism and crime, with 63.8 percent of the respondents assigning the issue the highest importance rating ("very important"), and more than one-third of the respondents rating this as their most important issue. Following this is the perennial conflict over abortion, with over one-half of the respondents rating it as very important, and one-fourth judging abortion to be the most important issue before the Supreme Court. Perhaps most interesting is the relatively low salience of issues of homosexuality, affirmative action, and even so-called tort reform, none of which attracts a very large constituency. Indeed, twice as many respondents ascribe the greatest importance to the issue of whether to allow religious displays on government property as compared to affirmative action. Homosexuality is even less significant to these respondents.

Table 4.2 also reports the respondents' positions on the judicial issue they deem to be most important. Considerable variability exists in the percentages of respondents adopting the modal position on each issue. For instance, a very large percentage (84.6 percent) of those rating the public display of religious symbols as most important wants to allow such displays. Similarly, most (73.1 percent) of those rating the civil liberties issue as most important would limit the government's right to monitor

[11] The question stem read: "As I read some issues the Supreme Court may rule on over the coming years, please tell me how important each issue is to you personally. Are court decisions on [INSERT ITEM] very important, somewhat important, not very important, or not important at all to you?"

citizens' telephone calls and e-mail. But, those who mention abortion as the most important issue are closely divided between those who would restrict abortion rights versus those who would expand them (with the remainder not wishing to change current policy). These figures are of course not for the population as a whole, but are rather the preferences of those who rate the specific issue as the most important on the list.

Finally, table 4.3 reports the respondents' perceptions of Judge Alito's position on the issue they consider to be most important.[12] Again, this table reports only the views of those who rate the issue as most important to them. So, for instance, among those viewing the religious display issue as most important, 43.2 percent view Judge Alito as inclined to favor allowing such displays, which is of course the preferred position of nearly all of those who assign priority to this controversy (see table 4.2, facing). Generally, the modal perception on five of the six issues is conservative, with the somewhat puzzling exception that 50.3 percent of those rating issues of homosexuality as most important asserting that an "Alito Court" would expand gay rights (in contrast to 42.1 percent who believe gay rights would be reduced—data not shown).[13] Interestingly, very large percentages of Americans believe they know Judge Alito's position on the

[12] The question read: "Assume for a moment that Judge Alito is confirmed and takes his seat on the Supreme Court. In your view, do you think that the decisions of the Supreme Court would [READ RESPONSE OPTIONS]?" The options for the various issues are:

- Considerably expand the right to abortion
- Somewhat expand the right to abortion
- Stay about the same as they are now
- Somewhat restrict the right to abortion
- Considerably restrict the right to abortion

- Expand the use of affirmative action
- Reduce the use of affirmative action

- Expand the rights of homosexuals
- Reduce the rights of homosexuals

- Limit the amount of money courts can award in personal injury lawsuits
- Not limit the amount of money

- Allow religious displays on government property
- Prohibit religious displays on government property

- Not limit the government's right to record the telephone calls and monitor the e-mail of private U.S. citizens in order to prevent people from planning terrorist or criminal acts
- Limit the government's right to record the telephone calls and monitor the e-mail of private U.S. citizens in order to prevent people from planning terrorist or criminal acts

[13] This finding likely reflects the fact that only 4.7 percent of the respondents rated gay rights issues as most important to them.

TABLE 4.2.
The Distribution of Issue Importance

Issue	*Percentage Rating as Very Important* [a]	*Percentage Rating as Most Important* [b]	*Modal Position*	*Percentage Favoring Modal Position*
Abortion	57.5	25.3	Restrict abortion rights	43.1
Affirmative Action	44.2	7.5	Expand the use	68.0
Issues related to homosexuality	33.7	4.7	Reduce gay rights	62.6
The amount of money courts can award in personal injury lawsuits	44.8	8.5	Limit awards	69.8
Whether to allow religious displays on government property	41.9	14.8	Allow displays	84.6
The government's right to record the telephone calls and monitor the e-mail of private U.S. citizens in order to prevent people from planning terrorist or criminal acts	63.8	36.8	Limit government rights	73.1

[a] The question read: "As I read some issues the Supreme Court may rule on over the coming years, please tell me how important each issue is to you personally. Are court decisions on [INSERT ISSUE] very important, somewhat important, not very important, or not important at all to you?"

[b] The question read: "Of the issues I just mentioned, which single one is the most important to you?"

issue of greatest importance to them (even if not necessarily on all issues). The largest exception to this pattern is on the issue of religious displays, but even here, of those rating this issue as most important, nearly three-fourths believe they can identify Judge Alito's position. At the other extreme, only 6.9 percent of those rating abortion as most important are uncertain about the judge's stance on that judicial policy.

Putting these various data together, we were able to score virtually all respondents on the degree of perceived agreement with the "Alito Court" on the policy matter to which the respondent assigned the highest priority. We differentiate in this analysis between ordinary disagreement and strong disagreement by distinguishing between those who take an entirely contrary position to Alito (e.g., expand versus restrict civil liberties) and those who differ only in that either the respondent or Alito favors "no change" in current policy, while the other favors a change in substantive position. The distribution of the variable is as follows:

In agreement with Alito— 41.2 percent
Disagreement with Alito— 11.1 percent
Strong disagreement with Alito— 34.5 percent
Uncertainty over Alito— 13.3 percent
Total— 100.0 percent

TABLE 4.3.
Perceptions of Alito's Position, *Most Important Issue*

Issue	*Perceived Position — Modal Position*	*Percentage Perceiving Modal Position*
Abortion	Restrict abortion rights	56.1
Affirmative Action	Reduce the use	53.1
Issues related to homosexuality	Expand gay rights	50.3
The amount of money courts can award in personal injury lawsuits	Limit awards	39.8
Whether to allow religious displays on government property	Allow displays	43.2
The government's right to record the telephone calls and monitor the e-mail of private U.S. citizens in order to prevent people from planning terrorist or criminal acts	Not limit government rights	45.6

The question read: "Assume for a moment that Judge Alito is confirmed and takes his seat on the Supreme Court. In your view, do you think that the decisions of the Supreme Court would [READ RESPONSE OPTIONS]?"

Thus, specific policy agreement with Judge Alito is less widespread than general ideological congruence, with only four in ten Americans expecting a Court including Justice Alito to make the policy preferred by the respondent on her or his most important issue; however, only slightly more than one-third take a substantive policy view opposite of that which they perceive Judge Alito to hold. Once again, a remarkably high percentage of the American people believe they know the judge's position on the issue of greatest importance to them.

Finally, this finding of relatively high knowledge about Alito's policy positions seems to be at odds with the general conclusion that the American people know precious little about their courts and judges. It seems likely that our findings reflect our focus on the policy issues that are important to the individual respondent, rather than on issues that are preselected by the researchers. When we allow the respondents to tell us which issues are important to them, we touch on highly salient concerns and consequently find remarkably high levels of information about the perceived policy location of the nominee. Moreover, a new revisionist literature is developing that shows that the American people are vastly more knowledgeable about courts than heretofore thought (e.g., Gibson and Caldeira 2007). In our second-wave survey, for example, three knowledge questions were asked about the United States Supreme Court (how the justices are selected, the length of their terms, and who has the "last say" in interpreting the constitution). Fully 46 percent of the respondent gave correct answers to all three knowledge measures.

The Judiciousness Model

Judiciousness is an alternative to ideology as a criterion for preference-formation and is based on the qualities the respondent views as important for being a good judge.[14] We began consideration of the respondents' expectations with the following text: "Now I would like you to focus on thinking about the characteristics of a good Supreme Court judge, that is, what a good judge ought to be like. First, how important would you say it is for a good Supreme Court judge to [INSERT ITEM]?" The characteristics about which we queried the respondents were:

- Strictly follow the law no matter what people in the country may want
- Try to maintain the appearance of being fair and impartial no matter what the cost
- Be especially concerned about protecting people without power from people and groups with power
- Stay entirely independent of the president and the government
- Respect existing Supreme Court decisions by changing the law as little as possible
- Uphold the values of those who wrote our constitution two hundred years ago

Table 4.4 reports the importance the American people ascribe to these characteristics.

The data clearly reveal that Americans expect their Supreme Court justices to maintain the appearance of fairness and impartiality (75.5 percent), as well as, no doubt, to *act* in a fair and impartial way; to be especially concerned about protecting people without power from those with power (71.7 percent), and to uphold long-standing constitutional values (67.4 percent). Given the ballyhoo from elites about precedent and

[14] These questions are obviously based on role theory, which specifies that actors in particular positions are subject to expectations about how they ought to behave (and that such expectations are one factor influencing the actor's own beliefs about how he or she ought to behave—i.e., role orientations). Few governmental actors are subject to such all-encompassing and stringent expectations as judges. On role theory, see Gibson 1981. For a study of the expectations citizens hold of members of Congress, see Kimball and Patterson 1997.

TABLE 4.4.
Expectations of the Characteristics of a Good Supreme Court Justice

Characteristic	*% Rating It Very Important*	*Mean*[a]	*Std. Dev.*	*N*
Appear fair and impartial	75.5	3.66	.70	334
Protect people without power	71.7	3.62	.69	334
Uphold constitutional values	67.4	3.59	.68	335
Strictly follow the law	61.7	3.47	.80	334
Independent of president and government	60.9	3.47	.77	334
Respect existing decisions	37.3	3.11	.89	334
Represent the majority	36.0	2.84	1.10	334
Give my ideology a voice	32.9	2.95	.95	335
Base decisions on party affiliations	17.8	2.08	1.12	333

The items read:

"Now I would like you to focus on thinking about the characteristics of a good Supreme Court judge, that is, what a good judge ought to be like. First, how important would you say it is for a good Supreme Court judge to . . .

Try to maintain the appearance of being fair and impartial no matter what the cost.
Be especially concerned about protecting people without power from people and groups with power.
Uphold the values of those who wrote our constitution two hundred years ago.
Strictly follow the law no matter what people in the country may want.
Stay entirely independent of the president and the government.
Respect existing Supreme Court decisions by changing the law as little as possible.
Be involved in politics, since ultimately they should represent the majority.
Give [CONSERVATIVES/LIBERALS] a strong voice in how the constitution is interpreted.
Base their decisions on whether they are a Republican or a Democrat.

[a] The response varies from (1) Not at all important/Don't know to (4) Very important. Thus, higher mean scores indicate greater ascribed importance to the characteristic.

"superprecedents" during the Senate hearings on this nomination, perhaps the most surprising finding in these data is the relatively small weight the Americans give to respecting existing Supreme Court decisions (only 37.3 percent rate it as very important). Across the set of items, the average number of characteristics judged to be extremely important is 3.7 (with a median of 4). Virtually all respondents found something on our list to rate as very important.

These expectations are interesting in and of themselves and we will have more to say about them at a later point in our research. For the purposes of this analysis, however, the primary function of these variables is to allow an expectancy-based method of analyzing judiciousness. Consequently, we asked the respondents to evaluate Judge Alito on each of these criteria, and we used their replies to calculate an index of satisfaction/disappointment for each of the characteristics about which we asked. The index is scored only for those respondents rating the attribute as very important. Table 4.5 shows the results.

First, we note that uncertainty about Judge Alito is relatively rare, with none of the questions generating as much as 10 percent "don't know" responses. It seems from these data that Judge Alito was a reasonably well known quantity to most Americans.

Second, for none of the characteristics is there a great deal of certainty as to Judge Alito's likely actions. The greatest agreement is on whether Alito will try to appear to be fair and impartial, but only 41.2 percent of the respondents are quite certain that Judge Alito will act in this fashion.[15] In this sense, the American people seem somewhat less confident of what sort of justice Alito will become.

According to the index, disappointment is most widespread on whether Alito will be independent of the president and the government and whether he will be concerned to protect the powerless (on each, 10.5 percent scored as very disappointed), and is least widespread on whether the justice will uphold constitutional values (4.9 percent very disappointed, 42.0 percent very satisfied)—among those rating the attribute as very important. Table 4.6 reports the mean satisfaction/disappointment scores (with high scores indicating greater satisfaction). The column labeled "N" is the number of respondents on which the mean is based, which is the number of people rating the characteristics as "very important" in the role-expectations questions.

The data reveal that, in general, the Americans are reasonably satisfied with Judge Alito, since all the means are greater than .5 (which is the score for uncertainty about Alito). In every instance, Judge Alito is judged to be at least somewhat likely to behave as the respondent expects him to behave. With scores like these, it is little wonder that a majority of Americans favored Judge Alito's confirmation.

Table 4.6 also reports the bivariate correlation between the disappointment/satisfaction measure and opinions on whether Alito ought to be confirmed. Several interesting findings emerge from these coefficients. First, some variability exists across the attributes, ranging from a correlation of

[15] Note that the last two attributes in the table have no comparable expectation indicator since we assume that all respondents expect judges to act in a fair and impartial manner in making decisions, and since not all respondents necessarily see Alito as a conservative.

TABLE 4.5.
Perceptions of the Characteristics of Judge Alito

Characteristic	*% Don't Know*	*% Rating Him Very Likely To*	*Mean*[a]	*Std. Dev.*	*N*
Strictly follow the law	5.2	31.2	3.06	.80	335
Appear fair and impartial	4.6	41.2	3.20	.81	335
Protect people without power	7.1	21.2	2.79	.89	334
Represent the majority	4.5	32.7	3.01	.89	331
Independent of president and government	5.9	21.6	2.76	.89	332
Give my ideology a voice	6.8	27.9	2.88	.92	334
Respect existing decisions	6.4	24.8	2.95	.80	331
Uphold constitutional values	4.8	37.1	3.14	.82	335
Base decisions on party affiliations	5.7	30.4	3.01	.87	330
Base decisions on his conservatism	5.8	33.7	3.01	.82	334
Make fair and impartial decisions	5.8	33.7	3.08	.84	335

The items read:

Strictly follow the law no matter what people in the country may want.
Try to maintain the appearance of being fair and impartial no matter what the cost.
Be especially concerned about protecting people without power from people and groups with power.
Be involved in politics, since ultimately they should represent the majority.
Stay entirely independent of the president and the government.
Give [CONSERVATIVES/LIBERALS] a strong voice in how the constitution is interpreted.
Respect existing Supreme Court decisions by changing the law as little as possible.
Uphold the values of those who wrote our constitution two hundred years ago.
Base his decisions on the fact that he is a Republican.
Base his decisions on the fact that he is a conservative.
Make fair and impartial decisions.

[a] The response varies from (1) Not at all likely to (4) Very likely. Thus, higher mean scores indicate greater confidence that Alito will behave in the fashion indicated.

.53 for satisfaction that Alito will strictly follow the law, to a significantly smaller coefficient of .27 for respecting existing decisions. In general, the more an expectation is satisfied, the more likely the respondent is to support the confirmation of Judge Alito.

A very strong bivariate relationship exists between the average disappointment/satisfaction score and support for confirming Judge Alito

Table 4.6.
Disappointment/Satisfaction with Judge Alito

	Disappointment / Satisfaction			
Characteristic	*Mean*[a]	*Std. Dev.*	N	*Correlation with Confirmation Preference*
Strictly follow the law	.69	.29	207	.53
Appear fair and impartial	.74	.27	253	.42
Protect people without power	.60	.30	239	.43
Independent of president and government	.59	.31	201	.45
Respect existing decisions	.70	.29	122	.27
Uphold constitutional values	.73	.28	226	.44

The items read:

Strictly follow the law no matter what people in the country may want.
Try to maintain the appearance of being fair and impartial no matter what the cost.
Be especially concerned about protecting people without power from people and groups with power.
Stay entirely independent of the president and the government.
Respect existing Supreme Court decisions by changing the law as little as possible.
Uphold the values of those who wrote our constitution two hundred years ago.

[a] The disappointment/satisfaction measure ranges from (0)—completely dissatisfied to (1)—completely satisfied. High scores indicate the greater satisfaction of expectations.

to the U.S. Supreme Court: $r = .56$ (N = 321, $p < .000$). Those whose expectations of Alito are satisfied—in a "running tally" of a sort—are vastly more likely to support his confirmation. This is quite strong evidence in support of the expectancy model.

Summary

To this point in the analysis, we have developed three important independent variables and their associated hypotheses:

H_1: Support for Alito's confirmation is expected to be inversely related to the degree to which general ideological disagreement with Alito is perceived.

H_2: Support for Alito's confirmation is expected to be inversely related to the degree to which the citizen perceives policy disagreement with Judge Alito on the issue of greatest importance to the citizen.

H_3: Support for Alito's confirmation is expected to be positively related to the degree to which Judge Alito is perceived to satisfy the respondent's expectations of judiciousness.

We turn next to our analysis of confirmation preferences.

Determinants of Confirmation Preferences

We begin the analysis with a simple set of equations positing that confirmation preferences are no more than a function of ideological and partisan disagreement. Table 4.7 reports three nested regression models. Model 1 hypothesizes that confirmation preferences are a function of the general ideological distance (measured as a continuous variable) between the respondent and Judge Alito. Model 2 adds policy disagreements to the equation. Because we do not necessarily hypothesize linear effects of policy disagreements, we nominalized the variable and included in the equation three dummy variables: policy disagreement, strong policy disagreement, and uncertainty over whether disagreement exists with Judge Alito's policies. The excluded category for this set of dummy variables is agreement with Alito. Finally, in Model 3 we add the respondent's party identification (measured using the conventional seven-point scale) to the equation, hypothesizing that Democrats are less likely to prefer Alito than Republicans. Partisan self-identification was measured using the conventional seven-point scale.

Several telling conclusions emerge from the three models analyzed in table 4.7. First, ideological disagreement has a moderately strong impact on confirmation preferences: the greater the ideological distance between the respondent and Alito, the more likely the respondent is to oppose confirmation. Second, however, virtually no *independent* impact can be found from specific policy disagreement. A significant bivariate correlation between strong policy disagreement and opinions exists ($r = -.16$), indicating that greater policy disagreement is associated with less support for confirmation; but the effect of this variable is entirely subsumed in the multivariate equation by the measure of ideological distance. Opposition to Alito's confirmation therefore had less to do with any specific policy disagreements with the judge and more to do with broader ideological conflict (although of course the former is a component of the latter).[16]

[16] We have carefully considered whether these results are influenced by multicollinearity, and conclude that they are not. The strongest bivariate correlation among the independent variables is only .32, and the variance-inflation factors (VIF) only slightly exceed 1.0 (with the largest VIF of only 1.24). Clearly, multicollinearity is not a problem for this analysis.

TABLE 4.7.
Ideology and Policy Preferences as Predictors of Alito Confirmation Preferences

		Model 1			Model 2			Model 3		
Predictor	*r*	*b*	*s.e.*	*β*	*b*	*s.e.*	*β*	*b*	*s.e.*	*β*
Ideological Distance	–.37	–.02	.02	–.37***	–.02	.02	–.35***	–.02	.00	–.32***
Policy—Disagreement	–.01				.01	.22	.00	.06	.21	.02
Policy—Strong Disagreement	–.16				–.19	.16	–.07	–.13	.15	–.05
Policy—Don't Know	.05				.03	.26	.01	.02	.25	.00
Party Identification	–.32							–.16	.03	–.26***
Intercept		3.69	.08		3.74	.10		4.40	.17	
Standard Deviation—Dependent Variable		1.22			1.22			1.22		
Standard Error of Estimate		1.14			1.14			1.10		
R^2				.14***			.14***			.21***
N		293			293			293		

Note: Standardized Regression Coefficients (β): *** $p < .001$ ** $p < .01$ * $p < .05$

The contribution of Model 3 is to demonstrate that partisanship influences confirmation opinions over and above simple ideological disagreement. As expected, the independent effects of both ideological distance and partisanship on confirmation preferences are smaller than their bivariate effects; nonetheless, both variables exert a moderately strong impact on views of whether Alito should be confirmed. In this instance, partisanship and ideology are separate bases on which one might oppose or support the elevation of Judge Alito to the Supreme Court.

Thus, at this point in the analysis, it appears that opinions on the Alito confirmation are fairly simple: Democrats and those perceiving strong ideological differences with the judge (mainly, but not exclusively, liberals) tend to oppose him. The equation has reasonable predictive power (explaining 21 percent of the variance in confirmation preferences). But is this simple model of ideology and partisanship all there is to the confirmation controversy?

Adding Judiciousness to the Equation

To what degree does failure to satisfy the role expectations of the respondent influence confirmation preferences? As we have noted, the answer provided by these data is that preferences are strongly influenced by ex-

TABLE 4.8.
Ideology, Partisanship, and Role Expectations as Predictors of Alito Confirmation Preferences

	Model I			
Predictor	*r*	*b*	*s. e.*	*β*
Ideological Distance	–.38	–.01	.00	–.19***
Partisanship	–.31	–.10	.03	–.16***
Satisfaction of Role Expectations	.57	2.48	.27	.47***
Intercept		2.33	.26	
Standard Deviation—Dependent Variable		1.22		
Standard Error of Estimate		.96		
R^2				.39***
N		284		

Note: Standardized Regression Coefficients (β): *** $p < .001$ ** $p < .01$ * $p < .05$

pectations: $r = .56$. Those who perceived Judge Alito as satisfying their expectations are considerably more likely to favor his confirmation. Moreover, this relationship eclipses the ideology/partisanship equation in its ability to predict opinions.

Ideology and partisanship alone (excluding policy disagreement) can explain about 21 percent of the variance in confirmation preferences. When the measure of expectation satisfaction is added to that equation, *another 18 percent of the variance is explained* (for a total of 39 percent). Table 4.8 reports the full regression results.[17]

The addition of role expectations to the equation significantly reduces the impact of ideological distance and partisanship on preferences, although the relationships remain highly statistically and substantively significant. But the primary importance of table 4.8 is that it demonstrates an extraordinarily strong and independent impact of the satisfaction of role expectations on confirmation preferences. Those whose expectations of Alito are satisfied more strongly are *much more* supportive of his confirmation than those holding unrequited expectations. Thus, the conclusion to draw from this table is that confirmation preferences are a function of three major considerations: (1) whether Judge Alito is seen as having the characteristics of a good judge, as defined and perceived by the citizen;

[17] The strongest bivariate correlation among the independent variables is only –.34, and the variance-inflation factors (VIF) only slightly exceed 1.0 (with the largest VIF of only 1.18). Clearly, multicollinearity is not a problem in this analysis.

(2) the perceived ideological distance between Alito and the citizen; and (3) the citizen's partisanship. Perhaps the most important finding is that confirmation preferences clearly are shaped by much more than just ideology and partisanship.

Finally, we have considered whether the relationships depicted in table 4.8 are affected when a variety of demographic characteristics and other attitudes are added to the equation. Specifically, we control for: (1) whether the respondent is an African American; (2) gender; (3) level of education; (4) income; (5) age; (6) knowledge of the Supreme Court; and (7) confidence in President Bush. In this expanded equation, the coefficients for the three substantive variables reported in table 4.8 are virtually identical. The only control variable with a significant effect on the preference for whether Alito should be confirmed is gender; none of the other variables comes close to having a statistically or substantively significant independent impact. Ceteris paribus, men are more likely to support Alito. Because gender is uncorrelated with the independent variables of primary substantive interest in this analysis, the reduced equation, which has the virtue of simplicity, adequately and accurately represents these relationships.

We also investigate whether perceptions of Judge Alito's role orientation had any impact on support for his confirmation. As it turns out, 34.2 percent of the respondents perceived him as an activist, 48.0 percent as a "strict constructionist," and the remaining 17.8 percent was unsure. The addition of dummy variables for perceptions of activism and "don't know" responses to the equation reported in table 4.8 results in a significant but small change (1.7 percent) in the amount of variance explained. Those who perceive Alito as more of an activist are less likely to support his confirmation ($\beta = -.12$, $p = .013$), as are those who do not know whether Alito is an activist or a strict constructionist ($\beta = -.09$, $p = .069$). Because the increase in explanatory power is small—and because we do not have questions that directly measure whether the respondent prefers activist or constructionist judges—we have not included these indicators in the central portion of our analysis.

The Conditional Effect of Institutional Loyalty

The theory of positivity bias suggests that those with certain predispositions are likely to view confirmation disputes in particular ways. More specifically, those expressing strong attachment to the Supreme Court are likely to hold a distinct set of expectations of judges and are also predisposed to accept arguments by the nominee and her or his advocates about the importance of judiciousness, especially in contrast to policy preferences, ideology, and partisanship.

Testing this hypothesis requires that we develop a measure of loyalty to the U.S. Supreme Court, which of course we have produced in chapter 3, above. To recap, our measure of institutional loyalty is the conventional four-item index, and, conceptually, it varies from willingness to accept fundamental alterations in the structure and function of the institution to willingness to protect the integrity of the institution from disabling modifications.[18] We have computed two such indices, one indicating the average response to the four statements and another simply counting the number of supportive responses. Moreover, we calculate these loyalty indices from two sources: the 2005 survey (i.e., loyalty measured prior to the Alito nomination), and loyalty measured contemporaneously with the Alito questions (i.e., in the 2006 survey). The former of course have stronger claims to causality, but the relationships are attenuated by any change that might have occurred between the two interviews. The latter indicators should be stronger predictors since they are measured at the same point in time, but owing to that factor, confidence in the causal inference is clouded. Table 4.9 reports the bivariate correlations between institutional loyalty and the role-expectation questions.[19] From both sets of coefficients, perhaps we can get some purchase on the nature of the relationship.

Those who express loyalty toward the Supreme Court are more notable for what they do not emphasize than for what they do. The strongest correlations are negative. For instance, high institutional loyalty is associated with a lesser emphasis on the need for justices to represent the majority and to base their decisions on party affiliation (and to a lesser degree with giving voice to the citizen's ideology). Also interesting is the complete lack of correlation between institutional loyalty and the markers of traditional mechanical jurisprudence judging: strictly following the law, respecting existing decisions, upholding constitutional values. As reported

[18] The propositions (replies on which were collected via a five-point Likert response set) are:

- The right of the Supreme Court to decide certain types of controversial issues should be reduced.
- If the U.S. Supreme Court started making a lot of decisions that most people disagreed with, it might be better to do away with the Supreme Court altogether.
- The Supreme Court can usually be trusted to make decisions that are right for the country as a whole.
- The U.S. Supreme Court gets too mixed up in politics.

[19] These are the actual expectations questions (see table 4.4, above), which are unadjusted for perceptions of Judge Alito's characteristics.

TABLE 4.9.
Correlations of Expectations of the Characteristics of a Good Supreme Court Justice and Institutional Loyalty

Characteristic	*Institutional Loyalty, 2005*	*Institutional Loyalty, 2006*
Strictly follow the law	.00	.03
Appear fair and impartial	–.02	–.07
Protect people without power	–.02	.07
Represent the majority	–.20 ***	–.25 ***
Independent of president and government	–.03	.06
Give my ideology a voice	–.09 *	–.15 ***
Respect existing decisions	.02	.08
Uphold constitutional values	–.01	.07
Base decisions on party affiliations	–.18 ***	–.34 ***
Index of Judiciousness	.10 *	.12 *

N ≈ 333.

The items read:

Strictly follow the law no matter what people in the country may want.
Try to maintain the appearance of being fair and impartial no matter what the cost.
Be especially concerned about protecting people without power from people and groups with power.
Be involved in politics, since ultimately they should represent the majority.
Stay entirely independent of the president and the government.
Give [CONSERVATIVES/LIBERALS] a strong voice in how the constitution is interpreted.
Respect existing Supreme Court decisions by changing the law as little as possible.
Uphold the values of those who wrote our constitution two hundred years ago.
Base their decisions on whether they are a Republican or a Democrat.

The response varies from (1) Not at all important/Don't know to (4) Very important. Thus, higher mean scores indicate greater ascribed importance to the characteristic.

Note: Entries are bivariate correlation coefficients.
*** $p < .001$ ** $p < .01$ * $p < .05$, one-tailed test

in table 4.9, the correlations between institutional loyalty and the index of expectations of judiciousness are also relatively weak (although statistically significant). To some degree, this reflects the lack of variance in these expectations, but these data nonetheless suggest a slight amendment to our thinking about the myth of legality: Institutional loyalty in this case seems to be distinctive *less* with regard to adopting a strong commitment to a mythical understanding of the role of the judge, and *more* with regard to the rejection of an explicitly political definition of what constitutes a good judge. To the extent this interpretation is correct, our argument that the primary message of controversy-based socialization—that judges are different from politicians—receives at least some support from these data.[20]

To reiterate, the hypothesis we test is that those with preexisting loyalty to the U.S. Supreme Court will judge the confirmation process differently. More specifically, we expect those with high levels of loyalty to weigh judiciousness much more heavily than they weight partisanship and ideology, and more highly than those with low loyalty toward the Court. Table 4.10 reports the relevant data. In testing the conditional hypothesis, we cast our lot with improving internal validity: increasing the confidence in the causal inference (even though this works against the confirmation of the hypothesis). Therefore, institutional loyalty is measured in 2005, and all other variables associated with the confirmation are measured in 2006. The temporal sequencing of the data adds increased confidence to any causal inferences that we might make about the effect of preexisting attitudes on expectations, perceptions, and judgments of the confirmation process.

The coefficients in this table provide strong support for the hypothesized conditional effect of preexisting loyalty toward the Supreme Court. Those who score high on the loyalty index tend to weigh satisfaction of their role expectations (judiciousness) much more heavily in forming a confirmation preference than those who score low on institutional loyalty ($b = 3.46$ versus $b = 1.97$). The difference of regression coefficients is highly statistically and substantively significant. Institutional loyalty makes little difference in how much weight is accorded ideological distance and partisanship (the coefficients between citizens with high and low loyalty do not differ). Thus, the consequence of institutional support is that loyalty points the citizen toward judging the process on the basis of judiciousness, and the satisfaction of one's expectations of judges has

[20] This is an important finding, about which we will have more to say at a later point in the analysis of these data. It seems that those with strong loyalty to the Court expect an institution that is not necessarily mechanical in its approach to decision making, but that nonetheless is not characterized by the demons of "partisan bickering," self-interestedness, et cetera, that are perceived to dominate decision making in Congress (e.g., Hibbing and Theiss-Morse 2002). This suggests that the American people might indeed be willing to recognize discretion in judicial decision making—even accepting the inevitability that judges must make the law, not just interpret it—without threats to the legitimacy of courts. So long as the exercise of discretion is principled (and, we suspect, grounded in concepts such as fairness and justice, the very important complements to legality), people may accept it as legitimate. Indeed, it also seems possible that when the strict adherence to *stare decisis* produces decisions perceived to be unfair, strong legitimacy threats emerge from following the law (e.g., "legal technicalities"), since for most Americans fairness most likely trumps legality. Much more analysis must be done of the expectations people hold of law and courts in the United States.

TABLE 4.10.
The Conditional Effect of Institutional Loyalty on Alito Confirmation Preferences

	Low Loyalty				High Loyalty			
Predictor	*r*	*b*	*s. e.*	β	*r*	*b*	*s. e.*	β
Ideological Distance	−.40	−.01	.00	−.23***	−.37	−.02	.01	−.22**
Partisanship	−.23	−.09	.04	−.15*	−.41	−.07	.04	−.11
Satisfaction of Role Expectations	.50	1.97	.35	.39***	.68	3.46	.43	.59***
Intercept		2.70	.33			1.48	.43	
Standard Deviation — Dependent Variable		1.19				1.27		
Standard Error of Estimate		.99				.88		
R^2				.32***				.53***
N		169				113		

Note: Standardized Regression Coefficients (β): *** $p < .001$ ** $p < .01$ * $p < .05$

When a single, interactive equation is estimated for all respondents, the results are:

Y = 3.57 + (.74 * Role Expectations) – (.01 * Ideological Distance) – (.07 * Partisanship) – (.67 * Institutional Loyalty) + (.88 * Expectations-Loyalty Interaction)

a very large effect on confirmation preferences, even if loyalty does not totally eliminate considerations of ideology and partisanship.

Table 4.10 provides a useful means of illustrating these important differences. A more efficient method of testing the interactive hypothesis is available, however.[21] We estimated a single equation that included as predictors: (1) ideological distance, (2) partisanship, (3) satisfaction of role expectations, (4) institutional loyalty, and (5) the interaction of loyalty and role expectations. We tested the hypothesis using two separate indicators of loyalty: the mean response to the four items and a count of the number of supportive replies to the four propositions. The results of this formal test of interaction strongly support our hypothesis, and it matters little which of the indicators of loyalty is used.[22] Since the count variable employs the most intuitively accessible metric (the number of items

[21] When we tested for interactive effects between loyalty and ideological distance and loyalty and partisanship, we found absolutely no evidence of such relationships. Given the similarity of the coefficients for these two variables shown in table 4.4, above, this is an entirely predictable finding.

[22] When the interactive term is entered into the equation, R^2 increases by 5 percent, which is statistically significant at $p < .000$. Thus, the hypothesis of linearity is rejected; an interactive relationship does indeed exist. On the analysis of interactions see Cohen et al. 2003.

on which support is expressed, varying from zero to four), we use that variable to illustrate the results of the hypothesis test.

The regression coefficient for the interaction term is .88 (see table 4.4, at the bottom, for the full equation). Thus, the slopes of the satisfaction of role expectations variable, according to level of institutional loyalty (number of items endorsed), are:

Items Endorsed	Slope
0	.74
1	1.62
2	2.51
3	3.39
4	4.27

These figures clearly document that the impact of the satisfaction of role expectations on confirmation preferences increases rather dramatically over the range of degrees of institutional loyalty.[23] The most loyal citizens place an exceptional degree of emphasis on the judiciousness of the nominee when considering whether to support the nomination to the High Bench.[24]

Discussion and Concluding Comments

The analysis presented in this chapter has produced some reasonably strong support for the theory of positivity bias in public reactions to Supreme Court decisions and events. Most specifically, we have shown that those who express loyalty toward the U.S. Supreme Court form their judgments about nominees to the Court on the basis of specific criteria: satisfaction by the nominee of expectations of judiciousness. Among the most loyal, failure to satisfy role expectations is strongly associated with opposition to confirming Judge Alito, just as satisfying such expectations is strongly connected to approval of his confirmation. These citizens do not eschew entirely issues of ideology, policy, and partisanship—and in that sense they differ little from those who express low loyalty toward the Court—but the dominant factor in their decision making focuses on

[23] The satisfaction variable varies from 0 to 1, with a mean of .68 (standard deviation = .23).

[24] The direct interrelationship between loyalty and satisfaction is small, $r = .10$. This means that those who are more loyal to the Supreme Court tend only modestly to hold role expectations that were satisfied by Judge Alito. The effect of the loyalty variable is rather to enhance the role of satisfaction in shaping confirmation opinions, not necessarily to shape directly perceptions of the nominee.

whether the nominee has the characteristics of a good judge. This is evidence, we argue, of a preexisting attitude (loyalty) establishing a frame of reference for evaluating judicial nominees. This frame provides the criteria for judging the candidates. We place an unusually high degree of confidence in these findings because they make use of panel data in which loyalty to the Supreme Court is measured well before the variables associated with perceptions and judgments of the confirmation process, a particularly tough test of the hypothesis.

These findings give succor to those who have long labored toward understanding the causes and consequences of institutional legitimacy. Our evidence indicates that legitimacy matters. Whether citizens accord legitimacy to institutions like the Supreme Court has highly significant consequences for a variety of aspects of judicial politics.

Moreover, this analysis also provides considerable support for the theory of framing. We have demonstrated that preexisting attitudes shape evaluations of contemporary events. These attitudes activate criteria against which perceptions of facts are evaluated. Without the frame, matters of judiciousness are less relevant to citizens in their assessments of Supreme Court nominees. This seems to us to be a classic example of the power of frames, although we certainly recognize that more work on the process involved here is in order. Nonetheless, the empirical results are encouraging.

Our findings have important consequences for the confirmation process itself, quite apart from any theoretical implications. We begin with the basic empirical fact that the U.S. Supreme Court has a very large supply of institutional legitimacy. Owing to that legitimacy, a large proportion of the American people are predisposed to judge confirmation controversies in terms of criteria of judiciousness, apart from normal partisan or ideological politics. The *presumption* is that judiciousness is the most relevant criterion. Of course, candidates can be defeated on issues of judiciousness, of which perhaps Harriet Miers's nomination is a classic example. It turned out that it was not difficult to challenge Miers's judicial credentials.[25] Indeed, in her case, many did not reach consideration of the dimension of ideology and partisanship, so suspect were her judicial qualifications. Once the presumption of judiciousness was disestablished as the principal relevant criterion, issues of ideology and partisanship could be effectively raised. Of course, the withdrawal of Miers's nomination by President Bush perhaps had more to do with politics within the Republican Party than with ordinary citizens, but we nonetheless perceive

[25] Since Miers had never served as a judge, she was not entitled to be referred to as "Judge Miers" during the debates over her candidacy, and therefore this aspect of judicial symbolism was denied to her.

some of the same processes at work here. If a president is shrewd enough to nominate someone who is even minimally qualified to be a Supreme Court justice, then the debate can often be centered on issues of judiciousness, as it was for Judges Alito and Roberts.

The job of the opposition to a nominee is to try to substitute an alternative frame through which the debate can be conducted. That frame of course focuses on ideology, issues, and partisanship. We have seen, however, just how difficult it is for substitute frames to be effective. We attribute this to the wellspring of legitimacy enjoyed by the Supreme Court, and the consequence of this legitimacy, which is the belief that judges are different from ordinary politicians, and that therefore nominees ought to be evaluated on the basis of legal, not political, criteria. As long as the Supreme Court maintains its reservoir of goodwill—and if presidents are cagey enough to nominate candidates for whom an easy prima facie case for judiciousness can be made—it seems unlikely that political forces can be effectively mobilized to deny presidents their choices.

We close this chapter by reiterating the view that institutional legitimacy is an enormously important source of political capital. The conventional hypothesis is that legitimacy is significant because it contributes to acquiescence to decisions of which people do not approve (e.g., Gibson, Caldeira, and Spence 2005). We have devoted considerable effort toward investigating that hypothesis throughout the world. But to the extent that we are correct in our analysis of the theory of positivity bias, we suggest here that legitimacy has an even more significant role in the political process: citizens who extend legitimacy to the U.S. Supreme Court are characterized by a whole set of attitudes that frame a variety of expectations and choices. These frames provide a standing decision that is very difficult (although not impossible) to rebut in contemporary American politics. This consequence of institutional legitimacy is perhaps the most significant of all.

CHAPTER FIVE

A Dynamic Test of the Positivity Bias Hypothesis

As we observed earlier in this analysis, few studies of attitudes toward political institutions have adopted a dynamic perspective. Either implicitly or explicitly, most studies seem to presume that citizen beliefs about institutions are inculcated early in the life-cycle, perhaps even in adolescence, and change little over time (hence the great interest in research on political socialization—e.g., Caldeira 1977). Under this assumption, the question of change does not seem interesting.

It seems to us, however, that the assumption of stasis is untenable. Bits and pieces of empirical evidence support our view, as in the changes at the aggregate level in the support African Americans extend to the U.S. Supreme Court (e.g., Gibson and Caldeira 1992) or in the increase in Court support by Republicans (again, at the aggregate level) after the Court's decision in *Bush v. Gore*. Indeed, the hypothesis that institutional legitimacy is affected by both short-term and long-term forces seems entirely plausible.

Consequently, the purpose of this chapter is specifically to test hypotheses about the causes of changes in attitudes toward the Supreme Court. Because confirmation fights attract the attention of the American people, an opportunity arises for citizens to revise and update their attitudes toward the Supreme Court and its institutional legitimacy. Confirmation processes stimulate attitudes toward law and courts to emerge from their hibernation. Our general hypothesis in this chapter is that when citizens pay attention to the Supreme Court, they are taught something about the structure and function of the institutions, and generally that these lessons tend to reinforce the legitimacy of the institution.

The theoretical underpinning of the analysis in this chapter is, of course, the theory of positivity bias. As we have explicated it in the earlier chapters of this book, that theory asserts that almost anything that causes people to pay attention to courts—even highly controversial events—enhances institutional legitimacy because citizens are simultaneously exposed to legal symbols that portray the judiciary as a unique institution and that therefore impart and reinforce judicial legitimacy. Thus, the overriding hypothesis of this research states that confirmation fights—even politicized ones—may not undermine the legitimacy of the United States Supreme

Court. Since that theory is so central to our analysis, it is useful to begin by discussing how it might apply to politicized confirmation processes.

Applying the Theory of Positivity Bias to Confirmations

Positivity theory offers an explanation of how citizens update their attitudes toward political institutions. The theory becomes relevant when exogenous events cause ordinary people to pay attention to the United States Supreme Court. Confirmation hearings and highly controversial court rulings are examples of such events. Such episodes "wake up" existing institutional attitudes, providing an opportunity for those attitudes to change. Attitudes come out of hibernation.

In the contemporary United States, the attitudes that are aroused by salient judicial events tend strongly to favor the Supreme Court, which is little more than to point out that the Court attracts the esteem of a quite considerable proportion of the American people (e.g., Gibson, Caldeira, and Baird 1998; Gibson 2007a). This residue of earlier salient events—what some refer to as a "running tally" (e.g., Taber, Glather, and Lodge 2001), a sort of summary score of earlier positive and negative evaluations of the Court—becomes susceptible to updating when events cause citizens to pay attention to the Supreme Court.

The fear of many is that politicized confirmation processes will detract from the legitimacy of the Supreme Court. During confirmation fights, citizens are offered the opportunity to get a view of how the Supreme Court actually operates. Since many actors are debating the ideology of the nominee, considerable potential exists for citizens to see the Supreme Court as an ordinary political institution (or perhaps even in partisan terms). As we have argued, such a view tends to undermine judicial legitimacy.

Extant Research on Change in Attitudes toward the Supreme Court

The most telling design for assessing the impact of the nomination processes on the legitimacy of law and courts is a pre- /post-survey centered on a highly salient confirmation event. Unfortunately, resignations and deaths of Supreme Court justices typically occur without much advance notice, and, consequently, we know little about how citizens view confirmation fights, and even less about how attitudes toward the institution affect and are affected by the process. Since practical issues of timing make it extremely difficult to design and implement a rigorous research design, scholars have been forced to rely upon data collected for other purposes (e.g., Gimpel and Ringel 1995), and in particular on extremely weak measures of the concept "legitimacy." For instance, as clever as their research is, Gimpel and Wolpert (1996) are faced with two substantial limitations in their analysis of mass opinion on the Rehnquist, Bork, Souter, and Thomas nominations: (1) the data sources available include only cross-sectional ("snapshot") polls, and (2) the questions asked in the surveys are limited to simple opinion-holding and approval of each of the nominees. No valid measures of the perceived legitimacy of the Court itself are included in any of the earlier analyses of confirmation fights (note that Gibson, Caldeira, and Spence 2003b have shown that the commonly used "confidence in the leaders of the Supreme Court" indicator is far from being a valid and reliable indicator of the concept of institutional legitimacy). Consequently, little if any research has considered how perceptions of confirmation controversies affect preexisting commitments to the Supreme Court (even if speculation about the effects of such events is commonplace).

Thus, the central purpose of this chapter is to assess the impact of confirmation processes on the legitimacy of the United States Supreme Court in the eyes of the American people, using our three-wave panel survey. The value of a panel survey is that it allows the assessment of individual change over time (something not possible with repeated cross-sections),[1] and the crucial dependent variable (the perceived legitimacy of the Supreme Court) is measured outside the nomination season (and thus is not contaminated with variance properly assigned to the independent variables—the confirmation stimuli). Since the central hypotheses of this research concern the effects of the nomination process on individual citizens, no other research design would produce probative data.

Measuring Change in Attitudes toward the U.S. Supreme Court

Legitimacy Theory is a crucial component of contemporary thinking about the role of courts in American society, ranging from macrolevel theories about the ability of courts to bring about social change (e.g., Rosenberg 1991) to microlevel theories about the willingness of citizens to comply with law (e.g., Tyler 1990), and broader issues of judicial independence and accountability (e.g., Kramer 2004; see also Friedman 2004). Especially in an ideologically divided society like the United States, courts must be able to persuade people to accept outcomes with which

[1] This point is made and illustrated in the context of analysis of both cross-sectional and panel data on anti-Semitism in Russia in Gibson and Howard 2007.

they strongly disagree, and most scholars acknowledge that legitimacy is a crucial component of that process.[2]

Our most recent thoughts on how institutional support should be measured were published in 2003 in the *American Journal of Political Science* (Gibson, Caldeira, and Spence 2003b). In that article, we discussed alternative measures of attitudes toward courts and then presented what we consider to be a useful measure of loyalty toward (or institutional support for) high courts. Across all three waves of the survey, we included four core indicators of institutional loyalty, based on those findings:

- If the U.S. Supreme Court started making a lot of decisions that most people disagree with, it might be better to do away with the Supreme Court altogether.
- The right of the Supreme Court to decide certain types of controversial issues should be reduced.
- The Supreme Court can usually be trusted to make decisions that are right for the country as a whole.
- The U.S. Supreme Court gets too mixed up in politics.

Both the t_2 and t_3 interviews included two additional measures:

- Judges on the U.S. Supreme Court who consistently make decisions at odds with what a majority of the people want should be removed from their position as judge.
- The U.S. Supreme Court has become too independent and should be seriously reined in.

Finally, one additional statement was used only in the t_3 survey:

- The U.S. Supreme Court ought to be made less independent so that it listens a lot more to what the people want.

As reported in table 5.1, at the aggregate level, these four items seem to indicate a) reasonably high levels of support for the Court,[3] and b) a great deal of stability in responses across the waves of the panel. The correlations of the four-item indices of support (simply the mean response to the four items) vary from .40 ($t_1 - t_3$) to .53 ($t_2 - t_3$).

The four indicators available at t_1 are reasonably reliable: Cronbach's alpha = .70.[4] Although the four items are markedly less reliable at t_2 and

[2] We have investigated the relationship between perceptions of institutional legitimacy and willingness to accept unfavorable court decisions in several contexts. See Gibson 2004, 1991; Gibson, Caldeira, and Spence 2005; Gibson and Caldeira 2003, 1995.

[3] For a cross-national perspective on the relative legitimacy of the Supreme Court, see Gibson, Caldeira, and Baird 1998. For analysis of support within the United States over time, see chapter 3, above.

[4] The t_1 survey was not primarily focused on the legitimacy of the United States Supreme Court, and hence the number of support indicators available is limited.

TABLE 5.1.
Loyalty toward the Supreme Court, 2005–2006

		Level of Diffuse Support for the Supreme Court					
		Percentage					
Item	*Year*	*Not Supportive*	*Undecided*	*Supportive*	*Mean*	*Std. Dev.*	*N*
Do away with the Court							
	t^1	17.1	9.1	73.8	3.7	1.0	251
	t^2	15.5	6.2	78.3	3.8	1.0	251
	t^3	11.0	7.7	81.4	3.9	.9	251
Limit the Court's jurisdiction							
	t^1	32.4	15.3	52.3	3.2	1.1	251
	t^2	38.6	11.2	50.2	3.2	1.1	249
	t^3	36.1	9.3	54.6	3.2	1.2	251
Court can be trusted							
	t^1	17.9	13.0	69.1	3.6	.9	251
	t^2	16.9	7.8	75.3	3.7	.9	251
	t^3	20.1	9.1	70.8	3.6	1.0	251
Court gets too mixed up in politics							
	t^1	45.0	16.1	38.9	2.9	1.0	251
	t^2	50.1	10.6	39.3	2.9	1.3	251
	t^3	48.3	12.0	39.8	2.9	1.2	250
Number of items endorse							
	t^1				2.3	1.3	251
	t^2				2.4	1.2	251
	t^3				2.5	1.1	251
Index Average							
	t^1				3.4	.7	251
	t^2				3.4	.7	251
	t^3				3.4	.7	251

Note: The percentages are based on collapsing the five-point Likert response set (e.g., "agree strongly" and "agree" responses are combined). The means and standard deviations are calculated on the uncollapsed distributions. Higher mean scores indicate more institutional loyalty.

The propositions are:

Do away with the Court:
If the US Supreme Court started making a lot of decisions that most people disagree with, it might be better to do away with the Supreme Court altogether.

Limit the Court's jurisdiction:
The right of the Supreme Court to decide certain types of controversial issues should be reduced.

Court can be trusted:
The Supreme Court can usually be trusted to make decisions that are right for the country as a whole.

Court gets too mixed up in politics:
The U.S. Supreme Court gets too mixed up in politics.

t_3 (alpha = .48 and .47, respectively),[5] the six-item pool at t_2 has an alpha of .67, and the set of seven indicators at t_3 produces a coefficient of .73. Thus, using all available measures at each of the interviews results in indices of institutional loyalty of roughly equal reliability (.70, .67, and .73). In terms of the t_1—t_3 correlations, using all seven indicators at t_3 strengthens the relationship, but not greatly when compared to the four-item index (.40 versus .43). The t_2—t_3 correlation increases, however, from .53 to .68 when all available items are used in the t_2 and t_3 indices. Because we wish to avoid the confounding influence of variables with different degrees of reliability at the three points in the panel survey, we have derived support indices from the maximum number available at each wave—four items at t_1, six items at t_2, and seven items at t_3.

Change in Loyalty toward the Supreme Court

As we have noted, the correlations of the indices are .46 for the t_1—t_2 pair and .68 for the t_2—t_3 scores. When the t_3 index is regressed on the two earlier measures, nearly one-half of the variance can be accounted for (R^2 = .48).[6] In terms of the simple number of supportive replies given on the four-item core set, 36.2 percent of the respondents became more supportive of the Court, 24.4 percent did not change in their level of support, and 39.4 percent became less supportive from the t_1 to the t_3 interview. Figure 5.1 reports these change data, with change in responses to two or more items being scored as "significant" change. By these measures, 11.5 percent of the respondents became significantly less supportive of the Court

[5] We are not exactly certain what accounts for the significantly lower reliabilities at t_2 and t_3. Perhaps what is happening here is that, in the absence of any specific information about the Court (recall that the t_1 interview was decidedly *not* focused on law and courts), people may respond to these propositions on the basis of fairly general and abstract attitudes. Thus, alpha is high because all of the reliable variability in the responses stems from a single latent construct. The unique content of any given item is not very high; most of the systematic variance originates in the general attitudes. But when information is readily available (owing to other questions in the interview), each item is evaluated more on the basis of its face content, which is affected by circumstances at the time and by the context of the survey. Hence the role of unique factors is greater, driving down the inter-item correlations. Think of it this way. Can the Court be trusted? If I have no specific thoughts readily available, I deduce a response from my general attitude toward the Court. But if I have been thinking about the Court in responding to earlier questions, I think "well, can they be trusted? After all, they have been making some pretty stupid decisions lately. So I'm not sure if they can be trusted." The point is that the idiosyncratic content under more salient conditions is stronger, and therefore the inter-correlations among items are weaker. Ironically, these responses in some sense reflect *more* informed answers to the questions (and therefore the role of the general attitude is lessened), even if reliability is penalized.

[6] The part coefficients for both the t_2 and t_1 measures of support are statistically and substantively significant in the multivariate regression.

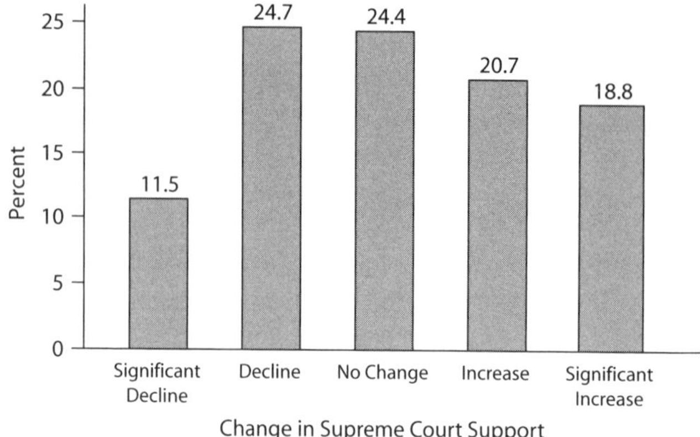

Figure 5.1. Change in Support for the Supreme Court, Before and After the Alito Nomination

from 2005 to 2006; 18.8 percent became significantly more supportive. Overall, these data reveal that substantial proportions of the respondents changed their views from before the Alito nomination to afterward.

In the analysis that follows, we measure attitudes toward the Court in several ways. First, we examine postconfirmation (t_3) Court support. Second, we analyze change in attitudes from the preconfirmation to the postconfirmation surveys (t_1 and t_3) using a variable that is the difference between Court support at t_3 and support at t_1. We also use as a measure of change a lagged dependent variable, controlling for Court attitudes at t_1. Thus, other than the first measure, all of the findings we report control for the original (pre-Alito) attitudes of the respondents. We do not also control for support at t_2, owing to the possibility that the t_2 variance in Court support was contaminated by the interview being conducted at the time of the confirmation hearings.[7] We also report for illustrative purposes simple variables indicating change between t_1 and t_3, as in change in the number of supportive replies to our queries, and, on occasion, the residuals resulting from regressing t_3 support on t_1 attitudes. We report these indicators for illustrative purposes only, and only after confirming relationships within the multivariate equations.[8]

[7] Since t_2 loyalty toward the Supreme Court was measured directly within the context of the Alito confirmation process, controlling for t_2 attitudes may in some sense overcontrol because the t_2 measure represents in part attitude change that may have taken place as a result of that process (and, if so, this would account for the quite strong relationship we observe between attitudes at t_2 and t_3). Thus, we are cautious in our use of t_2 attitudes as a control variable.

[8] The correlation between the residuals and the difference across the interviews in the number of supportive responses is .54; the correlation with the difference of mean responses

The Model of Change in Institutional Support

Our objective in this research is to account for how attitudes toward the Supreme Court might have changed as a result of exposure to the Alito controversy. To do so requires a model incorporating both factors associated with cross-sectional variability in support and factors that are expected to drive change in attitudes. So, in general, we hypothesize that support for the Supreme Court is influenced by two types of variables: first, attributes of the individual that predate the confirmation hearings, such as support for democratic institutions and processes more generally (e.g., Caldeira and Gibson 1995), and general political and ideological predispositions of the individual (e.g., party identification). The hypotheses here are well grounded in extant investigations of Court support.

Second, expectations, perceptions, and judgments of the Alito nominations may have influenced support for the Supreme Court. Since these influences have so rarely been considered in the political science literature, we pay careful attention in this investigation to any connections between these variables and institutional support. We then proceed to a single integrated analysis that simultaneously controls for all known influences on institutional support. To reiterate, change in support for the Court is measured by analyzing attitudes at t_1 and t_3. All of the variables associated with the Alito confirmation process were measured at t_2. Additional control variables were measured at various interviews in the panel survey (e.g., education at t_1). When a control was measured at multiple points in time (e.g., party identification), we have typically used the indicator at t_3—that is, contemporaneous with the t_3 measure of institutional support.

We begin the analysis with further consideration of the cross-sectional model.

The Origins of Attitudes toward Political Institutions

Earlier research on support for the United States Supreme Court has determined that those more strongly committed to democratic institutions and processes are more likely to support the Court (e.g., Caldeira and Gibson 1992; see also chapter 3, above). This body of research has also demonstrated that support for the Court is grounded in political knowledge (see Gibson and Caldeira 2007). Gibson, Caldeira, and Spence (2003a) assert that this relationship is connected to exposure to the legitimizing symbols

---

at t_1 and t_3 is .70. The t_3–t_1 residuals vary from −.48 to +.50, with 14.6 percent scoring at less than 1 standard deviation below the mean, 30.3 percent scoring at one standard deviation below the mean, 30.8 percent at one standard deviation above the mean, and 18.3 percent at more than one standard deviation above the mean.

of the judiciary: To know more about courts is to extend more support to them because to know more about courts is to have been exposed to the highly symbolic trappings of the judiciary (e.g., robes, "your honor," the marble temple). Furthermore, political knowledge is associated with greater support for democratic institutions and processes (Gibson 2007a; Gibson and Caldeira 2007). Thus, it seems that knowledge is an important independent variable not primarily because information underpins support, but because knowledge is indicative of processes of socialization to democratic values and exposure to legitimizing symbols. From the 2005 cross-sectional analysis we reported in chapter 3, above, we provided this understanding of the processes involved:

> The causal process involved here seems relatively clear. Citizens who are better educated learn more about the Supreme Court and the democratic theory in which the Court is embedded and sustained. We suspect that the primary content of the learning is to stress that "courts are different." They are relatively nonpolitical, and judges make decisions on the basis of principled criteria—impartiality, for instance—without regard to self-interest (even the self-interest of being re-elected or reappointed). This knowledge predisposes people to accept the viewpoint that courts have a distinctive role in democracy and that role is not necessarily to mollify the preferences of the majority. The reason why democratic values and court support are so closely connected is that supporting a court—an institution that often tells the majority that it cannot do that which it very much wants to do—requires a relatively sophisticated understanding of democratic theory. As it turns out, a reasonable number of Americans understand this, and therefore support for the Court is quite high.

Earlier research (including that reported on chapter 3, above) has also decidedly rejected the hypothesis that the legitimacy of the United States Supreme Court is shaped by partisan and ideological considerations. The Court draws its support nearly equally from liberals and conservatives, Democrats and Republicans.[9] Nonetheless, in the preliminary model, we include indicators of these political identities.[10] Other variables for which we control include education, race, gender, age, and social class (home ownership). As an additional control variable, the equation incorporates the respondent's expressed confidence in President Bush. These attributes are measured at t_3.

[9] In this analysis of data from 2005, Gibson (2007a) also discovered that support for the Court is related to political efficacy and race, while African Americans extend significantly less support to the institution.

[10] Indeed, since our chapter 3 analysis is of the t_1 data set, we include the precise indicators incorporated in that equation (see table 3.4, above).

Our best measures of democratic values are found in the t_1 survey (on measurement, see chapter 3, above). In addition, we use these pre-Alito indicators so as to minimize causal confusion. Since it is possible that these attitudes changed systematically over the short term, perhaps even as a result of the Alito process itself, the most conservative strategy is to employ measures of commitment to democratic institutions and processes that predate the confirmation process itself. We draw the same conclusion about the indicator of political knowledge, and thus use the t_1 index.

The cross-sectional model has been well honed in previous research. Exposure to and evaluations of the Alito hearings provide the engine for possible change in our model. Since these variables have not been at all well investigated in previous research, we consider this portion of the model in more detail.

Independent Variables: Evaluations of the Alito Confirmation Process

Our primary hypotheses concern the impact of the Alito confirmation process on broader loyalty toward the U.S. Supreme Court. Can events like confirmation hearings shape people's views of the Supreme Court as an institution? We begin consideration of this question by reviewing the advertising campaigns that mobilized in response to Judge Alito's nomination.

According to data collected by the Campaign Media Analysis Group (CMAG), 1,190 individual advertisements were aired during the course of the Alito confirmation dispute (see table 5.2).[11] The ads ran from November 1, 2005, through January 27, 2006. Apparently, most interest groups saw little additional benefit in running advertisements during the week prior to the vote in the Senate.

According to the CMAG data, four organizations ran ads during the Alito confirmation fight. On the anti-Alito side were IndependentCourt .org (a coalition of interest groups), MoveOn.org, and People for the American Way. Progress for America was the only group sponsoring ads in support of the confirmation of Judge Alito.[12] The opponents spent

[11] Through CMAG, all advertisements concerning nominees to the Supreme Court were captured from the public airwaves and analyzed. Analysis of the ads, as well as copies of the "storyboards" (television images captured every few seconds, and the full text of the ad and the "paid for by" information) are available from the Brennan Center at New York University. Appendix 5.A (online) reports the storyboards for each ad broadcast during the battle over the confirmation of Judge Alito.

[12] For details on the organizations, see *http://progressforamerica.org/* (accessed 5/18/2006; *http://independentcourt.org/* (accessed 5/18/2006); *http://moveon.com/* (accessed 5/18/2006); and *http://www.pfaw.org/pfaw/general/* (accessed 5/18/2006). We have been unable to locate a website for Progress for America, except one that has little content on it.

Table 5.2.
Advertisements For and Against the Confirmation of Judge Samuel Alito

Sponsor	*Advertisement Name*	*Number of Times Broadcast*
IndependentCourt.org		
	Right Wing Takeover	235
	Alito If	27
	Alito Keep Your Word	158
	Alito Wiretapping	26
	Alito Your Rights	380
MoveOn.org		
	Plays One on TV	110
People for the American Way		
	Alito Radical Right	51
Progress for America		
	Alito Fair Vote	48
	Alito Praise	8
	Know Him Best	11
	Shameful	69
	Steady Drip	67

$1,515,067 on seven ads, aired 987 times on cable and additionally in individual media markets in Portland, Maine; Providence, Rhode Island; Washington, D.C.; Denver, Colorado; Little Rock, Arkansas; and Dayton, Ohio.[13] The proponents produced five advertisements and broadcast them 203 times, primarily on cable (N = 191) and in about a dozen individual markets, with a total expenditure of $1,019,335. Thus, considerably more resources and effort were expended in trying to block Alito's confirmation. Interestingly enough, with the important exception of cable television and a single airing in Little Rock, Arkansas, in no media market were citizens exposed to both pro- and anti-Alito advertisements. The pro-Alito campaign began on November 1, 2005, and lasted through January 27, 2006, while the anti-Alito campaign began slightly later, on November 7, 2005, and terminated on January 23, 2006.

The ads run in support of and in opposition to Alito's confirmation pulled no punches. For instance, consider the following transcript of an IndependentCourt.org ad:

[13] Although no full account of other sorts of advertisements is available, IndependentCourt.org also prepared for broadcast at least three radio advertisements opposing the confirmation of Judge Alito.

[Narrator]: Washington: the Right Wing has taken over the West Wing. George Bush gave extremists the veto over Supreme Court nominations. And they chose Samuel Alito. As a judge, Alito ruled to make it easier for corporations to discriminate, even voted to approve the strip-search of a ten-year-old girl. As a government lawyer Alito wrote, "The Constitution does not protect a right to abortion." The Right Wing has already taken over the West Wing. Don't let them take over your Supreme Court. [PFB] IndependentCourt.org.[14]

The most widely run pro-confirmation ad said the following:

[Announcer]: Everyday, desperate liberals make up a steady drip of attacks against Judge Samuel Alito. Want the truth? Respected Supreme Court analyst, Stuart Taylor of the non-partisan *National Journal: Alito* (quote) [*sic*] "is widely admired by liberals, moderates, and conservatives who know him well as fair-minded, committed to apolitical judging, and wedded to no ideological agenda other than restraint and the exercise of judicial power" (end quote) [*sic*]. Confirm Judge Samuel Alito. [PFB] Progress for America.[15]

A fair conclusion is that all ads broadcast, for and against Alito's confirmation, had a distinctly "political" tone.

Were the ads effective?[16] This is, of course, an extremely difficult question to answer, although we do have some data relevant to drawing a conclusion. First, a substantial portion of our respondents (62.5 percent) reported seeing or hearing an advertisement (on TV, radio, in newspapers, or elsewhere) "concerning whether Judge Alito should be confirmed by the U.S. Senate."[17] The modal response to this question was "saw a few" ads (42.3 percent), although 4.9 percent reported seeing many such ads

[14] Creative Id: 4176684, Issue/IC Right Wing Takeover, IndependentCourt.org (B329). See Appendix 5.A (online). "PFB" means "Paid for by."

[15] Creative Id: 4242787, Issue/PFA Steady Drip, Progress for America Org (B329). See Appendix 5.A.

[16] To recap our findings from chapter 4, above: A majority of respondents (59.9 percent) followed the Senate debate on Alito either "very" or "somewhat" closely, and a majority of respondents (65.7 percent) favored Alito's confirmation.

[17] As with all national surveys, not every state is represented by respondents included in the survey. In our case, there were five states in which pro-Alito ads were broadcast; respondents were interviewed in each of these states. In the case of anti-Alito ads, however, our respondents hail from only two of the six states (including Washington, D.C.) in which these ads were shown. Thus, 17.5 percent of our respondents live in states where pro-Alito ads were run (although it should be noted that the ads were not necessarily or even typically run statewide), but only 5.0 percent live in states where anti-Alito ads were broadcast. Recall, however, that most ads were broadcast on cable TV, which is of course a national market.

and 15.4 percent saw some. That something close to two-thirds of the American people were exposed to advertisements regarding whether Alito ought to be confirmed is striking and somewhat unexpected.[18]

A moderate relationship exists between overall attentiveness to the confirmation process and seeing advertisements.[19] For instance, 59.5 percent of those who did not follow the process reported seeing no ads, whereas only 25.0 percent of those very closely paying attention did not see an ad. The most significant distinction is between those who claimed not to follow the process and everyone else—even among those who said they did not pay much attention to the Alito confirmation, 62.8 percent nonetheless reported seeing an ad about the dispute. Thus, it seems that advertising was sufficiently prolific that people with fairly low thresholds of political interest and attentiveness were nonetheless exposed to information about the confirmation controversy.[20]

Is ad exposure simply a function of one's own position on whether Judge Alito should be confirmed to the Supreme Court? With one exception, generally not. Of those believing Alito should definitely not be confirmed, 34.6 percent saw no ads, compared to 33.3 percent of those definitely supporting Alito's confirmation. Ad exposure is somewhat related to intensity of opinion among the opponents, but not among the supporters. The big (and unsurprising) difference is among those unable to form an opinion about whether to confirm Alito, with 60.9 percent of these respondents reporting seeing no ads.

The 60-plus percent of the respondents who were exposed to Alito advertisements were asked a series of questions about their judgments of the ads they saw or heard. Among those seeing an ad, nearly a majority (49.0 percent) reported that the ads favored Alito's confirmation. Some said that nearly all of the ads did so (14.8 percent), while others said most but not all favored the confirmation (34.3 percent). This stands in contrast to the 14.0 percent who claimed to have seen ads nearly all of which opposed the confirmation, and 22.6 percent who said most of the ads they saw

[18] There is virtually no relationship between living in a state in which anti-Alito ads were shown and responses to this question on the survey. This no doubt reflects the fact that the bulk of the advertising was done on national cable TV, and that the question we asked referred to radio, TV, and newspapers.

[19] The question asked is: "As you may know, President Bush has nominated Judge Samuel Alito (Ah-lee-tow) to serve on the U.S. Supreme Court. The U.S. Senate has just been debating whether Judge Alito ought to be confirmed to the Supreme Court. How closely would you say you have been following news about the appointment of Samuel Alito to the U.S. Supreme Court: very closely, somewhat closely, not very closely, or not at all closely?"

[20] We also note that the difference in ad exposure between those who followed the confirmation events "very" and "somewhat" closely is slight indeed, a finding that suggests that the reply "somewhat closely" is a meaningful and valid reply and not just a socially acceptable cover for inattentiveness to the confirmation process.

opposed confirmation. Another 6.2 percent saw a balanced mix of ads. Only 8.1 percent of those exposed to an advertisement could not recall whether the ad favored the confirmation or not. As we have noted above, in terms of the number of airings of ads, 987 were shown in opposition to the nomination and 203 in support of confirming Alito. In terms of just nationwide cable ads, however, 133 anti-Alito spots were aired, in contrast to 191 pro-Alito spots. Although we have no direct data on the point, it seems likely that our respondents were reporting exposure primarily to the national cable ads, where the ad content was to some degree evenly balanced.

We also asked the respondents about their judgments of three characteristics of the ads they saw. Substantial majorities viewed the advertisements as at least somewhat negative (61.8 percent) and at least somewhat partisan (77.4 percent). But perhaps surprising is the finding that the respondents also viewed the ads as fair. A substantial majority (59.1 percent) judged the ads they saw as somewhat fair, and another 8.3 percent rated them as extremely fair. When we regress perceived ad fairness on the other perceptions and preferences, we find that the single greatest component of unfairness is perceived partisanship ($\beta = -.26$); those who judge the ads to be more partisan rate the ads in general as less fair. The other three variables (including the respondent's own preference for whether Alito ought to be confirmed) have trivial (and statistically insignificant) influences upon perceived fairness.[21] For these respondents, the dominant meaning of unfair procedures is partisanship, even if many respondents saw the process as both partisan and fair.

In the analysis that follows, we test several specific conjectures about the consequences of the confirmation process for attitudes toward the Court:

- Since attentiveness to judicial events is inevitably associated with exposure to legitimizing legal symbols, those who paid more attention to the Alito confirmation controversy are expected to experience an increase in support for the Supreme Court.
- Those satisfied with the confirmation process are expected to become more supportive of the Court. Satisfaction is indexed both by outcome (preference that Alito be confirmed) and by process satisfaction (perceptions that the confirmation process was fair).
- As we have noted, the ad campaigns of opposition interest groups strongly emphasized Alito's ideology, not his judiciousness. We therefore hypothesize that those exposed to more advertisements became less supportive of the Court.

[21] Note that the correlation between perceived partisanship and perceived negativity is only .11, so these results are completely unaffected by multicollinearity.

FINDINGS

Table 5.3 reports three equations. Model 1 does not include a control for institutional attitudes at t_1 and therefore should be considered as an account of variation from low to high support for the Court after the close of the battle over the nomination. Model 2 simply adds the control for attitudes at t_1 to Model 1, and thus is a model of change in attitudes. Model 3 analyzes the difference between support before and after the fight and therefore is also an analysis of change in attitudes toward the Supreme Court.[22] Each of these equations provides some analytical purchase on the nature of attitudes toward the Supreme Court.

We begin our analysis with consideration of the variables that have no consequences whatsoever for institutional loyalty. The most significant such variables are the respondent's party and ideological identifications. After the fight, Democrats and Republicans were indistinguishable in their levels of support for Court; similarly, they changed their attitudes toward the Court in a roughly comparable fashion. There is clearly much more to attitudes toward the Supreme Court than partisanship and ideology.

Neither does Asian ethnicity, political knowledge, or even general levels of attentiveness to the nomination have much influence on either levels of or change in support for the Court. Although political knowledge has a healthy bivariate correlation with Court support, the independent effect of knowledge is reduced to insignificance in the multivariate equation, largely owing to the correlations between knowledge and democratic values. The data do reveal a slight correlation between being black and increasing support for the Court, and between being Hispanic and level of support after the nomination, but these relationships are weak, based on few respondents, are inconsistent across the models, and are therefore perhaps of little substantive significance. Level of education is associated with Court attitudes in the bivariate case, but the relationship is small-to-trivial in the various multivariate equations. As in previous research, political efficacy is an important control variable.

The various measures of democratic values are related both to levels of support and changes in levels of support. The strongest relationship is with attitudes toward a multiparty system. It is worth reiterating

[22] Model 2 is based on a measure of change between responses to the seven-item set at t_3 and the four-item set at t_1. As we noted above, the advantage of this form of analysis is that the dependent variable is measured with greater reliability. When we restrict the change measure to exactly the same four items at t_1 and t_3, however, the results are virtually identical to those reported in table 5.3. This is not surprising inasmuch as the correlation between the two versions of the change variable exceeds .9.

TABLE 5.3.
The Impact of the Alito Confirmation Process on Support for the U.S. Supreme Court

	Model I				Model II			Model III		
Predictor	*r*	*b*	*s.e.*	*β*	*b*	*s.e.*	*β*	*b*	*s.e.*	*β*
Support for Multiparty System	.34	.04	.02	.18*	.05	.02	.22**	.07	.02	.27***
Political Tolerance	.33	.03	.01	.16*	.02	.01	.11	.00	.02	.00
Support for Rule of Law	.16	.01	.02	.05	–.01	.02	–.03	–.04	.02	–.16*
Liberty versus Order	.32	.00	.02	.01	–.01	.02	–.06	–.04	.02	–.17
Political Knowledge	.26	–.00	.01	–.01	–.01	.01	–.05	–.02	.01	–.11
Level of Education	.36	.02	.01	.16*	.01	.01	.10	.00	.01	.00
Political Efficacy	.35	.27	.08	.24***	.27	.08	.24***	.27	.09	.22**
Whether Black	–.09	–.02	.04	–.03	.02	.04	.03	.08	.04	.12*
Whether Hispanic	–.05	–.09	.04	–.16*	–.06	.04	–.11	–.00	.04	–.01
Whether Asian	.07	.06	.07	.07	.08	.06	.08	.09	.07	.09
Number of Advertisements Seen	–.19	–.04	.02	–.17**	–.04	.01	–.19**	–.05	.02	–.20**
Attention to the Confirmation Process	.17	.02	.01	.10	.02	.01	.09	.01	.02	.07
Assessment of Process Fairness	.02	–.00	.02	–.02	–.02	.02	–.10	–.06	.02	–.23***
Alito Confirmation Preference	.04	–.00	.01	–.00	.01	.01	.05	.02	.01	.14*
Confidence in President Bush	–.02	.00	.01	.02	–.01	.01	–.08	–.02	.01	–.23**
Party Identification	–.03	.00	.01	.04	–.01	.01	–.02	–.01	.01	–.12
Ideological Identification	–.12	.00	.01	.00	–.00	.01	–.03	–.01	.01	–.08
Support for the Supreme Court t_1	.38	—	—	—	.34	.07	.33***	—	—	—
Intercept		.37	.08		.27	.08		.08	.09	
Standard Deviation — Dependent Variable		.19			.19			.21		
Standard Error of Estimate		.16			.15			.18		
R^2				.32***			.39***			.31***
N		240			240			240		

Note: Significance of standardized regression coefficient (β): *** $p < .001$ ** $p < .01$ * $p < .05$

that we do not believe that support for a multiparty system per se generates allegiance to the Supreme Court. Instead, those who support political parties—especially in this strongly antiparty age—are those who possess a more sophisticated understanding of the nature of the American political system. To accept parties is associated with accepting the distinctive role of the judiciary in the American scheme. In short, those who are sophisticated enough to realize that democracy without parties is unthinkable are also sophisticated enough to recognize a unique role for the Supreme Court.

Those most supportive of the rule of law became less supportive of the Supreme Court over the course of the confirmation process, at least when the difference measure is used as the dependent variable. The rule-of-law relationship may be significant to the extent that it indicates that the confirmation antics were viewed as in conflict with rule-of-law principles. Unfortunately, no additional data are available to aid in the interpretation of this relationship.

In general, the Model 1 equation does a reasonable job of predicting support for the Court after the confirmation controversy concluded: nearly one-third of the variance can be explained. Among the best predictors of support for the Court are general political efficacy, and *not having been exposed to ads during the Alito dispute*. Effects are also seen of democratic values (support for a multiparty system and political tolerance),[23] and level of education.

The most substantively interesting portion of table 5.3 concerns the effects of the confirmation process on attitudes toward the Supreme Court. As the data indicate, a number of confirmation-related variables significantly influence change in support for the Court. Perhaps most telling, those who saw a greater number of advertisements became substantially less supportive of the Court. This finding is consistent across all three models. Exposure to the ads is associated with lower levels of support for the Court, as well as a decline in support for the institution. This is one of the strongest relationships we observe in these data.

Paying attention to the Alito hearings is positively associated with Court support in the bivariate case, but the coefficient becomes marginal in the multivariate equations. Nonetheless, attentiveness to the process seems not to have the same effect on judicial attitudes as exposure to the ads. [24]

The coefficient for perceptions of process fairness is strangely signed in Model 3 (and not statistically significant in the other two models): those who saw the process as more fair became less supportive of the Court, even if their level of support at the conclusion of the process was neither

[23] Caution must be taken in understanding the role of any particular democratic value since considerable multicollinearity exists among the four values. We are not much concerned about that, however, since our goal here is to investigate the effect of the Alito confirmation process on Court support within the context of a fully specified equation.

[24] The correlation between paying attention to the confirmation debate and exposure to ads is only .32.

particularly high nor low.[25] Similarly, those with the greatest confidence in President Bush became less supportive of the Court, even while supporters of Judge Alito became slightly more confident in the institution. The bivariate correlation between preferences (measured at t_2)[26] and Court support (measured at t_3) is a mere .04.[27] Alito supporters did develop greater allegiance to the Court as an institution, but the coefficient just barely achieves statistical significance ($p = .053$).[28] Thus, simply winning or losing a confirmation fight does not seem to undermine respect for the Court as an institution. It is unclear to us why process fairness in particular did not affect Court attitudes, although we conjecture that the procedural fairness may have more to do with attitudes toward the Senate and perhaps even the mass media. Thus, we note that neither satisfaction with the outcome nor the process caused much change in loyalty toward the Supreme Court.

From the point of view of the theory being investigated in this chapter, the most interesting finding of this analysis is that being exposed to advertisements during the Alito battle seems to undermine support for the Court. This is true in both the bivariate and multivariate equations, and for levels of support and change in support. At the same time, however, attentiveness to the nomination process does *not* erode support. The more people paid attention to the confirmation battle, the more supportive they were of the Court, although attentiveness has only a marginal and insignificant effect on increases in Court support. These relationships are depicted in figure 5.2, using the t_3—t_1 support residuals as the dependent variable. For exposure to the ads, the bivariate correlation between degree of exposure and change in support is –.22, with those having more exposure declining in support for the Court. The correlation with attentiveness is much weaker, and not statistically significant, although positive: as attentiveness increases, so, too, does Court support. These relationships are puzzling and require further investigation.

[25] The respondents were asked: "How would you rate the overall fairness of the process? Would you say it has been extremely fair, somewhat fair, not very fair, or not at all fair?"

[26] For ease of presentation, when we refer to bivariate relationships we consider both the bivariate correlation between the independent variable and support at t_3 and the multivariate relationship between the independent variable and t_3 support, controlling for t_1 support. If the findings are not consistent we always make explicit reference to that fact.

[27] Even when we substitute preferences (remembered at t_3), the correlation is only .08.

[28] We also find no relationship whatsoever between the ideological distance from the respondent to Judge Alito (a strong predictor at t_2 of Alito confirmation preferences; see chapter 4, above). We do not enter this variable into the multivariate equation owing to the fact that the variable has higher than average missing data (since it is a compound variable expressing the difference between the respondent's own ideological position and her or his perception of Alito's ideological location).

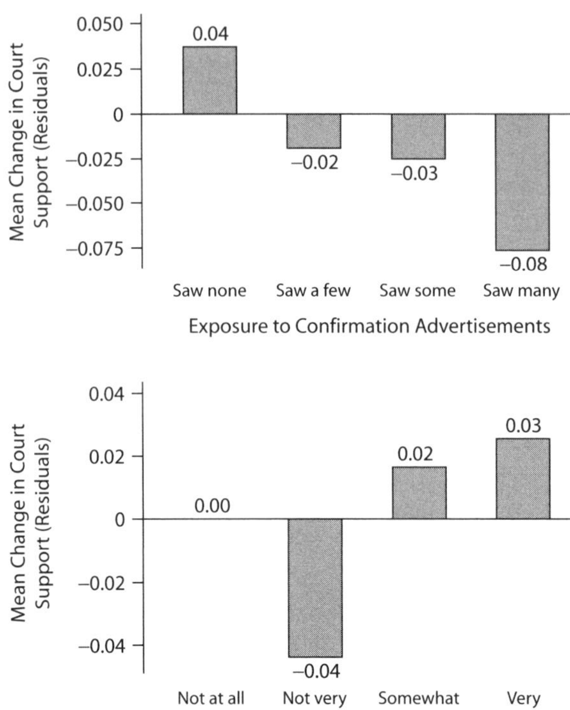

Figure 5.2. The Impact of the Alito Events on Change in Support for the Supreme Court

Perhaps the most interesting relationship—or lack thereof—has to do with ad exposure and overall assessments of the fairness of the confirmation process. Given the corrosive effect of ad exposure on institutional support, one might hypothesize that the ads caused people to view the process as unfair. Such is not at all the case.[29] Yet, as attentiveness to the confirmation hearings increases, so too do judgments of process fairness. Apparently, most Americans were able to distinguish between the confirmation process itself and the ads broadcast in conjunction with that process. The ads themselves apparently had an independent effect on how

[29] We do find that those who reported seeing "many" ads judged the process as somewhat less fair. Too few people saw many ads, however, so their effect on the overall measure of association is minimal.

people see the Supreme Court, an effect that is distinctive from and even contrary to observations of the confirmation debate within the Senate.[30]

Since the influences of ad exposure and process attentiveness are contrary to each other, the hypothesis of an interactive effect becomes reasonable. That is, one might hypothesize that the influence of attentiveness is mitigated as the citizen is exposed to more advertisements. Similarly, the effect of these advertisements may be diminished to the extent that the respondent paid attention to the confirmation process in the Senate. These hypotheses can be assessed with the data at hand.[31]

Across the four levels of attentiveness, the impact of exposure to ads on Court support changes little. The regression coefficients representing the effect of exposure from low to high attentiveness (in an equation controlling for attitudes at t_1) are: −.22, −.08, −.19, and −.26, respectively. The coefficient for the "not very closely" group (−.08) is anomalous, and without explanation, but generally these data provide no support for the expectation that the impact of exposure on change in support declines with increasing attentiveness to the confirmation process.

The alternative way of looking at this relationship is to examine the impact of attentiveness across the levels of ad exposure. Because so few respondents saw "many" ads, we have collapsed those people with those seeing "some" ads for the purposes of this analysis. The regression coefficients in an equation including attitudes at t_1, varying from low ad exposure to some ad exposure, are: .25, .16, and −.05, respectively. That is, among those respondents viewing practically no ads related to the confirmation, greater attention to the process is associated with increasing support for the Supreme Court ($\beta = .25$). Among those viewing some or many ads, however, attentiveness has no impact on Court support ($\beta = -.05$). Thus, we see the power of exposure to these ads. Even high attentiveness to the confirmation process does not mitigate the derogatory effect of seeing the ads; at the same time, high ad exposure completely neutralized any salutary efforts of paying attention to the confirmation

[30] The correlation between ad exposure and perceptions of fair process is a mere −.04.

[31] All of the interactive analyses we report in this chapter must be regarded as producing only tentative results. This is because the total numbers of cases available for analysis is relatively small, with the consequence that many of the subdivisions of the data (e.g., by degree of ad exposure) generate fairly small numbers of observations, and, in some instances, skewed distributions of the variables. As a consequence of the small Ns, our results are not always stable across different model specifications, and in particular between specifications based on Models 2 and 3 (as reported in table 5.3). Our most basic conclusion—that exposure to ads broadcast for and against Alito's confirmation undermined support for the Court—is well supported by the data and is *not* sensitive to model specifications. All other conditional results ought to be regarded as requiring confirmation by future research.

process in the Senate. This analysis makes it all the more important to try to isolate specifically which characteristics of these ads and exposure to them threaten the legitimacy of the United States Supreme Court.

Ad Content

Given that exposure to these ads is associated with a decline in institutional support, something about the ads themselves must have been unsettling to many respondents. The ads either taught lessons incompatible with the legitimacy of courts, or perhaps they violated expectations about the nature of the confirmation process. Perhaps that lesson was that "courts are *not* different." The ads attest to the conclusion that courts are just about the same as any other political institution. Because courts are political, they are not worthy of the special esteem judicial institutions normally attract. If this is so, then the confirmation process is quite damaging to the Supreme Court. Thus, the consequences and correlates of being exposed to these ads must be considered further.

In order to assess the impact of perceptions of the attributes of the advertisements on institutional support, we created a set of dummy variables and entered them into equations both with and without the control for Court attitudes at t_1. The excluded category is those who reported seeing no ads, and therefore the significance tests evaluate the hypothesis that those who saw particular kinds of ads differ in their support from those who saw none. We first consider the impact of overall ad fairness.

Only two of the dummy variables achieved statistical significance in the regressions. Those who judged the ads they saw as somewhat fair or extremely fair tended to be *less* supportive of the Court and to have *declined* in their support from the t_1 to the t_3 interview. Obviously, this finding is not consistent with the hypothesis. Indeed, the finding suggests that we may have gotten the causal structure reversed, with ad perceptions being endogenous rather than exogenous. We will consider this possibility further below.

The perceived partisanship of the ads has little systematic impact on Court support. Those who saw the ads as "somewhat" partisan tend to have lower support for the Court, but did not become less supportive over time. Moreover, those who judged the ads as "extremely" partisan (a more extreme point along the continuum) were neither less supportive nor did their support decline. In terms of perceptions of the negativity of the ads, those judging the ads as *not* negative tended to have lower support for the Court, and for those respondents, support declined. Moreover, those judging the ads as to any degree negative differ insignificantly from those who saw no ads. Thus, these tests also fail to support the hypothesis.

These findings suggest to us the conclusion that perceptions of the ads may be endogenous in the sense that they are strongly influenced by expectations. Variation in ad judgments most likely reflects the influence of two factors: perceptions of the ads and expectations about them. Individuals likely differ in their assessments of what is "too partisan," "too negative," or "unfair." Consider, for instance, one who believes strongly in the apolitical nature of the judiciary. For that person, any mention of ideology or party is likely to be judged to be inappropriate. The endogeneity of ad perceptions is all the more strongly suggested by the nature of the attitudes we are investigating here, having to do, for example, with whether the Supreme Court is different from other political institutions and thereby worthy of respect and esteem. Thus, whether an ad is considered to be fair depends upon the interaction between one's standards of fairness and perceptions of the content of the ad. If this is so, then ad evaluations are endogenous to the model, not exogenous.

We have no direct indicator of what sorts of ads the respondents view as appropriate and legitimate. But following our earlier analysis (in chapter 4, above) of the process by which opinions on Alito's confirmation are based—where we argued that prior institutional loyalty gave rise to a strong weight being attached to the criterion of judiciousness in evaluating Alito's candidacy—we suspect that those with strong loyalty toward the Supreme Court would subscribe to the view that confirmation advertisements should be civil and relatively nonpolitical. Institutional legitimacy provides a frame through which ads are judged. Thus, under this process, one might expect that support for the Court at t_1 causes the respondents to judge the ads they viewed during the confirmation harshly.

That is precisely what the data indicate. Support at t_1 is correlated with judging the ads to be unfair ($r = -.08$), negative ($r = .19$), and partisan ($r = .11$). That these relationships are not stronger is most likely a function of the imperfect relationship between institutional support and expectations. And all of these relationships are stronger among opponents of the confirmation as compared to among supporters of the confirmation. The most compelling difference is on the perceived fairness of the ads. Among Alito's opponents, institutional loyalty (t_1) is strongly connected to perceptions (t_2) of unfairness ($r = -.44$), whereas the relationship is trivial among those supporting the confirmation ($r = .01$).

Perhaps the key consideration here is whether the ads violated the expectations of citizens, thereby causing people to reevaluate how they feel about the Supreme Court. Consider a citizen who is also a typical political scientist specializing in judicial politics and process. Such a citizen likely believes the following. (1) The Supreme Court makes public policy. (2) Supreme Court justices have a great deal of discretion in casting their votes in cases. (3) Within limits, the president has the right to name whom he wants to the Supreme Court. (4) Those limits are defined by a) technical competence, b) broad ideological agreement, and c) extremism. Liberal conservative presidents have the right to name liberal conservative judges, so long as they are not extremists. (5) Therefore, ideological and political considerations are an appropriate part of the confirmation process. Such a citizen is unlikely to become disoriented by a moderately politicized confirmation process in which the ideology of the nominee is widely discussed.

Others, however, may view the Supreme Court as being "above" politics (can one be "below" politics?) and therefore ads focusing on the ideology of the candidate are inappropriate. For these citizens, the ad campaigns presented by both supporters and opponents of Alito's confirmation most likely seemed offensive. Thus, expectations may play a key role in this process.

The Judiciousness Submodel

As we noted in chapter 4, above, judiciousness is an alternative to ideology as a criterion for preference-formation and is based on the qualities the respondent views as important for being a good judge. We began consideration of the respondents' expectations with the following text: "Now I would like you to focus on thinking about the characteristics of a good Supreme Court judge, that is, what a good judge ought to be like. First, how important would you say it is for a good Supreme Court judge to [INSERT ITEM]?" The characteristics about which we queried the respondents were:

- Strictly follow the law no matter what people in the country may want
- Try to maintain the appearance of being fair and impartial no matter what the cost
- Stay entirely independent of the president and the government
- Respect existing Supreme Court decisions by changing the law as little as possible
- Uphold the values of those who wrote our constitution two hundred years ago

To reiterate the findings of chapter 4, the data clearly reveal that Americans expect their Supreme Court justices to maintain the appearance of fairness and impartiality, and to uphold long-standing constitutional values. Perhaps the most surprising finding in these data is the relatively small weight the Americans give to respecting existing Supreme Court decisions.

The interactive hypothesis is that as greater emphasis is placed on legalistic expectations of judges, the corrosive effects of the ads on institutional support will be stronger. Using a simple measure of the number of these expectations rated as "extremely important,"[32] we first examine the bivariate correlations of ad exposure and institutional support. Across the levels of legalistic expectations, the correlations are: +.18, −.04, −.19, −.23, and −.51, from low to high legalistic expectations. Thus, *as expectations emphasize legalistic criteria more, the corrosive effect of ad exposure on institutional support increases*. The same conclusions emerge from multivariate analysis. In an equation controlling for attitudes at t_1, the coefficient for the interaction between expectations and ad exposure is statistically and substantively significant ($\beta = -.49$), and that coefficient remains significant in the fully controlled model ($\beta = -.34$). Those who expect judges to adhere to strict standards of legality were more likely to have been affected by the ads they viewed. And as a result, their support for the Supreme Court declined.

Discussion and Concluding Comments

Despite a fairly complex and ambitious research design, the principal findings of this research are fairly simple. Politicized nomination processes do in fact subtract from the legitimacy of the United States Supreme Court. The corrosive effect seems not to be associated with the proceedings in the Senate—after all, Senate hearings on nominees tend to be civil to a considerable degree, especially when the nominee is a sitting judge and therefore is addressed as such. Instead, the damage to institutional support is associated with the advertisements produced by interest groups. At least in the case of Judge Alito, these ads were framed in terms of politics. One who viewed the ads might well assume that they were referring to a normal political appointee. That the effect of attentiveness to the Senate process is opposite that of ad exposure adds to our confidence that the specific content of the ads was the culprit in eroding support for the Court.

We are also impressed that the impact of the confirmation events on attitudes toward the Court persisted for several months after Alito was confirmed. One often sees studies of short-term attitude change (e.g., experiments embedded within surveys) and wonders whether attitude change is lasting. For these citizens, it seems that the confirmation process made a lasting impression on their views of the Supreme Court.

The driving mechanism for change in institutional support has to do with whether the Supreme Court is seen as an ordinary political institution or whether it is judged to be distinctive. To the extent that people

[32] Because so few respondents rated none of these as extremely important, we have collapsed the two lowest categories.

believe the Court is a relatively nonpolitical institution, support for it is more easily generated. Anything that drags the Court into ordinary politics damages the esteem of the institution.

We have written extensively about positivity bias, the process through which exposure to the judicial process tends to enhance support. In the analysis of this chapter, we uncovered evidence of negativity. To the extent that citizens are exposed to the Supreme Court and its processes and procedures, we believe citizens learn the message that the Court is different and worthy of esteem. To the extent, however, that low politics is associated with the Court, that esteem is threatened. Everything seems to depend on the content of the messages Americans receive when they start paying attention to the Supreme Court.

Attitudes toward the Court have much to do with the expectations citizens hold of judges. Support for the Court suffers most among those whose expectations are violated during politicized confirmation processes. These people expect legalism from judges; when the process is portrayed as political, they adjust their attitudes toward the Court itself. Of course, we do not know whether this effect persists over long periods of time, but unrequited expectations seem to undermine the legitimacy of the Supreme Court. Is the Court an ordinary political institution or is it not?

Much more about these processes must be understood. But this initial inquiry into how confirmation processes affect attitudes toward the Supreme Court demonstrates that the legitimacy of the institution is not obdurate. Future research would profit, therefore, from far more dynamic research designs than have characterized investigation of public attitudes toward the institution in the past. Change is important and needs to be much better understood.

CHAPTER SIX

Concluding Thoughts, Theory, and Policy

In the research presented in this book, we have provided one of the most comprehensive investigations ever undertaken of public attitudes toward the process of confirming a nominee to the United States Supreme Court. Our overall framework is dynamic: We ask what role do preexisting attitudes toward the Court play in shaping perceptions and evaluations of confirmation politics, as well as consider the impact such politics have on the evolution of those attitudes. Since most extant research on public attitudes has adopted a static view, our research is perhaps the first comprehensive, national effort to understand how attitudes are updated in response to salient judicial events.[1]

On the basis of this research design we have learned much about Americans' attitudes toward their Supreme Court. Perhaps a recap is in order. We begin with a recitation of fairly conventional findings and move toward the more unexpected conclusions from the dynamic portion of our analysis.

The Supreme Court enjoys a great deal of legitimacy among the American people. This finding is entirely in line with conventional wisdom; the political institution most respected and trusted by the American people is the United States Supreme Court.

Attitudes toward the Supreme Court do not suffer from partisan or ideological polarization. Many aspects of politics and policy in the contemporary United States exhibit signs of polarization. While we are not of the view that polarization in ordinary politics is necessarily deleterious to democracy, we do believe that democracies profit from a consensus on the rules of the game, and that the primary political institutions of a democracy must be supported and respected by all. In some respects, institutions represent procedural, in contrast to distributive, justice. If the venues in which we fight with each other over substantive ends are not

[1] We readily acknowledge Hoekstra's very important work (2003) on the impact of Supreme Court decisions on the attitudes of those in communities from which the case was drawn. Her study makes a very innovative use of a panel research design. It is not, however, nationally representative.

legitimate, then our conflicts can spill over to threaten the system itself. Fortunately, from the point of view of the political stability of the United States, support for the Supreme Court does not vary much by the party or ideological attachments of the American people.

The American people know far more about the Supreme Court than has heretofore been documented and appreciated. We do not want to overclaim on these findings. From the point of view of having detailed information about the structure and function of the Supreme Court, most Americans are undoubtedly ill-informed, wrongly informed, and/or naive. But from the viewpoint of the conventional wisdom asserting the woeful ignorance of the American people, these findings are revolutionary. Most people may not know much about the "emanations and penumbras" that undergird *Roe v. Wade*, but they do know that those who make the most important public policy on the issue of abortion are not held accountable for their policy making through elections. Perhaps an important element of this has to do with descriptive representation. Perhaps citizens pay attention to political institutions that include people "like them." And we would add one further heresy to this list, albeit with the recognition that it is not necessarily strictly grounded in our data: not only do the American people know something about law and courts, it appears they can also learn as these institutions and their actions become salient.

Knowledge enhances institutional legitimacy: to know courts is to love them, or at least to respect them. Political knowledge is associated with political support. As we have argued, this relationship is not, however, entirely as it seems. Knowledge per se does not produce support. Instead, knowledge gives rise to an understanding of the distinctive role of the judiciary in the American political system, reinforcing the view that "courts are different." Knowledge also comes from exposure to courts, and exposure to courts means exposure to the highly legitimizing symbols of law. To reiterate, the message these symbols advance is that courts are not run-of-the-mill political institutions. They are different, and they are special, and they are therefore worthy of esteem.

Whether people support the Supreme Court has consequences for how they view and judge important legal controversies. We have noted that knowledge of courts actually represents something more than knowledge. It represents socialization into the view that courts are different, which then frees courts from the disregard and cynicism many Americans seem to hold for their political institutions. But to expand the causal model a bit, to know about courts is to "know" that judges use principled processes of decision making. Why is the U.S. Congress held in low regard? Because its members are thought to be too heavily influenced by self-interest, be it the self-interest of getting re-elected, or even the self-interest of "feathering their own congressional nests." But judges are different. We are impressed that many, if not most, Americans do not seem to believe in strict mechanical jurisprudence. Most Americans recognize that judges engage in policy making, that policy making involves discretion that is only weakly bounded by law and *stare decisis*, and that judges are more than legal automatons. The notion that judges do (or even should) make legal decisions through strict syllogisms is not widely accepted by the American people. Judges are discretionary policy makers and the American people seem to understand that.

But it is how that discretion gets utilized that is important, since members of Congress also enjoy a great deal of discretion in policy making. Many believe that members of Congress sell their votes to the highest K Street bidder; few believe that about judges. Knowledge of courts imparts the viewpoint that judges engage in the *principled* exercise of discretion. The American people do not reject granting judges discretion. They support law and courts to the extent that the discretion is exercised in a principled, non-self-interested fashion—which some might describe with the term "impartiality."

The Alito nomination was judged differently by those most supportive of the United States Supreme Court. Support for the Supreme Court is indicative of the presence of a syndrome of beliefs about law and courts, and that syndrome provides a frame through which salient judicial events are perceived and judged. In the case of the Alito nomination, we refer to that frame as one of "judiciousness." Court supporters were predisposed to evaluate Judge Alito in terms of his judicial characteristics, in part because judges are different from ordinary politicians. For many Americans, Alito passed the test of judiciousness. His temperament seemed appropriate for a judge and his background on the federal bench seemed to qualify him for a position on the Supreme Court. We suspect that for a considerable portion of the American people, Alito was a fairly easy case. Those most supportive of the Court weighted judiciousness as a criterion in forming an opinion on Alito's confirmation much more heavily than did those less supportive of the Court.

Even those who paid more attention to Alito's ideological credentials generally concluded that, while conservative, Alito was not an extremist. We are impressed by our finding that Alito was judged by most Americans to occupy an ideological space reasonably close to their own. Our own view is that Alito is far more conservative than perceived by the American people; but in this confirmation fight, it was their views, not ours, that were important. Judge Alito was confirmed to the United States Supreme Court because strong Court supporters judged him on criteria of judiciousness, and found his record satisfactory, and because weak Court supporters judged him on ideological criteria, but found him to be a mainstream conservative. To reiterate, whether one emphasizes judiciousness or ideology depends to a considerable degree upon preexisting attitudes toward the Supreme Court and its role in the American democracy.

But attitudes toward the Supreme Court are not impervious to exogenous influences. Support for the Court can change. We have several times cited the slow deterioration of support among African Americans, as they came to view the Court not as a friend, but as a foe. In this instance, we speculate that the reservoir of goodwill ran dry owing to sustained dissatisfaction with the policy decisions of the Court.[2] But not all disliked policy decisions undermine Court support. We have repeatedly referenced our findings about the effect of *Bush v. Gore* on Court attitudes, arguing that if ever a single decision would threaten institutional legitimacy, it would be this one. Support for the Court seemed to grow among Republicans in the aftermath of this decision, although that is hardly surprising. What is surprising is that support did not decline among Democrats, or among African Americans. The losers in *Bush v. Gore* did not punish the Court by lowering the esteem they hold for the institution. This represents a phenomenal store of political capital for the Supreme Court. It may not be able to "get away with murder," and sustained disappointment with the institution may have negative consequences, but given the legitimacy that the institution currently enjoys, we doubt that any single ruling can seriously threaten the integrity of the institution.

That said, the Alito campaigns, pro- and anti-confirmation, did indeed seem to do some damage to the legitimacy of the Supreme Court. Again, we do not want to overstate our findings—the campaigns were not disastrous for the Court. But our statistical evidence is that those who viewed more advertisements by the interest groups urging support or opposition to the nomination came away from the controversy with less support for the Supreme Court. It was not simply paying attention to the battle over

[2] Although we know of no data on this score, an ironic possibility is that some of the erosion of support within the African American community may actually reflect the Court's unwillingness (at least until now) to turn back the clock on *Roe v. Wade* and abortion rights. It is assumed that African Americans dislike the Court owing to its retreat on civil rights issues, but we are unaware of any rigorous evidence, one way or the other, on the precise nature of the policy disagreement.

Alito that damaged legitimacy. Apparently, people can fight over matters such as whether to confirm a nominee, and fight vigorously, without affecting the legitimacy of the institution itself. But the advertisements run as part of the confirmation battle seemed to have framed the fight in different terms, terms that were explicitly political (even if, it should be recalled, the ads were not viewed as unfair). The lesson the ads taught is that "courts are not different." Those exposed to the ads lessened their support for the institution largely, we believe, because they came to see the Supreme Court as just another political institution. This is perhaps the most important finding of our research.

The effect of nominees on institutions. We are also impressed by the "spillover" from a controversy over a single nominee to the High Bench to the institution itself. One might not have predicted such a consequence. In our view, attitudes toward Alito were almost irrelevant. What seemed to happen is that the confirmation controversy caused people to pay attention to the judiciary, "waking up" attitudes that had been in hibernation. Paying attention in turn taught people lessons about the nature of the institution itself. The candidate was the stimulus making the Supreme Court salient; the way various elites debated the nomination provided citizens with insights into the judiciary more broadly. Confirmation controversies provide civics lessons, even if the lessons learned are not always civic, and the primary lesson is not about the nominees themselves.

Caveats, Puzzles, and Questions

All of the findings and conclusions of this book must be placed in a quite specific context: we analyze the perceptions and expectations of ordinary people. Some will no doubt question whether the "average Joe" is (or should be) of any particular relevance to the process of selecting people to serve on the United States Supreme Court. After all, most people are woefully ignorant of the structure and function of the Supreme Court, and nearly all would not know a good judge if they saw one (unless they were told by elites that the judge was good). While advocates of this view will surely have quit reading this book long prior to this point, we nonetheless feel obliged to offer some rebuttal to this critique.

We do not gainsay that elites are important. Indeed, in our view, it was elite politics that scuttled the nomination of Harriet Miers to the Supreme Court. Ordinary folks played a small role in that imbroglio. And in general, elites dominate the outcome of confirmation struggles.

But we conceive of the mass public as a form of political capital. How does one defeat a nomination? There is more to confirmation politics than reasoned discussion of judicial qualifications among senators and legal elites. Opponents inevitably seek to pressure senators to vote one way or the other, and a natural pressure point is through the mobilization of constituents—who are, by and large, ordinary people. The Alito nomination succeeded in considerable part owing to the failure of interest groups to mobilize public opinion against the nomination. The mass public is of course not determinative of the outcome of a confirmation battle. But we contend that the views of ordinary people are far from irrelevant to the outcome of the process.

More generally, how ordinary people feel about their political institutions is of considerable importance. Again, while the views of the people were not dispositive, we believe Franklin Roosevelt's failure in his court-packing scheme in the 1930s was in part due to the institutional legitimacy the Supreme Court enjoyed among the American mass public. More contemporaneously, the many current efforts to curb the Court in various ways (e.g., Geyh 2006) have failed in part owing to the mass legitimacy the institution enjoys. Whether ordinary people support or oppose efforts to punish political institutions for their policy making is crucial to the efficacy of the institution.

The evidence of our analysis is that the attitudes of some Americans toward their Supreme Court changed as a result of the fight over Alito's nomination. This is strong evidence since we measured Court support months prior to and after the confirmation process itself. Indeed, few of the voluminous studies of attitudes toward the judiciary have had access to such direct measures of change.

We nonetheless remain uncertain as to how attitudes evolve over longer periods of time. Were citizens permanently changed by the nomination campaigning? We do not know. Perhaps the "running tally" that people store in their memories was decremented by the events; perhaps, however, the next confirmation to the Supreme Court will be uncontroversial, leading to exposure to legitimizing symbols and resulting in a positive addition to the tally. We confess to knowing very little about how this larger dynamic process evolves. Ours is a study of opinion change over the course of a year; how opinions change over the course of a lifetime remains an enigma.

We do know, however, that a spiraling process is possible. That is, assume that Court support is lowered by a salient judicial event. This enhances the tendency to view the next judicial event in more political and less legal terms: the frame changes. In turn, with this new frame, events are likely to detract from Court support. This diminished support influences perceptions of the next judicial event. And so on. Because the "running tally" provides a frame for how subsequent events are evaluated, the deleterious effects of a politicized confirmation fight can reverberate into the future, even if slowly and incrementally.

Since attitude-updating is a dynamic process, longitudinal research designs are essential for further understanding how institutional legitimacy waxes and wanes. As we argued, the dominant design among scholars of courts and public opinion is static. We are not naive about the many difficulties and limitations associated with longitudinal designs, but, if nothing else, this research shows that attitudes change, and consequently that future research efforts would profit from the ability to analyze change.

Finally, we return to the central theoretical focus of this book—positivity theory. In our earlier investigations of Court support we have come close to arguing that virtually anything that stimulates citizens to pay attention to courts enhances institutional legitimacy. We argued this based on robust correlations between knowledge and support (e.g., Gibson, Caldeira, and Baird 1998), and with the corollary that increased exposure is associated with increased contact with legitimizing judicial symbols. It turns out from this research on the Alito nomination that we were wrong: there are indeed circumstances in which increasing exposure weakens legitimacy. These circumstances include (but are surely not limited to) the campaigns of interests groups that portray the judiciary as an ordinary and common political institution. We are, we contend, correct that most instances of the heightened salience of the judiciary involve exposure to legitimizing symbols. But not all events are focused on such symbols. We still assert that there is a bias—that when people pay attention to courts they are likely to be exposed to reinforcing legal symbols—but we now clearly recognize that citizens learn from events and that the content of some events portrays courts politically. Just as judiciousness is a presumption that can be overcome, the bias of positivity is not absolute.

The United States Supreme Court is among the most legitimate high courts in the world. That legitimacy constitutes a profound source of political capital. We are not exactly certain how the institution acquired this invaluable asset; we are certain, however, that legitimacy is not obdurate. The Court itself often worries about whether its decisions affect its legitimacy. Our most general conclusion is that they probably do not, to the extent that the judges cloak their actions in legal symbolism.

But exogenous events are another matter. As the Supreme Court becomes more enmeshed in the partisan and ideological politics of interest groups, dangers lurk. Should the legitimacy of institutions like the Supreme Court be lost, all Americans would lose. Understanding processes of change in attitudes toward political institutions should remain high on the agenda of law and politics scholars.

APPENDIX A

Survey Design: The 2005 Survey

This research is based on a nationally representative sample interviewed face to face during the summer of 2005. The field work took place from mid-May until mid-July, 2005. A total of 1,001 interviews was completed, with a response rate of 40.03 percent (AAPOR Response Rate #3). No respondent substitution was allowed; up to six call-backs were executed. The average length of interview was 83.8 minutes (with a standard deviation of 23.9 minutes). The data were subjected to some minor "poststratification," with the proviso that the weighted numbers of cases must correspond to the actual number of completed interviews. Interviews were offered in both English and Spanish (with the Spanish version of the questionnaire prepared through conventional translation/back-translation procedures). Samples such as this have a margin of error of approximately ± 3.08 percent.

During the course of the Alito confirmation process, we attempted to re-interview the respondents from the 2005 survey.[1] The fieldwork began on January 19, 2006, and was completed on February 13, 2006. A total of 335 individuals from the 2005 survey was re-interviewed.[2]

Since t_2 interviews were completed with only one-third of the original respondents, questions about the representativeness of the subsample naturally arise. We have considered this issue in some detail (see, appendix B, for the details of the statistical analysis). We draw two general conclusions from that analysis. First, the t_2 subsample is reasonably representative on its face, and second, with minor poststratification, the 2006 subsample closely mirrors the 2005 population from which it was drawn. We therefore believe inferences can confidently be drawn from our analysis, even if the confidence intervals of this relatively small subsample are larger than we might prefer.

The t_3 survey was in the field from May 24 through June 22, 2006, and resulted in 259 completed interviews. Only respondents interviewed at t_2

[1] We decided to exclude two categories of individuals from the second-wave project: (1) those for whom the initial interview was in Spanish, and (2) those living in areas decimated by Hurricane Katrina. This resulted in 969 individuals being eligible for re-interviewing.

[2] If we were to treat this as an entirely new survey, not a re-interview, and apply the AAPOR criteria to calculate the widely used Modified Response Rate #3, the rate would be 53.2 percent.

were eligible for inclusion in the t_3 re-interview survey (334 respondents), resulting in a 77.6 percent raw response rate, and a rate of 82 percent (AAPOR's Response Rate #3).

The question of how to weight the panel data is somewhat complicated. The t_1 survey was subjected to some slight poststratification so as to improve its representativeness. We then developed weights for the t_2 and t_3 surveys to improve the representativeness of these subsamples. The target for the t_2 and t_3 weighting was the characteristics of the t_1 survey. As a consequence, when we analyze the panel data, we use the t_3 weight, but when we consider only the t_1 data, we use the original weight variable.

A second issue has to do with the shifting N for the panel data. Instead of using the full t_2 sample when considering questions asked at t_2, we focus our analysis on those respondents interviewed in all three surveys. Even when we consider t_2 data alone, we use the t_3 weights because we are focusing on the restricted t_1 through t_3 sample. To do otherwise would make our analysis of change be based on different sets of respondents, thereby providing an alternative explanation of any change we observe. The exception is when we compare the t_1 data to earlier surveys; for this sort of analysis, we take advantage of all of the people interviewed in 2005.

APPENDIX B

The Representativeness of the Panel Sample

Owing to the shortness of the fieldwork period, and other factors, we were able to re-interview only roughly one-third of the original respondents in the 2005 survey. Therefore, it is necessary to investigate further the representativeness of the t_2 subsample.

One way in which the representativeness of the t_2 sample can be assessed is to determine whether those who were interviewed in the second survey differ from those who were not interviewed. The null hypothesis (H_0) is that no difference exists between the two subgroups.

We have investigated this hypothesis by examining the level of knowledge the respondents hold about the Supreme Court. Table B.1 reports the relevant statistical analysis. For instance, the first entry in the table reports that 72.8 percent of the respondents who were interviewed at t_2 knew that Supreme Court justices are appointed to the bench, whereas only 61.7 percent of those not interviewed were similarly informed. This difference is highly statistically significant ($p < .001$), but the strength of the relationship is not very strong (phi = .11).

Overall, the t_2 subsample is slightly more knowledgeable about the Supreme Court than those who were not interviewed. The differences are not great but neither are they trivial. Consequently, some statistical adjustments to the t_2 sample are necessary.

The initial 2005 sample was subjected to minor poststratification, adjusting the sample on a handful of demographic attributes (as is conventional these days). When we apply exactly the same methodology to the t_2 data, using the frequency distributions for the demographic variables from the 2005 survey, the gap between interviewed and not-interviewed reduces considerably. For instance, without t_2 weighting, the mean number of correct answers to the three knowledge questions among those who were interviewed is 2.03. With weighting, that mean reduces to 1.87, which is much closer to the mean of 1.72 for those who were not interviewed. Consequently, we have weighted the t_2 data by this factor, and, after doing so, the t_2 subsample is reasonably representative of the initial sample.

A second issue must be addressed. Most of the interviews were completed prior to the Senate vote on Alito's nomination (81.6 percent), but 18.4 percent were completed after the Senate decision. As it turns out,

TABLE B.1.
Differences between Those Interviewed and Those Not Interviewed in 2006

	t_2 *Outcome*	
Percentage knowing that[a]	*Not Interviewed*	*Interviewed*
Justices are appointed to the bench	61.7	72.8
Justices serve life terms	56.2	68.8
Supreme Court has "last say" on the constitution	54.4	61.6
Mean number of correct answers	1.7	2.0

[a] Knowledge was measured during the 2005 interview. These data are weighted by t_1 post stratification weights.

this seems to have made little if any difference in attitudes toward the confirmation. Of those interviewed prior to the vote, 62.0 percent support confirming Judge Alito, compared to 62.3 percent of those interviewed after the vote. Thus, we ignore the date of interview in the analysis reported in this paper.

APPENDIX C

The Supreme Court and the U.S. Presidential Election of 2000

WOUNDS, SELF-INFLICTED OR OTHERWISE?

James L. Gibson, Gregory A. Caldeira, and Lester Kenyatta Spence

The conventional wisdom about the U.S. Supreme Court and the 2000 presidential election is that the Court wounded itself by participating in such a partisan dispute.[1] By "wounded" people mean that the institution lost some of its legitimacy. Evidence from our survey, conducted in early 2001, suggests little if any diminution of the Court's legitimacy in the aftermath of *Bush v. Gore*, even among African Americans. We observe a relationship between evaluations of the opinion and institutional legitimacy, but the bulk of the causality seems to flow from loyalty to evaluations of the case, not vice versa. We argue that legitimacy frames perceptions of the Court opinion. Furthermore, increased awareness of the activities of the Court tends to reinforce legitimacy by exposing people to the powerful symbols of law. In 2000, legitimacy did indeed seem to provide a reservoir of good will that allowed the Court to weather the storm created by its involvement in Florida's presidential election.

The U.S. presidential election of 2000 reminds us once again of the importance of the legitimacy of political institutions. Consider this highly simplified view of the election.

This is slightly revised version of the following article: Gibson, James L., Gregory A. Caldeira, and Lester Kenyatta Spence. 2003. "The Supreme Court and the U.S. Presidential Election of 2000: Wounds, Self-Inflicted ot Otherwise?" *British Journal of Political Science* 33, 4 (October): 535–56.

[1] Gibson and Spence: Department of Political Science, Washington University, St. Louis; Caldeira: Department of Political Science, Ohio State University. This project would not have been possible without the support of the Weidenbaum Center on the Economy, Government, and Public Policy, Washington University, St. Louis, and The Ford Foundation (Grant Number 1015-0840). We are especially indebted to Steve Smith, Director of the Weidenbaum Center, for his encouragement of this work. An earlier version of this article was presented at the American Politics Workshop series at Columbia University. Professors Roger E. Hartley, Robert Erikson, and David Epstein made most useful comments on an earlier version of this article. We also appreciate the research assistance of Eric Lomazoff and Hannah Pierce of the Russell Sage Foundation.

A bitter political controversy arises. The dispute bounces around various institutions, with no definitive resolution. Finally, the U.S. Supreme Court intervenes and makes a decision. Many grumble about the ruling, but political elites call for it to be "respected," much if not most of the mass public seems to accept the decision, and the brouhaha ends. The country gets on with its business. Scholars then talk of the Court expending its "political capital," and wonder about the efficacy of the Court in future clashes, but the institution seems to have enough legitimacy to "get away with" its ruling and make it "stick."

The circumstances surrounding *Bush v. Gore* may well enter our textbooks one day as a stellar example of the power and efficacy of institutional legitimacy.[2]

The Supreme Court decision settling the outcome of the U.S. presidential election unleashed a torrent of criticism. Not only was the logic of the opinion assailed,[3] but many also judged the Court's opinion, and even the Court itself, as illegitimate.[4] For instance, 585 law professors placed an advertisement in the *New York Times* on January 13, 2001, condemning the Court's decision as illegitimate.[5] Perhaps for the first time, public opinion pollsters queried the American people using words like "legitimate" and "legitimacy."[6] Scholars complained about a "self-inflicted wound" on the Court,[7] as many questioned whether *Bush v. Gore* undermined the ability of the Court to rule on controversial issues in the future. In short, in the eyes of many, *Bush v. Gore* subtracted mightily from the institutional legitimacy enjoyed by the U.S. Supreme Court.

A great deal of hyperbole surrounded the U.S. election, and politicians, professors, and pundits made many outlandish empirical claims at the

[2] *Bush v. Gore*, 531 U.S. 98 (2000).

[3] Erwin Chemerinsky, "*Bush v. Gore* Was Not Justifiable," *Notre Dame Law Review* 76 (2001): 1093–1112.

[4] See, for instance, Peter Berkowitz and Benjamin Wittes, "The Professors and *Bush v. Gore*," *Wilson Quarterly* 25 (2001): 76–89; Vincent Bugliosi, *The Betrayal of America: How the Supreme Court Undermined the Constitution and Chose Our President* (New York: Thunder's Mouth Press/Nation Books, 2001).

[5] A copy of the advertisement, as well as much additional material and criticism, can be found at http://www.the-rule-of-law.com/ (12/7/2001).

[6] For instance, it was common for polling agencies to ask whether Bush won the presidency "legitimately," whether the outcome was "legitimate," or whether Bush's presidency is "legitimate." Pollsters rarely defined "legitimacy" for their respondents, although Zogby International did ask the following question: "If you define legitimacy as the will of the people, do you consider a George W. Bush presidency legitimate?" In response, 59 percent said yes and 37 percent said no. See Karlyn H. Bowman, *The 2000 Election: What the Polls Said*, available at www.aei.org/ps/psbowman6.pdf (accessed 11/23/2001).

[7] Frank Goodman ("Preface," in *Annals of the American Academy of Political and Social Science* 574 [2001]: 9–23) notes that the decision "generated a blizzard of criticism, much of it characterizing the *per curiam* decision as a grievous self-inflicted wound that threatens to diminish public respect for the Court." See the dissent of Justice Breyer, *Bush* v. *Gore*, 531 U.S. 98 (2000), 157–58, who also used the term in his opinion.

time. Terms like "legitimacy" were nearly always used loosely, without rigorous definition. Unfortunately, because serious scholarly inquiry into the Court's legitimacy has been limited, we have little systematic knowledge about how the election may actually have influenced the legitimacy of the Court.

The theoretical issues raised by this dispute are not, however, unfamiliar to scholars. Researchers have long been interested in the question of how an institution's performance affects its legitimacy, and in particular how the Supreme Court's decisions shape people's views of it.[8] Still, the relationship between judgments of particular decisions and more general attitudes toward political institutions such as the Supreme Court is underanalysed and poorly understood within political science.

How legitimate is the U.S. Supreme Court today, and how did the 2000 election affect the legitimacy of the institution? Though the question of change in support is difficult to answer, we adduce some new evidence on the Court's legitimacy in the period shortly after the conclusion of the presidential election. One purpose of this article is thus to provide empirical results on how Americans viewed the Court in the aftermath of the 2000 presidential election, based on a nationally representative sample interviewed at the beginning of 2001.

We have several additional objectives as well. First, because we draw our indicators of legitimacy from extant research, we are able to assess the degree to which the Court's legitimacy changed following its decision in *Bush v. Gore*. We do not have panel data, but we do have cross-sectional data from three surveys. Second, because our survey includes an oversample of African Americans, we are able to examine the attitudes African Americans hold toward the Court, both now and in comparison to earlier surveys. Third, we employ a variety of statistical techniques to untangle the causal relationship between views of the opinion in *Bush v. Gore* and more general loyalty to the Court as an institution. Finally, since our results are quite contrary to conventional wisdom, we reconsider extant theories of how people update their views toward political institutions, focusing in particular on the framing associated with incidents in which courts become salient. We begin with a brief review of Legitimacy Theory.

The Theory of Institutional Legitimacy

Considerable agreement exists among social scientists on most of the major elements of Legitimacy Theory. For instance, most agree that legiti-

[8] See, for example, Valerie J. Hoekstra, "The Supreme Court and Local Public Opinion," *American Political Science Review* 94 (2000): 89–100.

macy is a normative concept, having something to do with the right (moral and legal) to make decisions. "Authority" is often used as a synonym for legitimacy. Legitimate institutions are those with an authoritative mandate to render judgments for a polity.

Under the influence of Easton, scholars use "diffuse support" as a synonym for "legitimacy."[9] The concept refers to "a reservoir of favourable attitudes or good will that helps members to accept or tolerate outputs to which they are opposed or the effects of which they see as damaging to their wants."[10] Diffuse support is institutional *loyalty*, support *not* contingent upon satisfaction with the immediate outputs of the institution. Most analysts distinguish between approval of policy outputs in the short term and more fundamental loyalty to an institution over the long term. "Specific support" is satisfaction with the immediate policy outputs. Institutions without a reservoir of good will may be limited in their ability to go against the preferences of the majority, even when it is necessary or wise to do so.[11] Thus, a crucial attribute of political institutions, and courts in particular, is the degree to which they enjoy the loyalty of their constituents.

The Dynamics of Opinion: How Do People Update Their Views?

One of the most important unanswered questions for the field has to do with whether preexisting loyalty to the Court cushions the effect of unpopular decisions (such as that in *Bush v. Gore*), or whether highly charged decisions undermine an institution's basic legitimacy. Legitimacy Theory obviously suggests the former, but some important recent research suggests the latter.

For instance, Grosskopf and Mondak examine whether confidence in the Supreme Court "derives solely from stable factors such as core democratic values, or if citizens alter their evaluations to take into account their views of the Court's ruling."[12] They rightly note the importance of the

[9] David Easton, *A Systems Analysis of Political Life* (New York: Wiley, 1965); idem, "A Re-Assessment of the Concept of Political Support," *British Journal of Political Science* 5 (1975): 435–57.

[10] Easton, *A Systems Analysis of Political Life*, 273.

[11] Comparativists, such as George Tsebelis ("Veto Players and Institutional Analysis," *Governance* 13 [2000]: 441–74) focus on courts as "veto players" and have acknowledged that legitimacy is a necessary resource if courts are to play this role. See also James L. Gibson and Gregory A. Caldeira, "Defenders of Democracy? Legitimacy, Popular Acceptance, and the South African Constitutional Court," *Journal of Politics* 65 (2003): 1–30.

[12] Anke Grosskopf and Jeffrey J. Mondak, "Do Attitudes Toward Specific Supreme Court Decisions Matter? The Impact of *Webster* and *Texas v. Johnson* on Public Confidence in the Supreme Court," *Political Research Quarterly* 51 (1998): 633–34.

answer to this question: "If only core values matter, then a static depiction of support—treating it as a virtually inexhaustible resource—can be justified. However, if specific decisions can be shown to have an impact on support, then a dynamic view of legitimacy is more appropriate."[13] They conclude that confidence in the Court is very much a function of perceptions and evaluations of court opinions, and that *unpopular decisions erode the institution's political capital.* This finding directly challenges one of the central propositions of Legitimacy Theory.

At the level of the individual citizen, few longitudinal studies have investigated how information about the Supreme Court influences overall evaluations of the institution. Perhaps the best of these studies is Hoekstra's analysis of local reactions to Supreme Court opinions directly affecting several local communities.[14] She discovers that "satisfaction with [Court] decisions influences subsequent evaluations of the Court."[15]

Unfortunately, however, the conclusions of most earlier studies are limited because they employ indicators of Court support that are not valid measures of institutional legitimacy. For instance, Hoekstra's measure is: "In general do you approve or disapprove of the way the Supreme Court is handling its job? Do you approve/disapprove very strongly, strongly, or not strongly?"[16] Had this research a more valid measure of legitimacy, it might well have discovered that because the Court has a solid reservoir of good will, unpopular decisions generate ire that dissipates quickly and has no lasting consequence for the legitimacy of the institution, a possibility that Grosskopf and Mondak recognize.[17]

Thus, despite the acknowledged theoretical importance of this issue, we have a long way to go in understanding the relationship between institutional performance and legitimacy. Previous research has not been able to overcome measurement limitations, in part because it has not focused on actual Supreme Court decisions that are both controversial and salient

[13] Ibid., 634.

[14] Some experimental studies, based mainly on undergraduate students, also support the view that people update their opinions of institutions on the basis of their reactions to individual decisions. See, for instance, Jeffrey J. Mondak, "Institutional Legitimacy and Procedural Justice: Reexamining the Question of Causality," *Law and Society Review* 27 (1998): 599–608. See also Jeffrey J. Mondak, "Substantive and Procedural Aspects of Supreme Court Decisions as Determinants of Institutional Approval," *American Politics Quarterly* 19 (1991): 174–88; idem, "Institutional Legitimacy, Policy Legitimacy, and the Supreme Court," *American Politics Quarterly* 20 (1992): 457–77; and Valerie J. Hoekstra, "The Supreme Court and Opinion Change: An Experimental Study of the Court's Ability to Change Opinion," *American Politics Quarterly* 23 (1995): 109–29.

[15] Hoekstra, "The Supreme Court and Local Public Opinion," 97.

[16] Ibid., 99.

[17] Grosskopf and Mondak, "Do Attitudes Toward Specific Supreme Court Decisions Matter?," 641–42.

to the American people.[18] The Court's intervention in the Florida election provides an intriguing opportunity to advance our understanding of the connection between policy satisfaction and dissatisfaction and institutional legitimacy.

Previous Research on the Impact of Bush v. Gore *on Public Evaluations of the Court*

Most of the polls conducted in the aftermath of the presidential election used measures of confidence to assess the impact of the election on the Supreme Court. For instance, Harris Interactive used the conventional question employed by the General Social Survey, asking: "As far as the people running the U.S. Supreme Court are concerned, would you say you have a great deal of confidence, only some confidence, or hardly any confidence at all in them?" The results at the beginning of 2001 reveal only slightly less confidence than the results of a comparable survey conducted at the beginning of 2000.[19] Other poll data support a similar conclusion on the question of confidence.

Opinions are more evenly split over whether the Court based its decision on law or some combination of partisanship, politics, and the justices' own political preferences. A Hart-Teeter/NBC/*Wall Street Journal* survey, conducted December 7–10, 2000, reported that 34 percent of the respondents believed that the Court's decision in *Bush v. Gore* was based "mostly on the law" but that 53 percent believed the decision was based "mostly on politics." If one were forced to draw a conclusion from these and other fragmentary bits of survey evidence, one might conclude that the Court's ruling in *Bush v. Gore* diminished confidence in the Court little despite the fairly widespread view that the Court's decision was politically motivated.

The most rigorous analysis reported to date is Kritzer's. Based on a tracking poll in the field at the time of the election, he concludes that the Court's involvement in the dispute "had measurable consequences for the public's view of the Court, *at least in the short term*."[20] He also argues that views of the Court became more partisan as a result of the election, although his final judgment is that the impact of the ruling is perhaps not as great as many might have expected. Unfortunately, however, Kritzer's

[18] One justification for a study such as Hoekstra's is that, under most circumstances, ordinary people have insufficient information to form judgments of Supreme Court decisions. Such is clearly not the case with *Bush v. Gore*.

[19] Bowman, *The 2000 Election*.

[20] Herbert M. Kritzer, "The Impact of *Bush v. Gore* on Public Perceptions and Knowledge of the Supreme Court," *Judicature* 85 (2001): 32–38, 36 (emphasis in the original).

conclusions must be treated as not especially relevant to our work since his research was not designed to assess institutional legitimacy and therefore lacks a valid measure of the legitimacy of the Supreme Court.[21]

Thus, the limited data available do not produce a clear verdict on whether the Court's intervention in *Bush v. Gore* had any consequences, disastrous or otherwise, for the legitimacy of the institution. Fortunately, we specifically designed our survey to investigate the question of the linkage between judgments of the Court's decision and the legitimacy of the institution itself.[22]

Institutional Loyalty in the Aftermath of the Election

Our thinking about institutional loyalty follows a considerable body of research on conceptualizing and measuring mass perceptions of high courts.[23] That research treats institutional loyalty as opposition to fundamental structural and functional changes in the institution;[24] additionally, it is grounded empirically in the history of attacks by politicians against courts in the United States (for example, court-packing)[25] and elsewhere (for example, manipulation of appellate jurisdiction).[26] As Caldeira and Gibson describe it, those who have no loyalty toward the Supreme Court are willing "to accept, make, or countenance major changes in the fundamental attributes of how the high bench functions or fits into the U.S.

[21] Instead, the question on which his analysis relies measures approval of the job performance of the Court (*Bush v. Gore*, 531 U.S. 98 (2000), 34), not institutional loyalty.

[22] For technical details on the survey, see appendix C.1.

[23] Gregory A. Caldeira and James L. Gibson, "The Etiology of Public Support for the Supreme Court," *American Journal of Political Science* 36 (1992): 635–64; James L. Gibson, Gregory A. Caldeira, and Vanessa Baird, "On the Legitimacy of National High Courts," *American Political Science Review* 92 (1998): 343–58; Gregory A. Caldeira and James L. Gibson, "The Legitimacy of the Court of Justice in the European Union: Models of Institutional Support," *American Political Science Review* 89 (1995): 356–76; James L. Gibson and Gregory A. Caldeira, "The Legitimacy of Transnational Legal Institutions: Compliance, Support, and the European Court of Justice," *American Journal of Political Science* 39 (1995): 459–89; James L. Gibson and Gregory A. Caldeira, "Changes in the Legitimacy of the European Court of Justice: A Post-Maastricht Analysis," *British Journal of Political Science* 28 (1998): 63–91; Gibson and Caldeira, "Defenders of Democracy?"

[24] G. R. Boynton and Gerhard Loewenberg, "The Development of Public Support for Parliament in Germany, 1951–1959," *British Journal of Political Science* 3 (1973): 169–89.

[25] Gregory A. Caldeira, "Public Opinion and the Supreme Court: FDR's Court-Packing Plan," *American Political Science Review* 81 (1987): 1139–54.

[26] Herman Schwartz, *The Struggle for Constitutional Justice in Post-Communist Europe* (Chicago: University of Chicago Press, 2000).

TABLE C.1.
Indicators of Loyalty toward the U.S. Supreme Court, 2001

	Percentages (totalling to 100 %)					
	Not supportive of the Court	*Uncertain*	*Supportive of the Court*	*Mean*	*Std. Dev.*	*N*
Do away with the Court	12.9	4.4	82.7	4.23	1.16	1,418
Limit the Court's jurisdiction	28.3	11.0	60.7	3.55	1.34	1,418
Court can be trusted	17.0	5.1	77.8	3.89	1.17	1,418
Court favors some groups	43.7	14.4	41.9	3.02	1.37	1,409
Court gets too mixed up in politics	40.8	15.9	43.3	3.05	1.36	1,418
Court should interpret the Constitution	22.7	8.1	69.2	3.73	1.31	1,418

Note: The percentages are calculated on the basis of collapsing the five-point Likert response set (e.g., "agree strongly" and "agree" responses are combined). The means and standard deviations are calculated on the uncollapsed distributions. Higher mean scores indicate more institutional loyalty. The propositions are: (1) If the U.S. Supreme Court started making a lot of decisions that most people disagree with, it might be better to do away with the Supreme Court altogether. (2) The right of the Supreme Court to decide certain types of controversial issues should be reduced. (3) The Supreme Court can usually be trusted to make decisions that are right for the country as a whole. (4) The decisions of the U.S. Supreme Court favor some groups more than others. (5) The U.S. Supreme Court gets too mixed up in politics. (6) The U.S. Supreme Court should have the right to say what the Constitution means, even when the majority of the people disagree with the Court's decision.

constitutional system."[27] Loyalty is also characterized by a generalized trust that an institution will perform acceptably in the future. Loyalty thus ranges from complete unwillingness to support the continued existence of the institution to staunch institutional fealty.

Table C.1 reports the responses from the six statements we use to measure loyalty toward the U.S. Supreme Court. The first three columns of figures represent the frequencies after collapsing "strong" and not-so-strong responses, and the column labelled "Supportive of the Court" reports the percentage of respondents giving answers indicating loyalty to the institution, regardless of whether loyalty requires an "agree" or "disagree" reply. The means and standard deviations are based on the uncollapsed data, and in every instance higher scores indicate more loyalty toward the Supreme Court.

[27] See Caldeira and Gibson, "The Etiology of Public Support for the Supreme Court," 638, quoting from Gerhard Loewenberg, "The Influence of Parliamentary Behavior on Regime Stability," *Comparative Politics* 3 (1971): 177–200.

These data indicate at least a moderate level of loyalty toward the Supreme Court among most Americans. On average, 3.8 of the statements elicit support for the Court, and 77.7 percent of the respondents endorse at least three of the six statements (data not shown). Except for the two items on partisanship, strong majorities express support for the Court on four of the six statements. On the clearest measure of institutional loyalty, the first (but also easiest) item, support is extremely widespread: more than four out of five Americans assert that it would *not* be better to do away with the Court, even if there were fairly widespread displeasure with its decisions. Although a significant minority worries about politics and partisanship on the Court, over three-quarters of the sample asserts that the Court—not the leaders of the Court—can generally be trusted. These data indicate that the Supreme Court enjoys a reasonably solid reservoir of good will, even in the aftermath of the tumultuous presidential election of 2000. Placing these findings in the context of cross-national research, the U.S. Supreme Court is a fairly legitimate institution.[28]

The responses to these propositions are positively correlated, with an average inter-item correlation of 0.26, a decent level of intercorrelation given that these are survey data (with all the general problems of unreliability). Reliability is respectable, with a Cronbach's alpha (α an indicator of internal consistency) of 0.68. Deletion of any of the variables would not increase the alpha coefficient. The statement with the weakest relationship to the total item set (as indicated by its squared multiple correlation coefficient) is the last one, a complicated statement about whether the Court should be subservient to majority opinion. When factor analyzed, these six items generate a single significant factor (the eigenvalue of the second factor extracted is 0.91), with all of the indicators loading significantly on the factor. We have calculated an Index of Institutional Loyalty as the mean response to these six items. Thus, these measures appear to have excellent psychometric properties.

Change in Loyalty toward the Court

It is impossible in a cross-sectional survey to analyse individual-level change in opinions. However, two earlier national surveys employed similar measures of institutional loyalty, so we can derive some indication of the nature of macrolevel change.[29] Table C.2 reports a comparison of two

[28] For a cross-national comparison of responses to this item see Gibson, Caldeira, and Baird, "On the Legitimacy of National High Courts."

[29] This approach to assessing change is based on data availability and suffers from several important potential liabilities. For instance, it could very well be that by October 2000 support for the Supreme Court was at much higher levels than it was in 1987 or 1995, and that the election brought support down to more pedestrian levels. We know of no reason

of the items asked in 2001 with similar questions asked in 1987 in a national survey.[30] Since both studies included representative oversamples of African Americans, and since the election of 2000 had special relevance to African Americans, we report the findings according to the race of the respondent. Although the items put to the respondents are *not* identical, they are similar enough to be able to draw some inferences about change.[31]

Several aspects of this table are important. First, opinions toward the Court in 2001 are considerably more polarized. There are many fewer "uncertain" or "don't know" responses to our statements in 2001, surely reflecting the heightened salience of the Court during this period of political controversy.

Second, among white Americans, we find no evidence whatsoever of a diminution of support for the Court between 1987 and 2001. On the first statement, opinions changed insignificantly, perhaps due to a ceiling effect (opinion in 1987 was already about as positive as it could be). On the second proposition, if anything, support for the Court *increased*. For instance, 62.8 percent in 2001 would resist efforts to alter the jurisdiction of the Court; the comparable figure in 1987 was only 49.0 percent, and this difference is statistically significant. At least among white Americans, *Bush v. Gore* seems not to have undermined the Court's legitimacy.

Unexpectedly, the same is true of African Americans: there is no indication of an overall diminution of loyalty toward the Court between 1987 and 2001. There is certainly some evidence of increased opposition to the Court, but it is also clear that support for the institution grew as well, with nearly three of four African Americans in 2001, compared to two-thirds in 1987, declaring that the Court should not be eliminated even if it made a series of unpopular decisions. The difference is not large, but is statistically significant, and is also reflected in the difference of means between the two surveys. However, while the percentage of African Americans unwilling to limit the Court's jurisdiction increased significantly in 2001, approaching a majority, we observe an even larger increase in the percentage favoring such restrictions on the Court. The rather substantial decline between the two surveys in the percentage of African

---

why this potentiality might be so, but we also have no evidence with which to discount it. Further, the potential causes of change in attitudes between the current and earlier surveys are numerous; to attribute all temporal differences to the effects of the election might well overestimate the influence of that event. Ultimately, our goal is build a case for a conclusion based on a variety of bits of evidence, no single piece of which is dispositive.

[30] Caldeira and Gibson, "The Etiology of Public Support for the Supreme Court."

[31] As the notes to table C.2 make clear, the question wording in the two surveys is not identical. Thus, in assessing change, we focus on overall patterns rather than on any single question.

TABLE C.2.
Change in Loyalty toward the U.S. Supreme Court, 1987–2001

	Level of diffuse support for the Supreme Court					
	Not supportive† *(%)*	*Undecided*† *(%)*	*Supportive*† *(%)*	*Mean*	*Std. Dev.*	*N*
Do away with the Court						
African Americans						
1987	14.9	21.1	64.0***	3.68	1.0	436
2001	20.0	5.6	74.4	3.94	1.4	496
Whites						
1987	8.0	10.8	81.2	3.99	0.9	788
2001	10.5	4.7	84.8	4.31	1.1	807
Limit the Court's jurisdiction						
African Americans						
1987	28.7	31.7	39.5***	3.20	1.0	435
2001	41.6	10.3	48.1	3.12	1.5	494
Whites						
1987	28.3	22.7	49.0***	3.31	1.0	794
2001	26.3	10.9	62.8	3.64	1.3	807

† Allowing for rounding errors, these three columns total to 100 percent.
***$p < 0.001$.

Note: Question wording differed in the two surveys as follows:

1987: If the Supreme Court continually makes decisions that the people disagree with, it might be better to do away with the Court altogether.

2001: If the U.S. Supreme Court started making a lot of decisions that most people disagree with, it might be better to do away with the Supreme Court altogether.

1987: The right of the Supreme Court to decide certain types of controversial issues should be limited by the Congress.

2001: The right of the Supreme Court to decide certain types of controversial issues should be reduced.

Source: 1987—Gregory A. Caldeira and James L. Gibson, "The Etiology of Public Support for the Supreme Court," *American Journal of Political Science*, 36 (1992), 635–64, p. 641, Table 1.

Americans who are uncertain renders comparison slightly problematic, but the difference in means between the two surveys is small. Still, African Americans seem at least moderately committed to the Supreme Court. Most significantly, we find little evidence that the Court's involvement in the election changed basic attachments to the institution.

Substantial racial differences in opinions toward the Court existed in 1987 and persisted in 2001. African Americans are considerably less likely than whites to express loyalty toward the Court, with, for instance, a African American–white difference of 14.2 percentage points on the jurisdiction proposition in 2001 and a 10.1 percentage point difference on the institutional loyalty statement. No clear pattern of change in the differential in support between African Americans and whites is apparent. Though African American opinion may have polarized somewhat as a result of the presidential election, whites seem to have remained relatively loyal to the Court.

We can also compare the 2001 data to a similar survey conducted in 1995.[32] Table C.3 reports these results (the 2001 figures we report in table C.3 are identical to those reported in table C.1, above). Consider the mean scores first. In every instance, the mean is higher (more support) in 2001 than it was in 1995. The differences are not enormous, but they are in every instance statistically significant. From these data it is *impossible to conclude that loyalty toward the Supreme Court plummeted after the presidential election of 2000*. Indeed, the percentage of Americans saying the Court can be trusted is 12.5 percentage points higher in 2001 than it was in 1995. Americans were somewhat more likely to have an opinion toward the Supreme Court in 2001, and their opinions were more likely to be positive than in 1995.

Summary

This analysis yields several conclusions. First, the U.S. Supreme Court enjoys at least a moderate degree of loyalty from the American people—its "reservoir of good will" is certainly not shallow. Second, although African Americans continue to be less likely than whites to support the Court, loyalty toward the institution in the African American community is still fairly widespread. Third, support for the Court does not seem to have been depressed by the justices' involvement in the presidential election; it would be difficult indeed to conclude from these cross-sectional data that the basic legitimacy of the Court was threatened by the justices' involvement in the 2000 election imbroglio.

Views of the Court's Opinion in *Bush v. Gore*

Americans appear to have been bitterly divided during and immediately after the 2000 election. What is less clear is how they felt about the Supreme Court and whether they regarded the Court's involvement in the election as legitimate and proper. In our survey in early 2001, we explored

[32] This study included no oversample of African Americans. See Gibson, Caldeira, and Baird, "On the Legitimacy of National High Courts."

TABLE C.3.
Loyalty toward the Supreme Court, 1995–2001

	Level of diffuse support for the Supreme Court					
	Not Supportive† (%)	*Undecided*† (%)	*Supportive*† (%)	*Mean*	*Std. Dev.*	N
Limit the Court's jurisdiction						
1995	35.5	11.7	52.8	3.2***	1.1	803
2001	28.3	11.0	60.7	3.6	1.3	1,418
Do away with the Court						
1995	16.8	7.2	76.0	3.8***	1.0	803
2001	12.9	4.4	82.7	4.2	1.2	1,418
Court can be trusted						
1995	25.1	9.6	65.3	3.4***	1.0	804
2001	17.0	5.1	77.8	3.9	1.2	1,418

† Allowing for rounding errors, these three columns total to 100 percent. *** $p < 0.001$.

Note: The question wording in the two surveys was as follows:

Limit the Court's jurisdiction:
1995: The right of the Supreme Court to decide certain types of controversial issues should be reduced.
2001: The right of the Supreme Court to decide certain types of controversial issues should be reduced.

Do away with the Court:
1995: If the U.S. Supreme Court started making a lot of decisions that most people disagreed with, it might be better to do away with the Supreme Court altogether.
2001: If the U.S. Supreme Court started making a lot of decisions that most people disagree with, it might be better to do away with the Supreme Court altogether.

Court can be trusted:
1995: The Supreme Court can usually be trusted to make decisions that are right for the country as a whole.
2001: The Supreme Court can usually be trusted to make decisions that are right for the country as a whole.

Source: 1995—James L. Gibson, Gregory A. Caldeira and Vanessa Baird, "On the Legitimacy of National High Courts," *American Political Science Review*, 92 (1998), 343–58, pp. 350–1, table 4.

this issue with two questions about how our respondents felt about the Court's decision. We first asked:

> As you know, last month, a majority of the justices on the U.S. Supreme Court decided that the State of Florida could not have a hand recount of the votes in the presidential election. As a result, Al Gore conceded the election, and George W. Bush will become president of the United

States. Do you think the U.S. Supreme Court's decision in this case was fair or unfair?"

We followed this question with a query about the strength of the respondent's views on this matter.

Three things stand out clearly from the responses to this question. First, a majority of Americans (56.2 percent) judge the Court to have acted fairly in the dispute, even though a very large minority (41.9 percent) thought the decision unfair. Second, nearly all of our respondents (97.2 percent) have an opinion on this issue. Finally, opinions are firmly held, with the proportion of those holding strong views on the matter (80.5 percent) greatly outnumbering those with more moderately held opinions (16.6 percent). Those who disagreed with the decision are more likely to feel strongly about it than those who supported the outcome. The responses to this question confirm the sharp divisions that so characterized virtually every aspect of the 2000 presidential election.

Since there were so many allegations that the Court's decision was ideological, partisan, or otherwise unprincipled, we also asked the respondents their views of the criteria the Supreme Court used in making its decision.

> Do you think the justices of the U.S. Supreme Court who voted to end the recount in Florida did so mostly based on the legal merits of the case or mostly based on their own desire to have [George W.] Bush as the next president?

We assume that most Americans expect the justices to make decisions on the basis of the legal merits of a case and disapprove of the failure to do so; indeed, we suspect that most see a decision based on the justices' presidential preferences as procedurally unfair and improper.[33]

Most Americans (62.4 percent) believe that the Court based its decision on the legal merits of the case, not on the justices' desire to see Bush become president. The divisions here are less stark than on the first question, with only 29.0 percent denying that the decision was based on the case's legal merits. Not surprisingly, this question proved to be somewhat more difficult than the first, with 8.6 percent of the respondents unable to judge the basis of the Court's decision.

A fairly obvious hypothesis is that the responses to these two questions are closely connected, and, as table C.4 reveals, in fact they are. Those who believe the decision was based on the political preferences of the justices strongly tend to oppose the decision (86.4 percent); those who

[33] See John M. Scheb II and William Lyons, "The Myth of Legality and Public Evaluation of the Supreme Court," *Social Science Quarterly* 81 (2000): 928–40, on the use of legal criteria in Supreme Court decision making.

TABLE C.4.
The Relationship between Perceptions of Decisional Criteria and Judgments of the Court's Decision

	Perceived basis of Court decision		
Judgment of the decision	*Justices' desires*	*Don't know*	*Legal merits*
Disagree	86.4	55.4	18.1
Uncertain	2.7	9.1	1.9
Agree	10.9	35.5	80.0
Total	100.0%	100.0%	100.0%
Mean	1.5	2.6	4.2
Standard deviation	1.1	1.7	1.4
N	402	121	879

Note: The upper portion of the table reports percentages, based on collapsing "disagree strongly" responses with "disagree" responses and "agree strongly" with "agree" responses. The lower portion of the table is based on the uncollapsed responses to the question. The total N for this table is 1,402.

The two variables are related as follows: $r = 0.66$, $p < 0.000$.

assert that the decision was based on the case's legal merits are equally strongly likely to support the decision (80.0 percent). This is a substantial relationship indeed. Although we draw no conclusion about the direction of the causality connecting these two variables, how people perceive the decision to have been made has much to do with their evaluations of *Bush v. Gore*.

The causal structure connecting institutional loyalty with judgments of the decision may be that loyalty toward the Court causes one to perceive its decisions as legal and fair—loyalty acts as a frame within which to judge the opinion—or perhaps perceptions that the Court acted fairly and legally in *Bush v. Gore* lead to enhanced loyalty toward the Court. This is the eternal dilemma of cross-sectional studies—causality is inherently ambiguous. Yet, from the vantage of Legitimacy Theory, untangling the causality among these variables is of the utmost importance.

Investigating Causality

To examine reciprocal causality between perceptions of *Bush v. Gore* and loyalty toward the Supreme Court, we must first develop a model of the origins of these attitudes. Earlier research on attitudes toward the Court provides some useful hypotheses.

One of the strongest predictors of loyalty identified to date is support for the institutions and processes of democracy. Those who are more supportive of democracy in general are more likely to support the Supreme Court.[34] Consequently, we measured support for democratic institutions and processes along two major dimensions: (1) support for the rule of law, and (2) support for a multiparty system. We constructed indices representing each of these concepts, after confirming their unidimensionality through factor analysis.[35] We hypothesize that those more loyal to the Supreme Court hold values more supportive of democratic institutions and processes.

Earlier research has also strongly suggested that loyalty toward the Court is a function of exposure to its activities, as represented by awareness of and knowledge about the institution. The research literature has firmly established that to know more about the Supreme Court is to think more highly of it.[36] We employ two indicators here: (1) self-proclaimed awareness of the Supreme Court; and (2) knowledge of the Court, based on a three-item information test.

We incorporate in this model several measures of satisfaction with the performance of the Court, especially in conjunction with the election. *Bush v. Gore* essentially decided the outcome of the 2000 presidential election, giving the presidency to George W. Bush. Whether one viewed this as the proper outcome may depend in part on how one views the outcome of the balloting. Thus, we included two measures of election opinions—the respondent's judgment of who won the national election and of who won the election in Florida. We expect these variables to be strong predictors of the perceived fairness of the *Bush v. Gore* decision.

Conventional wisdom indicates that partisanship structures views of the Court;[37] given the circumstances, this may be especially true in the aftermath of *Bush v. Gore*. Thus, we hypothesize that loyalty is related to party identification and to affect toward George W. Bush (as measured through a feeling thermometer). We also expect that these variables will predict reactions to the Court decision. Finally, given our findings above, we hypothesize that African Americans will extend less loyalty to the Court and will disapprove more strongly of the Court's election decision.

Table C.5 reports the results of regressing judgments of the fairness of *Bush v. Gore* and loyalty toward the Court on these independent variables. Perhaps the most interesting finding in this table concerns the role

[34] Caldeira and Gibson, "The Etiology of Public Support for the Supreme Court."

[35] See appendix C.2 for the text of all the items used in this analysis.

[36] Gibson, Caldeira, and Baird, "On the Legitimacy of National High Courts"; Scheb and Lyons, "The Myth of Legality and Public Evaluation of the Supreme Court."

[37] Walter F. Murphy, Joseph Tanenhaus, and Daniel Kastner, *Public Evaluations of Constitutional Courts: Alternative Explanations* (Beverly Hills: Sage, 1973).

TABLE C.5.
Predictors of Judgments of the Court's Opinion and the Court Itself

	Perceived fairness of Bush v. Gore			*Loyalty to the Supreme Court*		
	b	*s.e.*	*β*	*b*	*s.e.*	*β*
Support for the rule of law	0.06	0.05	0.03	0.12	0.03	0.12***
Support for a multi-party system	0.05	0.04	0.02	0.13	0.03	0.13***
Party identification	0.18	0.02	0.22***	0.02	0.01	0.05
Perception of who won the national election	0.24	0.04	0.11***	–0.10	0.03	–0.08**
Perception of who won the Florida election	0.59	0.05	0.30***	0.06	0.03	0.07*
Affect for Bush	0.02	0.00	0.27***	0.01	0.00	0.22***
Awareness of the Court	0.19	0.05	0.07***	0.12	0.03	0.09***
Knowledge of the Court	–0.02	0.03	–0.01	0.11	0.02	0.15***
Whether African American	–0.32	0.10	–0.06**	–0.17	0.06	–0.07**
Intercept	0.67	0.27		1.53	0.16	
R^2			0.58***			0.24***
Standard deviation—dependent variable	1.82			0.80		
Standard error of estimate	1.18			0.69		
N	1,364			1,364		

*** $p \leq 0.001$; ** $p \leq 0.01$; * $p \leq 0.05$.

of values in predicting both judgments of *Bush v. Gore* and institutional loyalty. Those who support democratic institutions and processes are significantly more likely to express loyalty toward the Supreme Court, but they are no more or less likely to perceive the decision in *Bush v. Gore* as fair. This is particularly noteworthy, because one of the democratic values included in the equation is support for the rule of law. Those more strongly attached to the rule of law are *not* necessarily more critical of *Bush v. Gore*. These findings confirm an important conclusion from earlier research: institutional loyalty depends upon the relatively stable, "core" political values citizens hold.

We also note the weak independent influence of partisanship on institutional loyalty; no direct relationship between party identification and loyalty exists. Yet party identification is a strong predictor of the perceived fairness of the decision in *Bush v. Gore*. It appears that judgments of the fairness of the Court's decision and attitudes toward the Court itself are cut from different cloth.

Views of the outcome of the election influence judgments of decisional fairness, but have little impact on institutional loyalty. This is important evidence of the degree to which institutional support is insulated from contemporary events. Moreover, what little effects the two electoral variables have on institutional legitimacy go in opposite directions. As we expected, those who believe Bush won nationally and in Florida are more likely to judge *Bush v. Gore* fair. But those judging Bush to have won nationally are (slightly) less likely to express support for the Court, an unexpected relationship that we discount since it is so weak and only achieves marginal statistical significance.

The independent impact of affect toward George W. Bush is significant in both equations. It is difficult to know exactly how to understand this variable, however, in that its influence is independent of judgments of the outcome of the election and of party attachments. It is not surprising that this variable would influence judgments of the decision; that Bush supporters tend to express stronger loyalty toward the Court, irrespective of the election, most likely reflects satisfaction with the long history of conservative decisions by the Rehnquist Court. Perhaps affect for Bush captures a variety of types of variance.[38]

It is also noteworthy that perceptions of who won in Florida have a considerably stronger influence on judgments of the fairness of the decision than do perceptions of who won nationally. This differential effect no doubt reflects the direct connection of the Court decision to the Florida

[38] In order to try to tease out exactly how the Bush affect variable influences these attitudes, we experimented with adding measures of ideology to the equations reported in table C.5. When we add a seven-point self-identification scale to the two regressions, we discover that (a) R^2 increases insignificantly, (b) the regression coefficient for ideology in both instances is trivial and statistically insignificant, and (c) that the regression coefficients for affect toward Bush change only in the hundredth's digit. We obtain just about the same results when we use feeling thermometers for "liberals" and "conservatives," although there is a slight tendency for those feeling warmer toward liberals to extend more legitimacy to the Supreme Court (and of course this is an effect independent of affect toward Bush). The impact of feelings toward Bush thus seems to run through a process entirely independent of ideology. We have also examined table C.5 from the point of view of omitting the Bush affect variable. Doing so increases the influence of two variables (with the same pattern for both dependent variables): party identification and perceptions of who won the election in Florida. Thus, we understand the Bush affect variable as "electoral partisanship," which side one is on. It is connected to party attachments, but is not identical. It reflects perceptions of who won the election, but those perceptions also have an independent existence. If we had such a measure, electoral partisanship might also be connected to perceptions of how Bush handled himself during the election dispute.

election, as well as the confusion about who won nationally because of the biasing effects of the Electoral College.

We also confirm the conventional wisdom concerning knowledge and information: those who are more aware of the Court and know more about it tend to express more loyalty toward it. Both knowledge and awareness have independent influences on loyalty, with knowledge being a more powerful predictor than self-proclaimed awareness. Thus, the influence of awareness also extends beyond the effect of simple factual information, and may include, for example, attentiveness to the rituals associated with Supreme Court decision making.

Finally, we note that the independent effect of race on both attitudes is statistically significant, but small. This finding is not surprising since race is strongly related to the other independent variables included in the equation (for example, party identification and perceptions of who won the election).

Attitudes toward the rule of law have a direct effect on loyalty toward the Court. But support for the rule of law may also act as a conditional variable. That is, those more supportive of the rule of law may perceive everything about the election dispute in legalistic terms, thus moderating the relationships between the independent and dependent variables. This hypothesis can be investigated with the data at hand.

The Conditional Effect of Support for the Rule of Law

To test the intuition that attitudes toward the rule of law have a conditional effect on the relationships depicted in table C.5, we added terms representing the interactions of attitudes toward the rule of law and each of the independent variables. In the case of loyalty toward the Supreme Court as the dependent variable, the addition of the interaction terms to the linear equation results in a statistically significant increase in explained variance. However, only one of the interaction terms achieves statistical significance: as knowledge of the Court increases, the connection between support for the rule of law and support for the Court becomes stronger. The slope for the rule of law variable varies from - 0.16 among the weakest supporters of the rule of law to 0.15 among those most firmly committed to the rule of law. This conditional relationship makes sense to the degree that knowledge of the Court makes it easier to see the connection between what the Court does and the cherished value of legal universalism. For no other independent variable is there a statistically significant conditional effect.

In terms of the perceived fairness of *Bush v. Gore*, the change in explained variance brought about by the addition of the interactive terms barely achieves statistical significance (p = 0.04). The regression coefficients for two of the interactive variables—the rule-of-law interactions with awareness of the Court and with perceptions of who won the national election—are both significant at p = 0.02. As awareness of the Court increases, the relationship between support for the rule of law and perceived fairness becomes more negative. Among the most aware, there is a strong negative relationship between rule-of-law attitudes and judgments of the decision. Similarly, some interaction exists between rule-of-law attitudes and perceptions of who won the election. Among Gore supporters, the coefficient is 0.18; among those who are uncertain who won, it is 0.06; and among Bush supporters, the slope is - 0.06. These figures support two significant conclusions. First, rule-of-law attitudes are more important for forming judgments of the Court decision among Gore supporters, as one might expect. Second, among Gore supporters, greater support for the rule of law is associated with judgments that the Court *was fair.* None of these coefficients is particularly strong, but they nonetheless demonstrate the multiple pathways by which rule-of-law attitudes influenced perceptions of the Court's involvement in the dispute.

Two-Stage Least Squares

In order to estimate the direction of causality between perceptions of the Court's decision and institutional loyalty, we conducted a two-stage least squares analysis. The analysis is based on the hypotheses we put forth above, and uses the set of instruments drawn from the predictors of the perceived fairness of the opinion and loyalty to the Court (as reported in table C.5, above). The results are reported in table C.6. As hypothesized, the significant exogenous variables for perceptions of the opinion (party identification, perceptions of the national and Florida election outcomes, and affect for Bush) account for nearly all of the total explained variance (R_2 = 0.58); the significant hypothesized variables for loyalty (support for the rule of law, support for a multiparty system, affect for Bush, and awareness and knowledge of the Court) are also strong predictors of that variable (R^2 = 0.23). With only a single predictor significantly related to *both* of the endogenous variables, the first-stage analysis is strong enough statistically to support the second stage of the least squares.[39]

In the two-stage least squares, the findings for the variables predicting institutional loyalty and assessments of the decision differ insignificantly

[39] In two-stage least squares, the first-stage equations include all of the exogenous variables. Our point is that this technique is best able to disentangle reciprocal causation when (a) the first-stage equations strongly predict the endogenous variables, and (b) each endogenous variable is uniquely predicted by at least some of the endogenous variables. In this instance, these desiderata are satisfied.

TABLE C.6.
Two-Stage Least Squares Analysis of Loyalty and Opinion Satisfaction

	Perceived fairness of Bush v. Gore			*Loyalty to the Supreme Court*		
	b	*s.e.*	*β*	*b*	*s.e.*	*β*
Loyalty to the Supreme Court	0.46	0.13	0.20***	—	—	—
Perceived fairness of *Bush* v. *Gore*	—	—	—	0.05	0.03	0.11
Perception of who won the Florida election	0.56	0.05	0.29***			
Perception of who won the national election	0.28	0.05	0.13***			
Party identification	0.17	0.02	0.21***			
Affect for Bush	0.01	0.00	0.23***	0.01	0.00	0.19***
Whether African American	−0.22	0.11	−0.04*	−0.16	0.06	−0.07*
Support for the rule of law				0.12	0.03	0.11***
Support for a multi-party system				0.13	0.03	0.13***
Awareness of the Court				0.11	0.03	0.08***
Knowledge of the Court				0.12	0.02	0.17***
Intercept	0.29	0.42		1.51	0.15	
R^2			0.58***			0.24***
Standard deviation—dependent variable	1.82			0.80		
Standard error of estimate	1.19			0.69		
N	1,364			1,364		

*** $p \leq 0.001$; ** $p \leq 0.01$; * $p \leq 0.05$.

from those of the ordinary least squares analysis, so little further comment is required. The coefficients of greatest interest are those linking perceptions of the opinion and institutional loyalty. From the second-stage equation, these coefficients are:

Opinion Fairness = 0.29 + 0.46 x Institutional Loyalty + [the exogenous variables]

The coefficient for loyalty is highly statistically significant ($p < 0.000$, standard error = 0.13). For institutional loyalty, the equation is:

Institutional Loyalty = 1.51 + 0.05 x Opinion Fairness + [the exogenous variables]

The coefficient for fairness does *not* achieve statistical significance ($p > 0.05$, standard error = 0.03).

These results indicate that institutional loyalty influences judgments of the fairness of the decision in *Bush v. Gore*, but not vice versa. For instance, according to the two-stage least squares equation, the expected opinion fairness score for those with the lowest loyalty toward the Court (a score of 1) is 0.75, while those most strongly committed to the Supreme Court have an expected value of 2.59.[40] Loyalty strongly structures perceptions of the fairness of the decision in *Bush v. Gore*.

By contrast, when perceived fairness is at its lowest value, loyalty is expected to be 1.56; and when fairness is at the highest value, loyalty only increases to 1.76. Thus, the effect of assessments of the Court's election decision on enduring loyalty toward the institution itself is marginal indeed, reinforcing the conclusion that the Court may well have diminished its legitimacy by its ruling in *Bush v. Gore*, but only by a trivial amount. The reservoir of good will enjoyed by the Court greatly attenuated any negative effects of the ruling in *Bush v. Gore*. Indeed, institutional loyalty seems to have framed the decision, making it more palatable to those who objected to the outcome.

These findings comport well with our understanding of how people update their views toward institutions. We contend that established views toward an institution influence the way in which controversial decisions are perceived and evaluated. Some think of these "established views" as a sort of "running tally," a historical summary of how people have reacted to institutional decisions in the past. Any given adverse decision most likely does not dramatically alter these established views, but, as the statistical analysis implies, nor are reactions to highly controversial individual decisions of no consequence for how one feels about an institution. We are again attracted to the notion of "loyalty." Loyalty is not obdurate; it changes, even if slowly, in reaction to people's experiences. Loyalty shapes perceptions of individual events, but individual events also shape loyalty over the long haul. Our most important conclusion from this analysis is that even an enormously controversial decision like *Bush v. Gore* has little if any influence on institutional loyalty.

A Theoretical Explanation of the Findings: Positivity Frames

These results may reflect the bias of "positivity frames" when it comes to the Court (and perhaps judicial institutions in general), in the sense that exposure to courts—including exposure associated with controversial cir-

[40] Both loyalty and fairness range from 1 to 5. The respective means (and standard deviations) of the two variable are 3.58 (0.79) and 3.25 (1.82).

cumstances—enhances rather than detracts from judicial legitimacy, even among those who are disgusted with the Court's ruling. When courts become salient, people become exposed to the symbolic trappings of judicial power—"the marble temple, the High Bench, the purple curtain, the black robes."[41] When the news media covered the Court's deliberations surrounding the election, it generally did so with the greatest deference and respect. The contrast in images of the "partisan bickering" in Florida and the solemn judicial process in Washington could not be more stark. No matter how one judges the outcome in *Bush v. Gore*, exposure to the legitimizing symbols of law and courts is perhaps the dominant process at play. Thus, the effect of displeasure with a particular court decision may be muted by contact with these legitimizing symbols. To know courts is indeed to love them, in the sense that to know about courts is to be exposed to these legitimizing symbols.

One way to investigate this conjecture is to compare the views of partisans in 1987 and 2001.[42] Following the methodology reported in Kritzer,[43] we display in table C.7 the relationship between party attachment and a two-item loyalty index (based on table C.2, above). The correlation between loyalty and party identification in 1987 is 0.05; in 2001, it is 0.20. Thus, our findings comport with Kritzer's in the sense that attitudes toward the Court seem to be more partisan following the election of 2000—but not greatly so.

The more interesting evidence has to do with whether our conclusion that legitimacy changed little between 1987 and 2001 is due to off-setting tendencies among Democrats and Republicans. That is, if Democrats reduced their support for the Court as a result of *Bush v. Gore* and Republicans increased their support, then the overall level of support would appear not to have changed. Support would, however, be more closely related to partisanship. Most important, this would be evidence that people were adjusting their loyalty on the basis of the Court's ruling on the election. Table C.7 reports data of considerable relevance to the hypothesis that loyalty frames reactions to individual decisions and that unwelcome decisions contribute little to the diminution of institutional loyalty.

The evidence in table C.7 indicates that, between 1987 and 2001, support for the Court did *not* decline among Democrats, even as it increased somewhat among Independents and Republicans. In 2001, 46.6 percent of the Democrats gave two supportive replies to our questions; in 1987,

[41] Scheb and Lyons, "The Myth of Legality and Public Evaluation of the Supreme Court," 929.

[42] This analysis cannot be conducted with the 1995 data since party attachments were not measured in that survey.

[43] Kritzer, "The Impact of *Bush* v. *Gore* on Public Perceptions and Knowledge of the Supreme Court."

TABLE C.7.
Partisanship and Institutional Loyalty, 1987–2001

	Party identification		
Institutional loyalty	*Democrat*	*Independent*	*Republican*
2001			
No supportive replies	15.2	18.6	6.3
One supportive reply	38.5	26.7	27.5
Two supportive replies	46.4	54.7	66.2
Total	100.0%	100.0%	100.0%
N	673	172	571
1987			
No supportive replies	20.0	23.6	13.6
One supportive reply	36.9	42.9	40.5
Two supportive replies	43.0	33.6	45.9
Total	100.0%	100.0%	100.0%
N	639	140	427

this figure was *insignificantly* lower (43.0 percent). That Democrats in the aggregate seem not to have been affected by the adverse ruling in *Bush v. Gore* is a finding compatible with the general view that institutional loyalty inoculates against an unwelcome policy decision. The data also reveal that Republican support for the Court was boosted by the decision. Thus, these data are compatible with the conclusion that the Court profits from a bias of positivity frames in the sense that the Court gets "credit" when it pleases people, but that it is not penalized when its actions are displeasing.

Discussion and Concluding Comments

Several significant conclusions have emerged from this analysis. In terms of substantive politics, we have shown that the Supreme Court decision in *Bush v. Gore* did not have a debilitating impact on the legitimacy of the U.S. Supreme Court. Perhaps because the Court enjoyed such a deep reservoir of good will, most Americans were predisposed to view the Court's involvement as appropriate, and therefore dissatisfaction with the outcome did not poison attitudes toward the institution. This finding is an important corrective to popular and scholarly views of the politics of the election.

Nevertheless, no one can doubt that loyalty toward an institution is influenced by the policy outputs of that institution, at least in the long term.[44] Neither should any one doubt that loyalty toward an institution can cushion the shock of a highly controversial decision. Within any given cross-section, the causal relationship between perceptions of an opinion and loyalty is surely reciprocal.

Nonetheless, *Bush v. Gore* seems to have had a much smaller effect on the attitudes of Americans toward their Supreme Court than many expected. The various analyses presented in this article support the view that the weak effect of the Supreme Court's participation in the election is most likely due to preexisting attitudes toward the Court that blunted the impact of disapproval of the Court's involvement in the election. Thus, in general, the conclusions in which we have the greatest confidence are: (1) the ruling in *Bush v. Gore* did not greatly undermine the legitimacy of the Court, (2) probably because the effect of preexisting legitimacy on evaluations of the decision was stronger than the effect of evaluations on institutional loyalty, and (3) institutional loyalty predisposed most Americans to view the decision as based on law and therefore legitimate.

From a more theoretical viewpoint, we have posited the existence of a bias of positivity frames when it comes to popular perceptions of courts. In most areas of political and social life, negativity predominates. We have suggested that positive reactions result from exposure to the highly effective legitimizing symbols in which courts, and the Supreme Court in particular, typically drape themselves. Further research should more rigorously investigate exactly how—and under what conditions—symbols are effective at legitimizing judicial institutions.

Our analysis has reinforced a panoply of unanswered questions; three bear particular emphasis. First, only with more valid measures of institutional legitimacy can we make progress in unravelling the causal linkages between performance and legitimacy.[45] We despair in particular at the use of the standard confidence measures ("confidence in the leaders of the Supreme Court") for a variety of reasons, not the least of which is that

[44] James L. Gibson and Gregory A. Caldeira ("Blacks and the United States Supreme Court: Models of Diffuse Support," *Journal of Politics* 52 [1992]: 1120–45), based on a survey conducted in 1987, suggest that African Americans adjusted their views of the Supreme Court due to the declining success of African American litigants before the Burger and Rehnquist Courts. They did discover, however, a generation of African Americans defined by the Warren Court that still has an unusually strong attachment to the Supreme Court, despite dissatisfaction with current Court policies.

[45] See James L. Gibson, Gregory A. Caldeira, and Lester Kenyatta Spence, "Measuring Attitudes Toward the United States Supreme Court," *American Journal of Political Science* 47 (2003): 354–67.

confidence is too much affected by short-term forces. Secondly, we believe that cross-sectional analysis is inadequate to the task of addressing the question of how people update their attitudes toward institutions. We have pushed our cross-sectional data about as far as we dare, but answering the question of how people update their views of institutions requires a longitudinal research design—in particular, a panel. Alas, such designs are much too uncommon in research on judicial politics.

Finally, how do institutions build the sort of legitimacy enjoyed by the U.S. Supreme Court? Legitimacy is extraordinarily valuable to institutions, as *Bush v. Gore* has so clearly shown. Understanding how institutions acquire and spend legitimacy remains one of the most important unanswered questions for those interested in the power and influence of judicial institution.

Appendix C.1

Survey Design

This research is based on a survey conducted in early 2001 by the Center for Survey Research (CSR) at Ohio State University. The survey is based on a typical Random-Digit-Dial (RDD) sample of the American mass public and an oversample of African Americans. The fieldwork in the primary sample was conducted from January 5 through January 19, 2001, with 1,006 interviews completed during this period. Telephone interviewing was employed, utilizing an RDD sample purchased from Genesys Sampling Systems. The sample is representative of English-speaking households in the forty-eight contiguous U.S. states (and Washington, D.C.). Within households, respondents were selected by the "last birthday" technique.[46] The median length of interview was about twenty minutes.

Using the AAPOR standards,[47] several response rates were calculated. According to AAPOR Response Rate 5, our survey had a rate of 35 percent; according to Response Rate 1, the rate was 26 percent. Using AAPOR's Co-operation Rate 3, our co-operation rate was 49 percent; modifying this rate by taking into account all households in which it is certain that an interviewer spoke with the selected respondent, the co-operation rate climbs to 78 percent.

We also surveyed an oversample of African Americans. We sampled from census tracts in which the concentration of African American house-

[46] Paul J. Lavrakas, *Telephone Survey Research Methods: Sampling, Selection, and Supervision* (Thousand Oaks, CA: Sage, 1993), 7:111–13.

[47] *American Association for Public Opinion Research, Standard Definitions: Final Dispositions of Case Codes and Outcome Rates for Surveys* (Ann Arbor: University of Michigan Press, 2000).

holds was 25 percent or greater. The field work was conducted from January 22 through February 12, 2001. In all respects, the methods employed in the oversample were identical to those employed in the primary sample.

A total of 409 interviews with African American respondents were completed in the oversample. The response rates for the oversample are: AAPOR Response Rate 1: 30 percent; AAPOR Response Rate 5: 40 percent; AAPOR Co-operation Rate 3: 55 percent; and Modified AAPOR Co-operation Rate 3: 80 percent.

We have weighted these data to adjust for the unequal probabilities of selection (i.e., the oversample), and nonresponse.[48]

Given the rate of response, it is possible that our survey is not truly representative of the American population at the time of the survey. We are uncertain, however, about the nature of any possible bias. One line of thought suggests that the sample overrepresents those pleased with the performance of the Court since the displeased might refuse to participate in our survey out of disgust with the election. A contrary view is that those disgusted would welcome the opportunity to vent their views. Yet another perspective is that those who refused to be interviewed tend to be people who know and care little about politics and, were they interviewed about the Court, most of their answers would be either "don't know" or "don't care." Logical analysis can lead to many different conclusions.[49]

We have conducted some empirical analysis to determine whether the ease with which the respondent accepted the interview is related to attitudes toward the Supreme Court. We find no such relationship at all. This test is far from dispositive, but we can find no evidence in these data to suggest that those who readily responded to our questions differ in their attitudes toward the Supreme Court from those who were reluctant or initially refused to participate.

Appendix C.2

Measurement

Unless otherwise indicated, the response set for the following items is:

[48] Following the conventions of the American National Election Study, see Survey Research Center, "Post-Stratified Cross-Sectional Analysis Weights for the 1992, 1994 and 1996 NES Data" (Ann Arbor: Institute for Social Research, University of Michigan, n.d.), prepared by the Sampling Section Division of Surveys and Technologies, available online at http://www.umich.edu/ nes/studyres/nes1996/96wght.htm (accessed 2/25/2001).

[49] For an empirical study that concludes that low response rates do not necessarily result in biased substantive findings, see Scott Keeter, Carolyn Miller, Andrew Kohut, Robert M. Groves, and Stanley Presser, "Consequences of Reducing Nonresponse in a National Telephone Survey," *Public Opinion Quarterly* 64 (2000): 125–48.

1. Agree strongly
2. Agree somewhat
3. Neither agree nor disagree
4. Disagree somewhat
5. Disagree strongly

SUPPORT FOR THE RULE OF LAW

It is not necessary to obey a law you consider unjust.

Sometimes it might be better to ignore the law and solve problems immediately rather than wait for a legal solution.

The government should have some ability to bend the law in order to solve pressing social and political problems.

It is not necessary to obey the laws of a government that I did not vote for.

SUPPORT FOR A MULTIPARTY SYSTEM

What our country needs is one party which will rule the country.

The party that gets the support of the majority ought not to have to share political power with the political minority.

Our country would be better off if we just outlaw all political parties.

PARTY IDENTIFICATION

Generally speaking, do you usually think of yourself as a Republican, Democrat, Independent, or what?

1. Democrat [Go to Strength]
2. Republican [Go to Strength]
3. Other [Specify]
4. Independent [Go to Lean]

Do you think of yourself as closer to the Republican Party or to the Democratic Party?

1. Closer to Republican
2. Neither
3. Closer to Democrat

Would you call yourself a strong Democrat/Republican or a not very strong Democrat/Republican?

1. Strong
2. Not Very Strong

PERCEPTION OF WHO WON THE ELECTION

Which candidate do you think won the most votes nationwide—George W. Bush or Al Gore?

1. George W. Bush
2. Al Gore
3. CAN'T SAY [VOLUNTEERED]

From your point-of-view, which candidate do you think actually won the most votes in Florida—George W. Bush or Al Gore?

1. George W. Bush
2. Al Gore
3. CAN'T SAY [VOLUNTEERED]

AFFECT FOR GEORGE W. BUSH

Next, I would like to get your feelings toward some of our political leaders and groups. I'll read the name of a group and I'd like you to rate that group using something we call the feeling thermometer. You can use any number between 0 and 100 to express your feelings. Ratings above 50 degrees mean that you feel favorable and warm toward the group, while those below 50 degrees mean that you don't feel favorable toward the group. You would rate the group at the 50 degree mark if you don't feel particularly warm or cold toward it. If we come to a group whose name you don't recognize, you don't need to rate that group. Just tell me and we'll move on to the next one.

NOTE: THE ORDER OF PRESENTATION OF THE INSTITUTIONS AND GROUPS WAS RANDOMLY VARIED.

How do you feel about George W. Bush?

0–100 Degrees

AWARENESS OF THE SUPREME COURT

On a different subject, would you say that you are very aware, somewhat aware, not very aware, or haven't you heard of the U.S. Supreme Court?

1. Very Aware
2. Somewhat Aware
3. Not Very Aware
4. Have Never Heard

KNOWLEDGE OF THE SUPREME COURT

Some judges in the United States are elected; others are appointed to the bench. Do you happen to know if the justices of the U.S. Supreme Court are elected or appointed to the bench?

1. Appointed to the Bench
2. Elected
3. Other Answer

Some judges in the United States serve for a set number of years; others serve a life term. Do you happen to know whether the justices of the U.S. Supreme Court serve for a set number of years or whether they serve a life term?

1. Life Term
2. Set Number of Years
3. Other Answer

Do you happen to know who has the *last say* when there is a conflict over the meaning of the Constitution—the U.S. Supreme Court, the U.S. Congress, or the president?

1. U.S. Supreme Court
2. U.S. Congress
3. President
4. OTHER [VOLUNTEERED] [SPECIFY]

References

Abramowitz, Alan, and Kyle Saunders. 2005. "Why Can't We All Just Get Along? The Reality of a Polarized American." *The Forum* 3 (2), Article 1. http://www.bepress.com/forum/vol3/iss2/art1/ (Accessed May 30, 2006).

Ackerman, Bruce, ed. 2002. *Bush v. Gore: The Question of Legitimacy.* New Haven, CT: Yale University Press.

Alivizatos, Nicos. 1995. "Judges as Veto Players." In *Parliaments and Majority Rule in Western Europe*, ed. Herbert Doring. New York: St. Martin's, 566–91.

American Association for Public Opinion Research. 2000. *Standard Definitions: Final Dispositions of Case Codes and Outcome Rates for Surveys.* Ann Arbor, MI: AAPOR.

Annenberg Public Policy Center. 2006. "Fair and Independent Courts: A Conference on the State of the Judiciary, Georgetown Law Center, Washington, D.C., September 28–29, 2006." University of Pennsylvania. Available at http://www.annenbergpublicpolicycenter.org/Releases/Release_Courts20060928/Courts_Summary_20060928.pdf (Accessed January 1, 2007).

Aronson, Elliot, Phoebe C. Ellsworth, J. Merrill Carlsmith, and Marti Hope Gonzales. 1990. *Methods of Research in Social Psychology*, 2nd ed. New York: McGraw-Hill.

Baird, Vanessa A. 2001. "Building Institutional Legitimacy: The Role of Procedural Justice." *Political Research Quarterly* 54 (June): 333–54.

Baird, Vanessa A., and Amy Gangl. 2006. "Shattering the Myth of Legality: The Impact of the Media's Framing on Supreme Court Procedures on Perceptions of Fairness." *Political Psychology* 27 (August): 597–614.

Bell, Lauren Cohen. 2002. *Warring Factions: Interest Groups, Money and the New Politics of Senate Confirmation.* Columbus, OH: Ohio State University Press.

Bendor, Jonathan, Daniel Diermeier, and Michael Ting. 2003. "A Behavioral Model of Turnout." *American Political Science Review* 97 (May): 261–80.

Benesh, Sara C. 2006. "Understanding Public Confidence in American Courts." *Journal of Politics* 68 (August): 697–707.

Boynton, G. R., and Gerhard Loewenberg. 1973. "The Development of Public Support for Parliament in Germany, 1951–1959." *British Journal of Political Science* 3 (April): 169–89.

Brisbin, Richard A. 1996. "Slaying the Dragon: Segal, Spaeth and the Function of Law in Supreme Court Decision Making." *American Journal of Political Science* 40 (November): 1004–17.

Brooks, Deborah Jordan. 2006. "The Resilient Voter: Moving Toward Closure in the Debate over Negative Campaigning and Turnout." *Journal of Politics* 68 (August): 684–96.

———. 2007. "Beyond Negativity: The Effects of Incivility on the Electorate."*American Journal of Political Science* 51 (January): 1–16.

Caldeira, Gregory A. 1977. "Children's Images of the Supreme Court: A Preliminary Mapping." *Law and Society Review* 11 (Summer): 851–71.

———. 1986. "Neither the Purse Nor the Sword: Dynamics of Confidence in the U.S. Supreme Court." *American Political Science Review* 80 (December): 1209–26.

———. 1987. "Public Opinion and The U.S. Supreme Court: FDR's Court-Packing Plan." *American Political Science Review* 81 (November): 1139–53.

Caldeira, Gregory A., and James L. Gibson. 1992. "The Etiology of Public Support for the Supreme Court." *American Journal of Political Science* 36 (August): 635–64.

———. 1995. "The Legitimacy of the Court of Justice in the European Union: Models of Institutional Support." *American Political Science Review* 89 (June): 356–76.

Caldeira, Gregory A., Marie Hojnacki, and John R. Wright. 2000. "The Lobbying Activities of Organized Interests in Federal Judicial Nominations." *Journal of Politics* 62 (February): 51–69.

Caldeira, Gregory A., and Kevin T. McGuire. 2005. "What Americans Know About the Courts and Why It Matters." In *Institutions of American Democracy: The Judiciary*, ed. Kermit L. Hall and Kevin T. McGuire. New York: Oxford University Press, 262–79.

Caldeira, Gregory A., and Charles E. Smith, Jr. 1996. "Campaigning for the Supreme Court: The Dynamics of Public Opinion on the Thomas Nomination." *Journal of Politics* 58 (August): 655–81.

Caldeira, Gregory A., and John R. Wright. 1998. "Lobbying for Justice: Organized Interests Supreme Court Nominations, and United States Senate." *American Journal of Political Science* 42 (April): 499–523.

Casey, Gregory 1974. "The Supreme Court and Myth: An Empirical Investigation." *Law and Society Review* 8 (Spring): 385–419.

Choper, Jesse H. 1980. *Judicial Review and the National Political Process*. Chicago: University of Chicago Press.

Clawson, Rosalee A., Elizabeth R. Kegler, and Eric N. Waltenburg. 2001. "The Legitimacy-Conferring Authority of the U.S. Supreme Court: An Experimental Design." *American Politics Research* 29 (November): 566–91.

Clawson, Rosalee A., and Eric N. Waltenburg. 2003. "Support for a Supreme Court Affirmative Action Decision: A Story in Black and White." *American Politics Research* 31 (May): 251–79.

Cohen, Jacob, Stephen G. West, Leona Aiken, and Patricia Cohen. 2003. *Applied Multiple Regression/Correlation Analysis for the Behavioral Sciences*. 3rd ed. Mahwah, NJ: Erlbaum.

Cook, Thomas D., and Donald T. Campbell. 1979. *Quasi-Experimentation: Design and Analysis Issues for Field Settings*. Chicago: Rand McNally.

Cronbach, Lee J. 1946. "Response Sets and Test Validity." *Educational and Psychological Measurement* 6 (Fall): 475–94.

———. 1950. "Further Evidence on Response Sets and Test Design." *Educational and Psychological Measurement* 10 (Spring): 3–31.

Curtin, Richard, Stanley Presser, and Eleanor Singer. 2000. "The Effects of Response Rate Changes on the Index of Consumer Sentiment." *Public Opinion Quarterly* 64 (Winter): 413–28.

Dahl, Robert A. 1957. "Decision-Making in a Democracy: The Supreme Court as a National Policy-Maker." *Journal of Public Law* 6 (Fall): 279–95.

D.C.H e-Media. 2006. "U.S. Senate Judiciary Committee Hearing on Judge Samuel Alito's Nomination to the Supreme Court. Transcript of hearings from January 9 through January 13." Available at http://www.c-span.org/resources/courtwatch.asp (Accessed May 2, 2006).

Dean, John W. 2001. *The Rehnquist Choice: The Untold Story of the Nixon Appointment That Redefined the Supreme Court.* New York: Free Press.

Delli Carpini, Michael X., and Scott Keeter. 1996. *What Americans Know About Politics and Why It Matters.* New Haven, CN.: Yale University Press.

Dionne, E. J., Jr., and William Kristol, eds. 2001. *Bush v. Gore: The Court Cases and the Commentary.* Washington, D.C.: Brookings Institution.

Downing, Steven M. 1992. "True-False and Alternative-Choice Formats: A Review of Research." *Educational Measurement: Issues and Practices* 11 (September): 27–30.

Druckman, James N. 2004. "Political Preference-Formation: Competition, Deliberation, and the (Ir)relevance of Framing Effects." *American Political Science Review* 98 (November): 671–86.

Durr, Robert H., Andrew D. Martin, and Christina Wolbrecht. 2000. "Ideological Divergence and Public Support for the Supreme Court." *American Journal of Political Science* 44 (October): 768–76.

Dworkin, Ronald, ed. 2002. *A Badly Flawed Election: Debating Bush v. Gore, the Supreme Court, and American Democracy.* New York: New Press.

Easton, David. 1965. *A Systems Analysis of Political Life.* New York: John Wiley and Son.

———. 1975. "A Re-Assessment of the Concept of Political Support." *British Journal of Political Science* 5 (October): 435–57.

Ellmann, Stephen. 1992. *In a Time of Trouble: Law and Liberty in South Africa's State of Emergency.* New York: Oxford University Press.

Epstein, Lee, and Carol Mershon. 1996. "Measuring Political Preferences." *American Journal of Political Science* 40 (February): 261–94.

Epstein, Lee, and Jeffrey A. Segal. 2005. *Advice and Consent: The Politics of Judicial Appointments.* New York: Oxford University Press.

Epstein, Lee, Jeffrey A. Segal, Harold J. Spaeth, and Thomas G. Walker. 2003. *The Supreme Court Compendium: Data, Decisions, and Developments.* Washington D.C.: Congressional Quarterly.

Eskridge, William N., and Sanford Levinson. 1998. *Constitutional Stupidities, Constitutional Tragedies.* New York: New York University Press.

Fallon, Richard H., Jr. 2005. "Legitimacy and the Constitution." *Harvard Law Review* 118 (April): 1789–1853

Farnsworth, Ward. 2004. "The Regulation of Turnover on the Supreme Court." Boston: Boston University School of Law, Public Law and Legal Theory Working Paper Series, No. 04–18.

Fiorina, Morris P., with Samuel J. Abrams, and Jeremy C. Pope. 2006. *Culture Wars? The Myth of Polarized America*. 2nd ed. New York: Pearson Longman.

Flemming, Roy B., John Bohte, and Dan Wood. 1997. "One Voice Among Many: The Supreme Court's Influence on Attentiveness to Issues in the United States, 1947–92." *American Journal of Political Science* 41 (October): 1224–50.

Fletcher, Joseph F., and Paul Howe. 2000. "Canadian Attitudes toward the Charter and the Courts in Comparative Perspective." *Choices* 6 (May): 4–29.

Forsyth, C. F. 1985. *In Danger for their Talents: A Study of the Appellate Division of the Supreme Court of South Africa from 1950–80*. Cape Town: Juta.

Franklin, Charles H, and Liane C. Kosaki. 1989. "Republican Schoolmaster: The U. S. Supreme Court, Public Opinion, and Abortion." *American Political Science Review* 83 (September): 751–71.

———. 1995. "Media, Knowledge, and Public Evaluations of the Supreme Court." In *Contemplating Courts*, ed. Lee Epstein. Washington, D.C.: Congressional Quarterly, 352–75.

Franklin, Charles H., Liane C. Kosaki, and Herbert M. Kritzer. 1993. "The Salience of U.S. Supreme Court Decisions." Presented at the Annual Meeting of the American Political Science Association, Washington, D.C.

Frankovic, Kathleen, and Joyce Gelb. 1992. "Public Opinion on the Thomas Nomination." *PS: Political Science and Politics* 25 (September): 481–84.

Friedman, Barry. 2004. "The Importance of Being Positive: The Nature and Function of Judicial Review." *University of Cincinnati Law Review* 72 (Summer): 1257–1303.

Friedman, Barry. 2005. "The Politics of Judicial Review." *Texas Law Review* 84 (December): 257–337.

Friedman, Lawrence M. 1977. *Law and Society: An Introduction*. Englewood Cliffs, NJ: Prentice-Hall.

———. 1998. *American Law: An Introduction*, Revised and Updated Edition. New York: W. W. Norton.

Gerber, Scott G. 1996. "Judging Thomas: The Politics of Assessing a Supreme Court Justice." *Journal of Black Studies* 27 (November): 224–59.

Gewirtzman, Doni. 2005. "Glory Days: Popular Constitutionalism, Nostalgia, and the True Nature of Constitutional Culture." *Georgetown Law Journal* 93 (March): 897–938.

Geyh, Charles Gardner. 2003. "Why Judicial Elections Stink." *Ohio State Law Journal* 64 (1): 43–79.

———. 2006. *When Courts and Congress Collide: The Struggle for Control of America's Judicial System*. Ann Arbor, MI: University of Michigan Press.

Gibson, James L. 1981. "The Role Concept in Judicial Research." *Law and Policy Quarterly* 3 (July): 291–311.

———. 1989. "Understandings of Justice: Institutional Legitimacy, Procedural Justice, and Political Tolerance." *Law and Society Review* 23 (3) : 469–96.

———. 1991. "Institutional Legitimacy, Procedural Justice, and Compliance with Supreme Court Decisions: A Question of Causality." *Law and Society Review* 25 (3): 631–35.

———. 1995. "The Resilience of Mass Support for Democratic Institutions and Processes in the Nascent Russian and Ukrainian Democracies." In *Political Cul-*

ture and Civil Society in Russia and the New States of Eurasia, ed. Vladimir Tismaneanu. Armonk, NY: M. E. Sharp, 53–111.

———. 2004. *Overcoming Apartheid: Can Truth Reconcile a Divided Nation?* New York: Russell Sage Foundation.

———. 2007a. "The Legitimacy of the United States Supreme Court in a Polarized Polity." *Journal of Empirical Legal Studies* 4 (November): 507–38.

———. 2007b. "Changes in American Veneration for the Rule of Law." *DePaul Law Review* 56 (Winter): 593–614.

———. 2008a. "Challenges to the Impartiality of State Supreme Courts: Legitimacy Theory and 'New-Style' Judicial Campaigns." *American Political Science Review* 102 (February): 59–75.

———. 2008b. "The Evolving Legitimacy of the South African Constitutional Court." In *Justice and Reconciliation in Post-Apartheid South Africa*. Edited by François du Bois and Antje du Bois-Pedain. Cambridge University Press, 229–66.

———. 2008c. "Judicial Institutions." In *The Oxford Handbook of Political Institutions*. ed. R. A. W. Rhodes, Sarah A. Binder, and Bert A. Rockman. New York: Oxford University Press, 514–34.

Gibson, James L., and Gregory A. Caldeira. 1992. "Blacks and the United States Supreme Court: Models of Diffuse Support." *Journal of Politics* 54 (November): 1120–45.

———. 1995. "The Legitimacy of Transnational Legal Institutions: Compliance, Support, and the European Court of Justice." *American Journal of Political Science* 39 (May): 459–89.

———. 1998. "Changes in the Legitimacy of the European Court of Justice: A Post-Maastricht Analysis." *British Journal of Political Science* 28 (January): 63–91.

———. 2003. "Defenders of Democracy? Legitimacy, Popular Acceptance, and the South African Constitutional Court." *Journal of Politics* 65 (February): 1–30.

———. 2006. "Politicized Confirmation Processes and the Legitimacy of the U.S. Supreme Court." Paper delivered at the 64th Annual Conference of the Midwest Political Science Association, April 20–23, Palmer House Hilton, Chicago, Illinois.

———. 2007. "Knowing About Courts." Paper delivered at the 65th Annual National Conference of the Midwest Political Science Association, April 12–15, 2007, Palmer House Hilton, Chicago, Illinois.

Gibson, James L., Gregory A. Caldeira, and Vanessa Baird. 1998. "On the Legitimacy of National High Courts." *American Political Science Review* 92 (June): 343–58.

Gibson, James L., Gregory A. Caldeira, and Lester Kenyatta Spence. 2003a. "The Supreme Court and the U.S. Presidential Election of 2000: Wounds, Self-Inflicted or Otherwise?" *British Journal of Political Science* 33 (October): 535–56.

———. 2003b. "Measuring Attitudes toward the United States Supreme Court." *American Journal of Political Science* 47 (April): 354–67.

———. 2005. "Why Do People Accept Public Policies They Oppose? Testing Legitimacy Theory with a Survey-Based Experiment." *Political Research Quarterly* 58 (June): 187–201.

Gibson, James L., and Amanda Gouws. 2003. *Overcoming Intolerance in South Africa: Experiments in Democratic Persuasion.* New York: Cambridge University Press.

Gibson, James L., and Marc Morjé Howard. 2007. "Russian Anti-Semitism and the Scapegoating of Jews: The Dog That Didn't Bark?" *British Journal of Political Science* 37 (April): 193–223.

Gillman, Howard. 2001. *The Votes That Counted: How the Court Decided the 2000 Presidential Election.* Chicago: University of Chicago Press.

Gimpel, James G., and Lewis S. Ringel. 1995. "Understanding Court Nominee Evaluation and Approval: Mass Opinion in the Bork and Thomas Cases." *Political Behavior* 17 (June): 135–53.

Gimpel, James G., and Robin M. Wolpert. 1995. "Rationalizing Support and Opposition to Supreme Court Nominations: The Role of Credentials." *Polity* 28 (Autumn): 67–82.

———. 1996. "Opinion-Holding and Public Attitudes toward Controversial Supreme Court Nominees." *Political Research Quarterly* 49 (March): 163–76.

Grosskopf, Anke, and Jeffrey J. Mondak. 1998. "Do Attitudes Toward Specific Supreme Court Decisions Matter? The Impact of *Webster* and *Texas v. Johnson* on Public Confidence in the Supreme Court." *Political Research Quarterly* 51 (September): 633–54.

Haynie, Stacia. 2003. *Judging in Black & White: Decision Making in the South African Appellate Division, 1950–1990.* New York: Peter Lang.

Herzog, Don. 2005. "Dragonslaying." *University of Chicago Law Review* 72 (Spring): 757–76.

Hibbing, John R., and Elizabeth Theiss-Morse. 1995. *Congress as Public Enemy: Public Attitudes Toward American Political Institutions.* Cambridge: Cambridge University Press.

———. 1998. "The Media's Role in Public Negativity Toward Congress: Distinguishing Emotional Reactions and Cognitive Evaluations." *American Journal of Political Science* 42 (April): 475–98.

———. 2001a. "Process Preferences and American Politics: What the People Want Government to Be." *American Political Science Review* 95 (March): 145–53.

———. 2001b. *What is it About Government that Americans Dislike?* New York: Cambridge University Press.

———. 2002. *Stealth Democracy: Americans' Beliefs about How Government Should Work.* New York: Cambridge University Press.

Hoekstra, Valerie J. 1995. "The Supreme Court and Opinion Change: An Experimental Study of the Court's Ability to Change Opinion." *American Politics Quarterly* 23 (January): 109–29.

———. 2000. "The Supreme Court and Local Public Opinion." *American Political Science Review* 94 (March):89–100.

———. 2003. *Public Reaction to Supreme Court Decisions*. New York: Cambridge University Press.

Hoekstra, Valerie J., and Jeffrey A. Segal. 1996. "The Shepherding of Local Public Opinion: The Supreme Court and *Lamb's Chapel*." *Journal of Politics* 58 (November): 1079–1102.

Hojnacki, Marie, and Lawrence Baum. 1992. " 'New-Style' Judicial Campaigns and Voters: Economic Issues and Union Members in Ohio." *Western Political Quarterly* 45 (December): 921–48.

Hutchings, Vincent L. 2001. "Political Context, Issue Salience, and Selective Attentiveness: Constituent Knowledge of the Clarence Thomas Confirmation Vote." *Journal of Politics* 63 (August): 846–68.

Jennings, M. Kent, Jan W. van Deth et al. 1989. *Continuities in Political Action: A Longitudinal Study of Political Orientations in Three Western Democracies*. Berlin: Walter de Gruyter.

Johnston, Richard, Michael G. Hagen, and Kathleen Hall Jamieson. 2004. *The 2000 Presidential Election and the Foundations of Party Politics*. New York: Cambridge University Press.

Jost, John T., and Brenda Major. Eds. 2001. *The Psychology of Legitimacy: Emerging Perspectives on Ideology, Justice, and Intergroup Relations*. New York: Cambridge University Press.

Kam, Cindy D. 2006. "Political Campaigns and Open-Minded Thinking." *Journal of Politics* 68 (November): 931–45.

Keeter, Scott, Carolyn Miller, Andrew Kohut, Robert M. Groves, and Stanley Presser. 2000. "Consequences of Reducing Nonresponse in a National Telephone Survey." *Public Opinion Quarterly* 64 (Summer): 125–48.

Kimball, David C., and Samuel C. Patterson. 1997. "Living Up to Expectations: Public Attitudes Toward Congress." *Journal of Politics* 59 (August): 701–28.

Kinder, Donald R., and Thomas R. Palfrey, eds. 1993. *Experimental Foundations of Political Science*. Ann Arbor: University of Michigan Press.

Kosaki, Liane C., and Charles H. Franklin. 1991. "Public Awareness of Supreme Court Decisions." Paper presented at the Annual Meeting of the Midwest Political Science Association, April 18–20, Chicago, Illinois.

Kramer, Larry D. 2004. *The People Themselves: Popular Constitutionalism and Judicial Review*. New York: Oxford University Press.

Kritzer, Herbert M. 2001. "The Impact of *Bush v. Gore* on Public Perceptions and Knowledge of the Supreme Court." *Judicature* 85 (July–August): 32–38.

———. 2005. "The American Public's Assessment of the Rehnquist Court." *Judicature* 89 (November–December): 168–76.

Kritzer, Herbert M., and John Voelker. 1998. "Familiarity Breeds Respect: How Wisconsin Citizens View Their Courts." *Judicature* 82 (September–October): 58–64.

Landrum, R. Eric, Jeffrey R. Cashin, and Kristina S. Theis. 1993. "More Evidence in Favor of Three-Option Multiple-Choice Tests." *Educational and Psychological Measurement* 53 (September): 771–78.

Lavrakas, Paul J. 1993. *Telephone Survey Research Methods: Sampling, Selection, and Supervision*, Vol. 7. Thousand Oaks, CA: Sage.

Law, David S., and Lawrence B. Solum. 2005. "Judicial Selection, Appointments Gridlock, and the Nuclear Option." San Diego Legal Studies Paper No. 07–10, August 26. Available at http://ssrn.com/abstract=791244 (Accessed May 3, 2006).

Levinson, Sanford. 2006. *Our Undemocratic Constitution: Where the Constitution Goes Wrong (and How We the People Can Correct It)*. New York: Oxford University Press.

Lind, E. Allan, and Tom R. Tyler. 1988. *The Social Psychology of Procedural Justice*. New York: Plenum.

Loewenberg, Gerhard. 1971. "The Influence of Parliamentary Behavior on Regime Stability." *Comparative Politics* 3 (January): 177–200.

Loewenberg, Gerhard, and Samuel C. Patterson. 1979. *Comparing Legislatures*. Boston: Little, Brown.

Lovrich, Nicholas P., John C. Pierce, and Charles H. Sheldon. 1989. "Citizen Knowledge and Voting in Judicial Elections." *Judicature* 73 (June–July): 28–33.

Lupia, Arthur. 2006. "How Elitism Undermines the Study of Voter Competence." *Critical Review* 18 (12):217–32.

Markovits, Inga. 1995. *Imperfect Justice: An East-West German Diary*. New York: Oxford University Press.

Marshall, Thomas. 1989. *Public Opinion and the Supreme Court*. New York: Longman.

Mate, Manoj, and Matthew Wright. 2006. "*Bush v. Gore* and the Micro-Foundations of Public Support for the Supreme Court." Paper presented at the 2006 Annual Meeting of the American Political Science Association, September 2, Philadelphia, Pennsylvania.

McCarty, Nolan, Keith T. Poole, and Howard Rosenthal. 2006. *Polarized America: The Dance of Ideology and Unequal Riches*. Cambridge, MA: The MIT Press.

Merkle, Daniel, and Murray Edelman. 2002. "Nonresponse in Exit Polls: A Comprehensive Analysis." In *Survey Nonresponse*, ed. R. M. Groves, D. A. Dillman, J. L. Eltinge, and R. J. A. Little. New York: Wiley, 243–58.

Mishler, William, and Richard Rose. 1994. "Support for Parliaments and Regimes in the Transition Toward Democracy in Eastern Europe." *Legislative Studies Quarterly* 19 (February): 5–32.

Mondak, Jeffery J. 1990. "Perceived Legitimacy of Supreme Court Decisions: Three Functions of Source Credibility." *Political Behavior* 12 (December): 363–84.

———. 1991. "Substantive and Procedural Aspects of Supreme Court Decisions as Determinants of Institutional Approval." *American Politics Quarterly* 19 (April): 174–88.

———. 1992. "Institutional Legitimacy, Policy Legitimacy, and the Supreme Court." *American Politics Quarterly* 20 (October): 457–77.

———. 1994. "Policy Legitimacy and the Supreme Court: The Sources and Contexts of Legitimation." *Political Research Quarterly* 47 (September): 675–92.

———. 2001. "Developing Valid Knowledge Scales." *American Journal of Political Science* 45 (January): 224–38.

———. 2006. "Political Knowledge and Cross-National Research on Support for Democracy." Paper delivered at the LAPOP-UNDP Workshop on "Candidate Indicators for the UNDP Democracy Support Index (DSI)," Vanderbilt University, May 5–6, Nashville, Tennessee.

Mondak, Jeffery J., Edward G. Carmines, Robert Huckfeldt, Dona-Gene Mitchell, and Scot Schraufnagel. 2007. "Does Familiarity Breed Contempt? The Impact of Information on Mass Attitudes toward Congress." *American Journal of Political Science* 51 (January): 34–48.

Mondak, Jeffery J., and Belinda Creel Davis. 2001. "Asked and Answered: Knowledge Levels When We Will Not Take 'Don't Know' for an Answer." *Political Behavior* 23 (September):199–224.

Mondak, Jeffery J., and Shannon Ishiyama Smithey. 1997. "The Dynamics of Public Support for the Supreme Court." *Journal of Politics* 59 (November): 1114–42.

Morin, Richard. 1989. "Wapner v. Rehnquist: No Contest; TV Judge Vastly Outpolls Justices in Test of Public Recognition." *Washington Post*, June 23, A21.

Murphy, Walter F., and Joseph Tanenhaus. 1968. "Public Opinion and the United States Supreme Court." *Law and Society Review* 2 (May): 357–82.

———. 1990. "Publicity, Public Opinion, and the Court." *Northwestern University Law Review* 84 (nos. 3 and 4): 985–1023.

Murphy, Walter F., Joseph Tanenhaus, and Daniel Kastner. 1973. *Public Evaluations of Constitutional Courts: Alternative Explanations*. Beverly Hills: Sage.

Nicholson, Stephen P., and Robert M. Howard. 2003. "Framing Support for the Supreme Court in the Aftermath of *Bush v. Gore*." *Journal of Politics* 65 (August): 676–95.

Norris, Pippa, ed. 1999. *Critical Citizens*. New York: Oxford University Press.

Overby, Marvin L., Beth M. Henschen, Michael H. Walsh, and Julie Strauss. 1992. "Courting Constituents? An Analysis of the Senate Confirmation Vote on Justice Clarence Thomas." *American Political Science Review* 86 (December): 997–1003.

Pew Research Center. 2005. "Alito Viewed Positively, But Libby Takes a Toll." Washington D.C.: Pew Research Center.

Posner, Richard A. 2001. *Breaking the Deadlock: The 2000 Election, the Constitution, and the Courts*. Princeton: Princeton University Press.

Pound, Roscoe. 1908. "Mechanical Jurisprudence." *Columbia Law Review* 8 (December): 605–23.

Price, Vincent, and Anca Romantan. 2004. "Confidence in Institutions, Before, During, and After 'Indecision 2000.' " *Journal of Politics* 66 (August): 939–56.

Prior, Markus, and Arthur Lupia. 2006. "What Citizens Know Depends on How You Ask Them: Political Knowledge and Political Learning Skills." University of Michigan. Available at http://mpra.ub.uni-muenchen.de/103/01/MPRA_paper_103.pdf (Accessed December 12, 2006).

Republican Party of Minnesota et al. v. *Suzanne White, Chairperson, Minnesota Board of Judicial Standards et al.* 2002. 536 U.S. 765.

Robinson, Paul H., and John M. Darley. 1998. "Objectivist Versus Subjectivist Views of Criminality: A Study of the Role of Social Science in Criminal Law Theory." *Oxford Journal of Legal Studies* 18 (Autumn): 409–47.

Rosenberg, Gerald N. 1991. *The Hollow Hope: Can Courts Bring About Social Change?* Chicago: University of Chicago Press.

Schattschneider, Elmer E. 1942. *Party Government*. New York: Farrar Rinehart.

Scheb, John M., II, and William Lyons. 2000. "The Myth of Legality and Public Evaluation of the Supreme Court." *Social Science Quarterly* 81 (December): 928–40.

———. 2001. "Judicial Behavior and Public Opinion: Popular Expectations Regarding Factors That Influence Supreme Court Decisions." *Political Behavior* 23 (June): 181–94.

Scherer, Nancy, and Brett Curry. 2006. "What Impact Does Racial and Gender Diversity on the Federal Bench Have on Citizens' Support for the Judiciary?" Paper presented at the Annual Meeting of the Midwest Political Science Association, April 12–14, Chicago, Illinois.

Schwartz, Herman. 2000. *The Struggle for Constitutional Justice in Post-Communist Europe*. Chicago: University of Chicago Press.

Scott, Kevin M., and Kyle L. Saunders. 2006. "Supreme Court Influence and the Awareness of Court Decisions." Paper presented at the 2006 Annual Meeting of the American Political Science Association, September 2, Philadelphia, Pennsylvania.

Segal, Jeffrey. 2006. "Perceived Qualifications and Ideology of Supreme Court Nominees, 1937–2005." State University of New York, Stony Brook. Available at http://ws.cc.stonybrook.edu/polsci/jsegal/qualtable.pdf (Accessed May 3, 2006).

Segal, Jeffrey and Albert Cover. 1989. "Ideological Values and the Votes of Supreme Court Justices." *American Political Science Review* 83 (June): 557–65.

Shapiro, Robert Y., and Yaeli Bloch-Elkon. 2006. "Political Polarization and the Rational Public." Paper presented at the Annual Conference of the American Association for Public Opinion Research, May 18–21, Montreal, Quebec, Canada.

Sheldon, Charles H., and Nicholas P. Lovrich, Jr. 1999. "Voter Knowledge, Behavior, and Attitudes in Primary and General Judicial Elections." *Judicature* 82 (March–April): 216–23.

Sinclair, Barbara. 2006. *Party Wars: Polarization and the Politics of National Policy*. Norman: University of Oklahoma Press.

Singer, Eleanor, John Van Hoewyk, and Mary P. Maher. 1998. "Does the Payment of Incentives Create Expectation Effects?" *Public Opinion Quarterly* 62 (Summer): 152–64.

Slotnick, Elliot E., and Jennifer A. Segal. 1998. *Television News and the Supreme Court: All the News That's Fit to Air?* New York: Cambridge University Press.

Sniderman, Paul M., and Sean M. Theriault. 2004. "The Structure of Political Argument and the Logic of Issue Framing." In *Studies in Public Opinion: Attitudes, Nonattitudes, Measurement Error, and Change*, ed. Willem E. Saris and Paul M. Sniderman. Princeton: Princeton University Press, 133–65.

Somin, Ilya. 2004. "Political Ignorance and the Countermajoritarian Difficulty: A New Perspective on the Central Obsession of Constitutional Theory." *Iowa Law Review* 89 (April): 1287–1371.

Spill, Rorie, and Zoe Oxley. 2003. "Philosopher Kings or Political Actors: How the Media Portray the Supreme Court." *Judicature* 87 (July–August): 22–29.

Sunstein, Cass R., and Richard A. Epstein, eds. 2001. *The Vote: Bush, Gore, and the Supreme Court*. Chicago: University of Chicago Press.

Survey Research Center. Sampling Section Division of Surveys and Technologies. N.d. "Post-Stratified Cross-Sectional Analysis Weights for the 1992, 1994 and 1996 NES Data." Ann Arbor: Institute for Social Research, University of Michigan.

Taber, Charles S., and Milton Lodge. 2006. "Motivated Skepticism in the Evaluation of Political Beliefs." *American Journal of Political Science* 50 (July): 755–69.

Taber, Charles S., Jill Glather, and Milton G. Lodge. 2001. "The Motivated Construction of Political Judgments." In *Citizens and Politics: Perspectives from Political Psychology*, ed. James H. Kuklinski. New York: Cambridge University Press.

Tanenhaus, Joseph, and Walter F. Murphy. 1981 "Patterns of Public Support for the Supreme Court: A Panel Study." *Journal of Politics* 43 (February): 24–39.

Tate, C. Neal, and Torbjorn Vallinder, eds. 1995. *The Global Expansion of Judicial Power.* New York: New York University Press.

Tedin, Kent L., and Richard W. Murray. 1979. "Public Awareness of Congressional Representatives: Recall Versus Recognition." *American Politics Quarterly* 7 (October): 509–17.

Thomas, Evan, and Michael Isikoff. 2000. "The Truth Behind the Pillars." *Newsweek*, December 25, 2000: 46–51.

Tsebelis, George. 2000. "Veto Players and Institutional Analysis." *Governance* 13 (October): 441–74.

Tversky, Amos. 1964. "On the Optimal Number of Alternatives at a Choice Point." *Journal of Mathematical Psychology* 1 (July): 386–91.

Tyler, Tom R. 1990. *Why People Follow the Law: Procedural Justice, Legitimacy, and Compliance*. New Haven: Yale University Press.

———. 2001. "A Psychological Perspective on the Legitimacy of Institutions and Authorities." In *The Psychology of Legitimacy: Emerging Perspectives on Ideology, Justice, and Intergroup Relations*, eds. John T. Jost and Brenda Major. New York: Cambridge University Press, 416–36.

———. 2006. "Psychological Perspectives on Legitimacy and Legitimation." *Annual Review of Psychology* 57: 375–400.

Tyler, Tom R., and Yuen J. Huo. 2002. *Trust in the Law: Encouraging Public Cooperation with the Police and Courts*. New York: Russell Sage Foundation.

Tyler, Tom R., and Gregory Mitchell. 1994. "Legitimacy and the Empowerment of Discretionary Legal Authority: The United States Supreme Court and Abortion Rights." *Duke Law Journal* 43 (February): 703–815.

Tyler, Tom R., and Kenneth Rasinski. 1991. "Legitimacy and the Acceptance of Unpopular U. S. Supreme Court Decisions: A Reply to Gibson." *Law and Society Review* 25 (3): 621–30.

Ura, Joseph Daniel, Patrick Wohlfarth, and Kaitlyn Sill. 2007. "Public Confidence and the Dynamics of Supreme Court Institutionalization." Paper presented at the 2007 Annual Meeting of the Midwest Political Science Association, April 12–15, Chicago, Illinois.

Vanberg, Georg. 2001. "Legislative-Judicial Relations: A Game-Theoretic Approach to Constitutional Review." *American Journal of Political Science* 45 (April): 346–61.

Vieira, Norman, and Leonard Gross. 1998. *Supreme Court Appointments: Judge Bork and the Politicization of Senate Confirmations*. Carbondale and Edwardsville, IL: Southern Illinois University Press.

Walker, Lee Demetrius. 2006. "Separation of Powers and Judicial Legitimacy in Latin America [*sic*] Presidential Democracies." Paper presented at the Annual Meeting of the Midwest Political Science Association, April 12–15, Chicago, Illinois.

Wolpert, Robin M., and James G. Gimpel. 1997. "Information, Recall, and Accountability: The Electorate's Response to the Clarence Thomas Nomination." *Legislative Studies Quarterly* 22 (November): 535–50.

Yates, Jeffrey L., and Andrew B. Whitford. 2002. "The Presidency and the Supreme Court After *Bush v. Gore*: Implications for Legitimacy and Effectiveness." *Stanford Law and Policy Review* 13 (1): 101–18.

Yoo, John C. 2001. "In Defense of the Court's Legitimacy." In *The Vote: Bush, Gore, and the Supreme Court*, ed. Cass R. Sunstein and Richard A. Epstein. Chicago: University of Chicago Press, 223–40.

Index